MW00680223

EDITOR

Delanyo Adadevoh, Ph.D.

INTERNATIONAL LEADERSHIP FOUNDATION
www.transformingleadership.com

ILF Library on Religion and Government
The African Church in Mission and Transformation is the second book published in the series *Guidance for Christian Leadership in Religion and Government.*

Our specific intention is to inspire and equip leaders of integrity in all walks of life in all parts of the globe. We sincerely appreciate hearing from our readers about our books and the part they have played in life, work and family.

The African Church in Mission and Transformation
Delanyo Adadevoh, Ph.D. – Editor

ISBN: 978-1-60000-024-9

Book cover and interior design by J. B. Dasalla
Cover image by iStockphoto.com

Printed in the United States of America

Contents

Contents

Acknowledgements

Many people have made this AFREG 2 Compendium possible. First, we need to thank the members of two very important committees of AFREG 2—the Planning Committee and the Host Committee. It is appropriate to extend special appreciation to Rev. George Mamboleo, Conference Coordinator, and Dr. Steve Kabachia, Chairman of the Host Committee, for their outstanding services.

We owe thanks to each participant who spent long hours in hard and thoughtful work to write the papers included in this compendium, as well as others who also made significant contributions.

Finally, this publication would not have been possible without the dedication demonstrated by the team of people who helped me with the final edits. They include Dr. Mike Wicker, Diana Langerock, Angela Simpson and Cindy Mitchell. The cover design, illustrations, and book layout are by our gifted photographer and graphic artist Joel Dasalla.

We pray that the impact of *The African Church in Mission and Transformation* will bring each reader a deep sense of satisfaction, and the encouragement to keep Africa moving forward.

Delanyo Adadevoh, Ph.D.
Editor

AFREG 2 Planning Committee Members

Dr. Delanyo Adadevoh, *Chairman*
Miss Diana Langerock, *Secretary*
Ven. Dr. Sola Igbari
Mrs. Elenestina Mwelwa
Rev. Dr. Setri Nyomi
Rev. George Mamboleo, *Coordinator*

AFREG 2 Host Committee Members

Dr. Steve Kabachia, *Chairman*
Mr. Hudson Mukunza, *Vice-Chairman*
Mr. Kibby Kariithi
Mr. Ezekial Mutua
Rev. John Wesley Nguuh
Mr. Charles Kilonzo
Dr. Bertha Kaimenyi
Rev. Esther Kiarie
Rev. Dr. Wilson Mamboleo
Rev. Canon Rosemary Mbogo
Mr. Ken Stravens
Mr. Isaac Kanyingi
Miss Wamaitha Muratha
Rev. Ignatius Nyaga
Mrs. Beatrice Omondi
Mr. David Sonye

Abbreviations

The Old Testament

Amos	Am
1 Chronicles	1 Chr
2 Chronicles	2 Chr
Daniel	Dn
Deuteronomy	Dt
Ecclesiastes	Eccl
Esther	Est
Exodus	Ex
Ezekiel	Ez
Ezra	Ezr
Genesis	Gn
Habakkuk	Hb
Haggai	Hg
Hosea	Hos
Isaiah	Is
Jeremiah	Jer
Job	Jb
Joel	Jl
Jonah	Jon
Joshua	Jo
Judges	Jgs
1 Kings	1 Kgs
2 Kings	2 Kgs
Lamentations	Lam
Leviticus	Lv
Malachi	Mal
Micah	Mi
Nahum	Na
Nehemiah	Neh
Numbers	Nm
Obadiah	Ob
Proverbs	Prv
Psalms	Ps
Ruth	Ru
1 Samuel	1 Sm
2 Samuel	2 Sm
Song of Solomon	Sg
Zechariah	Zec
Zephaniah	Zep

The New Testament

Acts of the Apostles	Acts
Colossians	Col
1 Corinthians	1 Cor
2 Corinthians	2 Cor
Ephesians	Eph
Galatians	Gal
Hebrews	Heb
James	Jas
John (Gospel)	Jn
1 John (Epistle)	1 Jn
2 John (Epistle)	2 Jn
3 John (Epistle)	3 Jn
Jude	Jude
Luke	Lk
Mark	Mk
Matthew	Mt
1 Peter	1 Pt
2 Peter	2 Pt
Philemon	Phlm
Philippians	Phil
Revelation	Rv
Romans	Rom
1 Thessalonians	1 Thes
2 Thessalonians	2 Thes
1 Timothy	1 Tm
2 Timothy	2 Tm
Titus	Ti

Other selected abbreviations used in the Compendium:

AACC	All Africa Conference of Churches
ACLCA	Association of Christian Lay Centres in Africa
AFREG	African Forum on Religion and Government
ALARM	African Leadership and Reconciliation Ministries, Inc.
ALMA	Africa Leadership and Management Academy
APRM	African Peer Review Mechanism
ARV	Antiretroviral Treatment
AU	African Union
BBC	British Broadcasting Corporation
CAN	Christian Association of Nigeria
CCZ	Council of Churches in Zambia
CICM	Centre for International Christian Ministries
CORAT	Christian Organization, Research and Advisory Trust
CPA	Comprehensive Peace Agreement
EPZ	Export Processing Zones
EFZ	Evangelical Fellowship of Zambia
FAWE	Forum for African Women Educators
GDP	Gross Domestic Product
GMT	Greenwich Mean Time
GHACOE	Ghana Congress on Women's Ministry
HCR	(UN) High Commission for Refugees
HDI	Human Development Index
HIPC	Highly Indebted Poor Countries
HSLDA	Home School Legal Defense Association
ICMZ	Independent Churches and other Ministries of Zambia
IDP	Internally Displaced People
ILF	International Leadership Foundation
ILU	International Leadership University
IMF	International Monetary Fund

Abbreviations

IPU	Inter-Parliamentary Union
KNUST	Kwame Nkrumah University of Science and Technology
LDC	Least Developed Countries
MDG	Millennium Development Goals
MMD	Movement for Multi-party Democracy
MVA	Manufacturing Value Added
NEPAD	New Partnership for Africa's Development
NGO	Non-Governmental Organization
ODA	Official Development Assistance
OECD	Organization of Economic Cooperation and Development
PDP	Peoples Democratic Party
PLWHA	People Living with HIV/AIDS
PRS	Poverty Reduction Strategies
TIC	Tanzania Investment Center
UN	United Nations
UNCRC	UN Convention on the Rights of the Child
UNDP	UN Development Programs
UNICEF	UN Children's Fund
UNIP	United National Independence Party
US	United States
USAID	US Agency for International Development
WCRC	World Communion of Reformed Churches
WAD	Women and Development
WEA	World Evangelical Alliance
WHO	World Health Organization
WID	Women in Development
WILDAF	Women in Law and Development in Africa
ZEC	Zambia Episcopal Conference for the Catholic Church

INTRODUCTION TO THE COMPENDIUM

Award Acceptance Speeches

H. E. Pierre Nkurunziza, President of the Republic of Burundi

In his acceptance speech for the *"President's Transforming Leadership Award,"* H. E. Nkurunziza provides a practical example of political leadership involvement in national transformation. Though he will be the first to agree his government is not perfect, he shares from the Burundi experience efforts made to enhance peace, stability, democracy, the alleviation of poverty, and provision for the weak in society.

Burundi has made some good decisions to provide free primary education, promote the study of English, French and Kiswahili (one of the African languages encouraged by the African Union) in elementary education, and to provide free health care for children and expectant mothers. The numbers of primary and secondary educational institutions established with volunteer leadership and labor also provide a good example for the rest of the continent. What we learn from the Burundi illustration is that development takes more than financial resources; it is more about creative and effective leadership.

Rev. Dr. William Okoye

On his part, William Okoye in accepting the *"National Transforming Leadership Award,"* provides an important account of the history of the African Forum on Religion and Government (AFREG). The Nigeria experience is an encouraging example of how AFREG can operate at the national level. Okoye finally challenges the organization of AFREG by advocating for a stronger leadership and administrative structure at national, regional and continental levels in order to sustain and ensure the growth of the AFREG movement.

Family, Gender and Youth

Dr. Bertha Kaimenyi
Healthy Family as Foundation for Societal Transformation

Kaimenyi, in her paper, identifies the starting place for the ambitious objective of societal transformation, particularly in the African context; she proposes that it all begins with personal discipline in lifestyle management. She focuses sharply on what she perceives to be the area of weakness in African lifestyles; Africans are religious and as such, are engaged in many spiritual activities. According to

Kaimenyi, Africans fail in the areas of personal life management, especially in maintaining a lifestyle that includes recreation, rest, good diet and regular exercise. Her appeal is for the African leader to see a link between personal discipline in the physiological aspect of life, and effectiveness in spiritual service. An unhealthy person ends up being an ineffective spiritual leader.

Her paper focuses on what she calls the *power of balance*. An effective leader must balance all four areas of life—intimacy with God, fulfilling career, healthy family and healthy body, i.e. the spiritual, professional, family, and physical dimensions of life. If one area is not doing well, all of life is out of balance. Kaimenyi holds the view that the education system caters to only 20 percent of a person's success, while 80 percent lies in the ability to manage our personality (character development). She raises a challenging question: "Why is the Church not making an impact on society? Could it be because we have emphasized the spiritual so much and left out issues of family and health?"

Victor M. Manyim
Equipping and Empowering Youth for Leadership and Development in Africa

Manyim argues powerfully for the development of a new generation of young leaders in Africa. He sees this as essential to breaking the current cycle of ineffective leadership paradigms and practices on the continent. According to Manyim, failure to break this cycle will mean sacrificing the next generation of Africans to the same selfish leadership that has plagued the continent. It is his contention that leaders today have lost the ability to believe that things can change radically because of the effects of accumulated failures from the past. To the contrary, young people are full of creative ideas, and ready to try new ideas. One challenge facing the youth is the traditional cautiousness of Africans to risk taking. Another challenge is the Western system of education that primarily focuses on intellectual and academic development with little emphasis on preparation for life. As a result, young people are equipped for career development, but are ill equipped for life as it relates to character and identity.

A third challenge identified by Manyim is the tendency of Africans to seek endorsement from elsewhere before implementing their ideas on the continent. For Africa to develop, she needs to rid herself of this inferiority complex. The development of a positive self-identity is essential for African youth so they are able to exercise the creativity and initiative needed to transform Africa.

Manyim sees three sources for the training of African youth: the Word of God, African tradition, and modern leadership theories.

Professor Leah T. Marangu
An Overview: The Current Contribution of Women to Development in Africa

Marangu advocates for the broadening of women's participation in decision-making and development from the home to all other sectors of society, including economy, politics and government, and education. Marangu views that two factors are contributing to the increase of women's involvement in the development of Africa: first, the general African population is tired of the corruption and general failure of men in leadership; and second, women can no longer watch their nations deteriorate under male rule.

Marangu acknowledges the progress already made by women's involvement in leadership and development on the continent. She cites many examples including the works of Wangari Maathai (environmentalist), Ellen Johnson-Sirleaf (President of Liberia), and Graca Machel (advocate for women and children's rights).

Despite this progress, Marangu raises concern regarding some worrying trends. Women are still not reaching the top of the ladder in leadership; they have assigned roles in society and few of them really reach top levels in government, corporations and other institutions. Less than ten percent of those who have titles to land are women; it is about one percent for agricultural land. Women still have lower incomes than men for the same amount of work, and too many women are confined to low paying jobs in the informal sector like housework and subsistence farming.

According to Marangu, to reverse these trends, the following changes need to take place:

- More girls having access to education
- A reduction in gender stereotyping, which limits women to particular roles, or levels of leadership, authority, and for that matter, access to opportunities and resources in both public and private sectors
- New labor laws put in place enabling women to have greater access to land, credits and other inputs

- Higher wages for women
- Ending laws and policies that violate women's rights
- Promoting laws and policies that ensure equal rights and opportunities for women in all sectors

Government

Honorable Minister Chief Ojo Maduekwe
Towards the Theology of the Christian State

Maduekwe begins by raising questions regarding the discussion itself: "Is it legitimate or proper to talk of a Christian State in a plural religious milieu? If so, how?" His work provides a useful definition of the State, both from the legal and biblical standpoints. He views the State as a guarantor of social peace and space for a flourishing life of dignity. He also sees the State as the entity that has monopoly to "legitimate violence" in a given territory.

According to Maduekwe, the failure of the nation of Israel led to a different perspective and expectation on the State on the part of the early Christians. The State was no longer relied upon for promoting righteousness and glorifying God; its function was simply limited to punishing evil deeds and rewarding good deeds. Now the State is called upon to create the environment for God's people to freely bid His will.

It is the view of Maduekwe that the plural nature of our modern world makes it impossible and impracticable to speak of a Christian State; we should speak of the secular State. At the same time, he recognizes that the rise of religious fundamentalism or extremism itself signifies the beginning signs of de-secularization. He argues that the truly modern State is religiously neutral, but that does not make it amoral. The modern State is still moral in as much as it pursues the promotion of certain ideals that are somewhat related, though indirectly, to religious doctrines.

Maduekwe sees the Universal Declaration of Human Rights as a secularization of Christian virtues. This shows how the modern secular State is finding its own way to clarify its function. He proposes at least three functions of the State: first is the entrenching of free and fair elections; second is the establishment of a culture of "rule of law" in private and public transactions; and third is the enhancement of the capacity for effective social delivery, with the aim of providing a good life for citizens.

Maduekwe encourages Christians to be involved in politics, which is highly entrenched in statecraft based on the inter-subjective communication of persons who have become autonomous. He calls on Christian leaders and church leaders in particular, to be model statesmen and stateswomen. He views that the modern State is part of God's State or kingdom, not the other way round.

H. E. Dr. Stephen Musyoka, Vice President, Republic of Kenya
Christianity and the Pursuit of Good Governance

H. E. Musyoka explains the continuum of the sacred and the secular. One end argues for complete separation between religion and the State; the other end calls for a fusion of religion and the State. Musyoka plainly argues in favor of democracy because all other forms of government, including theocracies, have not demonstrated effectiveness to the level of democracy. He argues against theocratic forms of government because each religious group in society deserves respect. Musyoka is obviously not only making a theoretical statement, but he is also speaking from experience as one involved in negotiating peace between the north and the south in Sudan. The religious element in the north-south conflict cannot be underestimated. Whether we are referring to Christianity or to Islam, theocracy is not the answer.

Musyoka advocates for a separation between religion and State that allows for religiously enlightened conscience in leadership and governance. He sees the role of government as one of safeguarding and promoting of the interests and wellbeing of the governed.

Many countries in Africa are familiar with the duties of governments and the merits of democracy, yet they are unable to take the necessary actions to realize these ideals. According to Musyoka, it is important to know values and principles—*responsibility, accountability, honesty, integrity, meritocracy* and *trustworthiness*, etc.—that can be utilized in translating the accepted ideals into reality. It is his view that the Bible provides both examples of the values and principles needed to realize democratic governance, as well as how to do so.

Musyoka makes the call for two approaches to leadership: *God-centered leadership* and *servant leadership*. Rationalistic and scientific resources are not adequate for good governance. God-centeredness brings God's favor into leadership; this "God-factor" makes a difference in leadership effectiveness.

Rev. Japhet Ndhlovu
Theology of a Christian Nation: The Case of Zambia's Declaration as a Christian Nation

Ndhlovu's contribution to the discussion about religion and State is significantly different from that of Musyoka. Drawing from the Zambian experience, he gives reasons for the possibility for a Christian State. He supports Chiluba's declaration of Zambia as a Christian nation as an affirmation of an existing reality. Chiluba was doing no more than stating the existing reality that Zambia is a Christian nation; her population is predominantly Christian. As such, Christian principles would guide the government of the country, which in any case allow for freedom of religious expression.

A second reason is that the peace Zambia enjoyed was attributable to the impact of the Christian faith. Thirdly, Chiluba viewed that when a nation entered into a covenant relationship with God, the nation could then experience the blessings of God. Therefore, development is linked to the nation's obedience to God and the following of His ways; disobedience would lead to punishment, which would have developmental implications. These are the realities, whether Zambia declared itself a Christian nation or not. God blesses nations built and governed on righteous principles. The Zambia declaration can be viewed as an invitation into a covenant that will ensure a conscious following of God's ways and a dependence on God for favorable development.

Ndhlovu explains that the declaration was not a discrimination against other religions. People of other faiths would have the freedom to freely worship, and individuals would have the right to choose their religion, but the principles of the majority religion would guide leadership and government. The declaration is not a call for a Church-run State in which non-Christians would go into hiding and would not play a part in the running of the government. Instead, it is an inclusive declaration, understood in covenant terms. Zambians freely chose to invoke God's blessing through the declaration.

The Zambian model is therefore a challenge to current democratic thinking, which adopts secularism as the alternative for predominantly Christian nations.

Religious Freedom
Rev. Dr. Andrea Z. Stephanous
Religious Freedom in a Pluralistic Society

In this work, Stephanous provides different theological perspectives on the concept of freedom. He draws examples from the Egyptian experience and aims to present an Arab perspective on human rights and freedom.

Stephanous derives his understanding of human rights from the Creation story and the teachings of Jesus Christ on the kingdom of God. According to him, two pillars serve as the base for the Christian concept of human rights: humans are created in God's image, and called to be active in the fulfillment of the kingdom. God's image, represented in humans through equality, creativity, and responsibility makes it possible for humans to achieve a society of justice and equality. He argues that every individual must have the freedom to believe without being under any pressure. Freedom of belief must include freedom of religious education and practice, as well as the individual's right to choose what to believe.

Stephanous makes it clear that Egyptian laws, as well as the constitution, speak to religious freedom and the equality of citizens. The problem of freedom in Egypt is with the practices of people, especially those influential in society. Several negative factors challenge the practice of freedom in Egypt. First, is the prioritization of religious loyalty above national loyalty and second, is the intentional effort, on the part of the media, to cast doubts on the doctrines of the Christian faith, which gradually leads to hatred and schisms in society. The third factor is the selective reading of history, which emphasizes friendly passages when that is the subject and discriminatory passages when differentiation is the objective. Collectively these negative factors result in societal instability, and a relative understanding of coexistence.

Reversing these negative factors will allow the practice of freedom to actually occur in Egypt resulting in stability, social integration and development.

Societal Transformation

Rev. Dr. Delanyo Adadevoh
The Whole Gospel to the Whole Person

Adadevoh provides some useful insights on biblical concepts of the "gospel." The main idea of his paper is to broaden current Christian understandings of the gospel. The core of the gospel message is the cross of Jesus Christ and the empty tomb; He died and rose again to provide salvation from the penalty, power, and presence of sin. The gospel is an announcement of God, come in the flesh, through the Messiah. The gospel also speaks to the good news of Jesus the Christ, as the King of the kingdom, both in the now and in the future.

According to Adadevoh, the message of the gospel should not be dissociated from the purpose and promise of the gospel. The gospel is about restoring saved humanity, and the rest of God's Creation, back to the original state of blessings that God intended at Creation. This happens through the reconciliation of all things back to God through Jesus Christ. The message of the gospel, therefore, includes both the saving act of God and the promised blessings of God.

In addition to encouraging a broadening of the message of the gospel, Adadevoh also argues for the Church to take seriously the implications of the gospel for missions. The gospel reconnects people relationally to God, realigns them to God's purposes, and then restores God's image in them. This process begins now, albeit with human imperfections, and reaches a climax when the Messiah returns to inaugurate the eternal kingdom. At that time, the imperfect gives way to the perfect and eternal.

Missions in the present should therefore, seek to reconnect people to God relationally, realign people to the purposes of God, and engage people in the process of experiencing the Spirit's on-going restoration into God's image. Missions should also address the implications of God's on-going reconciliation and restoration of the rest of Creation to Himself through His Son, Jesus Christ.

Rev. Dr. Célestin Musekura
Conflict Resolution, Transformation and Development in Africa

Musekura focuses on the kind of leadership needed to bring transformation and development to Africa. The transformation of Africa will require multi-faceted efforts that utilize diverse instruments. Africa's transformation cannot be achieved by addressing a few selected problems. To be effective, the approach to transformation has to be holistic.

Musekura references two kinds of perspectives on Africa, and two groups of people for that matter. The first are the pessimists, who see the problems of Africa so intricately and permanently tied to Africa that they do not really believe in change initiatives. The second are the optimists, who see the potential of Africa, mainly in terms of her natural resources, and believe change is possible. Musekura clearly identifies himself with the group of optimists as he argues that Africa's economic fortunes could turn around with the positive and effective management of her God-given resources.

According to Musekura, there are three causes of conflicts in Africa: internal, external and the impact or cost of conflicts. It is the firm conviction of Musekura that without peace and stability there can be no dream, hope, or development. To promote peace and stability, African leaders need to develop character and master the skills necessary for conflict resolution. Musekura provides a brief, but very useful, overview of approaches to conflict resolution.

He proposes five kinds of leadership needed to ensure a stable and developing Africa: *visionary leadership, peaceful leadership, protecting leadership, responsible leadership*, and *skillful leadership.*

To encourage effective leadership in Africa, the John F. Kennedy School of Government at Harvard University brought together a group of prominent African leaders who met in 2003 and 2004. These leaders established the African Leadership Council with an objective to strengthen, nurture and encourage high quality elected leadership in Africa. The council "promulgated a code of African leadership with 23 commandments, issued a Mombasa Declaration, promoting better leadership and proposed a series of courses to train their political successors in the art of good government" (Rotberg, 2004:16). The proposed curriculum has 25 topics that are relevant to current African realities. This list is a most useful contribution to the discussion regarding the kind of leadership needed to birth a new Africa. Thanks to Musekura for making it available.

Rev. Dr. Setri Nyomi
The Environment and Our Christian Calling

If Adadevoh provides a theological framework for missions and de-velopment, and Musekura provides a leadership framework for de-velopment, then Nyomi provides us with the theoretical framework for environmental stewardship and development. His paper calls on Christians to focus on God's reign and all He cares about, instead of being preoccupied with self-satisfaction. Nyomi offers a biblical un-derstanding of the call to subdue the earth in Genesis 1:28; it is a call to be stewards of God's Creation, rather than a permission to over-power Creation for our human benefit. Nyomi also provides another perspective on the invitation of Jesus to His followers not to worry. According to him, this does not mean that Christians should not be concerned about matters related to the rest of Creation. He views it rather as a call to prioritize the reign of God and the values of the kingdom of God above all other things that may concern us.

Christians need to evaluate their lifestyles and theological teach-ings, and question whether they are promoting good stewardship of the environment or destroying the environment for selfish reasons. Drawing powerfully from one of Calvin's sermons on caring for the environment, Nyomi reminds us that the call to stewardship has been a concern for the Church in past centuries; it is not a 21st cen-tury development.

Our call to care about the reign of God and the values of the king-dom of God should lead us to good stewardship of God's Creation. If we seek first the kingdom of God in this way, then all other things will be added to us.

Rev. Charlotte Opoku-Addo
The Role of the Church in Societal Transformation

Opoku-Addo begins her paper on *The Role of the Church in Societal Transformation* by providing basic working definitions of the con-cepts of "church" and "societal transformation." She proposes that the example of Jesus Christ calls the Church to not only preach the gospel, but to also engage in the transformation of society. Opoku-Addo is, however, careful to provide a clear priority for the preaching of the gospel.

The engagement in societal transformation is a secondary role of the Church. However, it is necessary for the effective accomplishing of the primary role of preaching the good news of Jesus Christ. The two roles are therefore, necessary and interdependent. She challenges the Church to end the selective reading of scripture and give due attention to the parts of scripture that address the issues of suffering and justice. She puts particular emphasis on the sufferings of women and children in African societies.

Opoku-Addo provides abundant statistics showing the poor situation of women and children in African societies, particularly the Ghanaian society. She also challenges the use of selected passages of scripture that seem to promote the supremacy of men and calls the Church to focus equally, if not more, on those passages speaking to the equality of men and women. Opoku-Addo calls for an intentional prioritization of the needs of women and children in the development initiatives of the Church.

She concludes her paper by giving practical illustrations of how GHACOE Women's Ministry, the organization she leads in Ghana, works to develop and empower women as dignified members and leaders in their communities. This may well be the strength of her contribution to the discussion on how the Church should engage in mission and transformation in Africa.

LEADERSHIP AWARD ACCEPTANCE

Speeches

H. E. Pierre Nkurunziza, President of the Republic of Burundi, graduated with distinction in Education and Sports in 1990 and became an assistant university lecturer in 1995 when Burundi faced a bloody civil war, stemming from tribal antagonism between Hutus and Tutsis.

After the late 2003 appointment of Nkurunziza as Minister of Good Governance and State Inspector General within the transitional government, this former rebel chief vied for the office of the president. He was elected to the position on August 26, 2005.

Nkurunziza inherited a country devastated by over a decade of civil war and dictatorship. His policies for reconstruction, reconciliation, economic recovery and political stability are significant contributions to Burundi's development. Nkurunziza was re-elected to a second term and sworn into office on August 26, 2010.

President Nkurunziza is married to Madam First Lady Denise Bucumi Nkurunziza and they have five children.

President's Transforming Leadership Award

Remarks by

His Excellency Pierre Nkurunziza
President of the Republic of Burundi

to the African Forum on Religion and Government
Limuru, Kenya, August 19, 2009

G lory to God for blessing this sacred meeting, and for giving us enough energy to work for the future of our brothers and sisters in Burundi, to transform and improve the continent and the world.

I am taking this happy opportunity to express my sincere gratitude to AFREG for this award! I personally feel proud and elevated, together with the Burundian people, with whom I share this joy.

Allow me to tell you that our elected government has been in office for four years, which is unprecedented in the history of Burundi, thanks to the combined efforts of my compatriots.

It is hard to take, hard to believe, but since Burundi achieved independence back in 1962, no elected government has lasted more than three months! Every elected government was followed by bloodshed, starting with the killing of the top leadership.

The fact that the institutions elected in 2005 have managed to rule the country until today shows that peace and security are now a reality in Burundi. That is why we have decided to help other countries by sending our troops to countries like Somalia, Sudan and Côte d'Ivoire.

The confidence you have put in me is therefore, a sign of sympathy and solidarity towards the people of Burundi, who have suffered more than a decade of civil war in their efforts of reconstruction and reconciliation. Now we have started National Consultations aimed at setting up the Truth and Reconciliation Commission, the last step of Burundi's Peace Process.

It is true that war has ended in Burundi; however, we are still facing some challenges relating to opportunities for development.

The future of Africa is in the hands of Africans themselves, because they are the ones who must ensure that development takes root on the continent. But, this requires good leadership, committed to work for the interest of the people. A human being would never achieve these goals without the help of the Almighty God, because without God, there is no life, and in knowing God, we can know life!

It is true that Africa's leadership must rely on faith in God. Yet, this faith should materialize into positive actions in favor of victims of those bad things that are hampering the development of Africa. As they say, "Faith without concrete actions is dead, inactive and ineffective."

As far as we are concerned, in Burundi, important measures have been taken in favor of the most vulnerable in society, such as children, women, and the disabled. Let me assure you that for me, this is only the beginning! This shows love and patriotism.

Since I took office in August 2005, our government has instituted free medical care for children under five, and free maternity care in public hospitals and public health clinics. Moreover, Burundi now offers free schooling in primary schools, some anti-malaria drugs are provided free and the Ministry of Health has embarked on a nationwide program aimed at distributing mosquito-nets; so far, seven provinces out of 15 have been covered.

A strategy of community works brings together all categories of the population, including the highest leadership of the country. Through these projects, during the school year 2007-2008, hundreds of secondary schools and 500 primary schools were built without help from our foreign partners. An environmental strategy enabled our citizens to plant around 15 million fruit trees in 2009 alone. These are initiatives by the Office of the President.

A Poverty Reduction Strategy that involves local forces and foreign fund donors in the execution of a long-term development strategy known as Burundi Vision 2025 has been put in place. The associated initiatives are driving projects in agriculture, water, energy, mining, education, health, and many more infrastructures. In addition, reforms have been made in our social and economic sectors for good governance.

Before I close these few remarks, I would like to reiterate my sincere thankfulness to the AFREG officials, who thought that I deserved something! It is a good surprise for me, for my family, and for the Burundian people.

My thanks also go to all those who, in one way or another, contributed for the realization of this event. To all those who chose to join us, in spite of their numerous obligations, I say thank you.

May God bless you.

Rev. Dr. William Okoye has served the citizens of Nigeria in various capacities, including: membership on the Presidential Advisory Council on Youth Affairs; membership in the National Political Reform Conference (1999-2007); Chaplain to two Nigerian Heads of State; and Pastor of Aso Rock Villa Chapel.

He was at the forefront of the establishment of the African Forum on Religion and Government, the first of which, took place in Nigeria in 2006.

Dr. Okoye is the General Overseer for the All Christian Fellowship Mission in Abuja. He also serves as Chairman of the Purpose Driven Network Nigeria.

National Transforming Leadership Award

Remarks by

Rev. Dr. William Okoye
General Overseer
All Christians Fellowship Mission

to the African Forum on Religion and Government
Limuru, Kenya, August 19, 2009

I feel greatly honored and challenged by the conferment on me of the National Transforming Leadership Award by the leadership of the African Forum on Religion and Government (AFREG) on the occasion of the second African Forum on Religion and Government (AFREG 2) held here in Limuru, Kenya. With gratitude to God, I sincerely thank the leadership of AFREG and the organizers of this conference for this important award. I am indeed grateful.

As part of the ceremony for the award, the organizers of the conference have asked me to speak for 30 minutes on "what has taken place in Nigeria since AFREG 1, as well as my vision for the future of AFREG."

This topic is divided into two distinct parts, i.e. "What has taken place in Nigeria since AFREG 1," and, "My vision for the future of AFREG." However, in order to do justice to the topic, I have chosen to put it in a wider context by adding yet a third part, "the historical background to the emergence of AFREG 1." This is because a meaningful discussion of what has taken place in Nigeria since AFREG 1, as well as a forecast into the future, must be anchored on our proper understanding of the process of the formation of the African Forum on Religion and Government.

The import of this lies in the fact that the lessons of history are not easily wished away, since the present is invariably a product of the past, while the future is largely rooted in the present. It is for this consideration that a historical overview of AFREG 1 becomes imperative for the analysis of developments in Nigeria since the maiden conference of AFREG 1 in July of 2006, as well as the vision for its future development.

Historical Background to AFREG 1

Sometime in 2004, a non-governmental organization known as Integrity Advocates, whose members include Professor Yusuf Turaki, Professor Jerry Gana, Chief Ojo Maduekwe, Dr. Peter Ozodo and me, William Okoye, conceived the idea of conveying an "All African Conference on Religion, Leadership and Good Governance." The idea was developed into a written proposal, which was submitted to His Excellency, Chief Olusegun Obasanjo, the then President of the Federal Republic of Nigeria, for consideration. Chief Obasanjo, on receipt of the proposal, referred it to His Grace, John Onaiykan, the Catholic Archbishop of Abuja and the Most Reverend Peter J. Akinola, Primate of the Church of Nigeria (Anglican Communion) for their comments and advice. The two religious leaders responded positively to the proposal and accordingly, recommended it to the President for implementation.

The purpose of the All African Conference on Religion, Leadership and Good Governance was to create a platform for African leaders of integrity, who are committed to the transformation of the continent, and to address the issue of institutionalizing the culture of good governance with a view to tackling the problems of corruption, poverty and underdevelopment in Africa.

While discussions and wide consultations were still going on over the formation of the All African Conference on Religion, Leadership and Good Governance, the President of Nigeria, Chief Olusegun Obasanjo went on a private visit to Ghana to speak at a Ghana National Prayer Breakfast. Professor Yusuf Obaje, the then Chaplain for Aso Rock Villa Chapel in Abuja accompanied the President on the visit. Professor Obaje was already aware of President Obasanjo's approval of the Integrity Advocates' proposal to organize an All African Conference on Religion, Leadership and Good Governance. While in Ghana, he shared the desire for the continental forum to address the role of religion in leadership, government and development with Dr. Dela Adadevoh. Dr. Adadevoh expressed interest in the idea of organizing a continental forum that would help African leaders address the role of religion in government and development. Following this, he joined the leaders of the Integrity Advocates to organize the first forum of African leaders to address the role of religion in leadership, government and development. Dr. Adadevoh later worked with me and other leaders of the Integrity Advocates to shape the proposed All African Conference on Religion, Leadership and Good Governance, which metamorphosed into the African Forum on Religion and Government (AFREG).

The formal launching of AFREG 1, by Chief Olusegun Obasanjo, took place in July 2006 at Abuja, Nigeria. The invaluable contributions of Dr. Adadevoh towards the successful launching of AFREG 1 are simply wonderful and commendable. I also wish to acknowledge the immense contributions of Sister Diana Langerock, Vice President of Operations, International Leadership Foundation (ILF), who helped in providing secretarial services for the effective organization of the conference. In fact, the historical account of AFREG 1 would be incomplete without acknowledging the presence and encouragement of His Excellency, President Pierre Nkurunziza of Burundi and his wife, Madam First Lady Denise Bucumi Nkurunziza at the formal launching of AFREG in Nigeria.

By the grace of God, AFREG was launched with ownership and sponsorship from Africa, and with the support of friends of Africa. AFREG 1 drew nearly 200 delegates from 27 African countries, the United States and Iraq.

Nigeria in the Post-AFREG 1 Period

Soon after AFREG 1, some key Nigerian Christian leaders, who attended the conference, decided to develop a one-page document on what we Christians believe about our faith and government. This is known as the *Nigerian Christian Creed on Governance*. We later developed four Bible studies to go along with the four paragraphs of the *Nigerian Christian Creed on Governance*. Subsequently, two books (a teacher guide and a student edition) were developed and used as instructional materials for Sunday School lessons in our churches. In addition, a three-day meeting of Christian leaders, under the auspices of the Christian Association of Nigeria (CAN), convened in Abuja, where leaders were taught about the *Nigerian Christian Creed*. The response of the leaders was overwhelming. After the meeting, participants received copies of video recordings of the teachings in order to help them teach the Creed at the state and local government levels.

Furthermore, Nigerian Christian leaders held similar meetings in Enugu, in the southeast of Nigeria, and conducted two outreach programs (organized for politicians in the region) under the umbrella of AFREG. The underlying objective of these meetings and programs was, and is, to help participants become leaders of integrity. I am happy to state that the outcome has been quite encouraging.

In the lead up to the 2007 general elections in Nigeria, AFREG leaders organized and conducted interviews with the major candidates who were contesting for the presidency. Since each of the three primary candidates was Muslim, specific questions were asked about their attitudes toward issues that are important to Christians. Their opinions about these issues became part of the public record.

By the grace of God, in 2008, I was appointed by the Nigerian Directorate of National Issues and Social Welfare for the Christian Association of Nigeria (CAN). The office handles socioeconomic and political issues as it affects Christians throughout Nigeria. In the performance of this responsibility, I have written to the Independent Corrupt Practices and other Related Offences Commission (ICPC), an anti-corruption body established by the Federal Government of Nigeria, indicating the desire of the Church in Nigeria to join with the government in a partnership to fight corruption. The matter is receiving the attention of the Commission and the details and modalities of operation are being worked out.

Additionally, I have put together a booklet titled, *Outward Reform Begins with Inward Renewal*, which I borrowed from John C. Maxwell's *Leadership Bible*, with the permission of the author. Because of the relevance of the message of the booklet to the Nigerian situation of today, we will distribute 500,000 copies of the booklet to political leaders across the country for use during Nigeria's 49th independence anniversary ceremonies on 1st October 2009. We trust that God's influence will be tremendous.

In another development, we are planning to bring together key Christian leaders in Nigeria to Abuja in March 2010 for three days to teach them how to apply biblical principles and values to bring about transformation in their spheres of influence. Similarly, we will help train Christian political leaders running for election in 2011, by teaching about the virtues of leading with integrity and a servant heart. The Church in Nigeria is therefore, rising to its social responsibility of partnership with the government in diverse ways to tackle the social and political problems facing our nation today.

The Future of AFREG in Nigeria and Africa

The African Forum on Religion and Government (AFREG) should be a neutral body, a platform for all African leaders who are burdened for the transformation of the continent from backwardness, deprivation, moral decadence, corruption, insecurity of lives and property, infrastructural decay and abject poverty into a First World continent, characterized by excellence based on God-centered values. AFREG should be a forum for raising African leaders of integrity with the passion to serve and not be served. AFREG should be the African think tank where African leaders of thought share ideas and pull resources together for the achievement of God's purpose for Africa and humanity in general.

From the beginning, AFREG has had a very specific focus. God has called us to a very specific ministry of positively influencing our governments and our cultures with our Christian convictions and values. We must not allow ourselves to be diverted into doing things that our churches and other organizations are already doing. Let us keep focused.

It should be noted, that since AFREG started, it has continued to operate on an *ad hoc* basis, without appropriate administrative structures. It is true that some of us are not disposed to the idea of a highly structured and formalized AFREG, however, even in the most fluid movement or organization, certain administrative structures are inevitable in order to keep such organization focused and effective. Accordingly, to facilitate the proper organization of AFREG, I recommend the immediate establishment of three levels of organizational structure and leadership positions for the forum as follows:

- National Leadership
- Regional Leadership
- Continental Leadership

Each of these administrative structures and leadership levels would have defined duties and responsibilities for the effective administration of the continental body called AFREG.

I feel confident that building on the foundation, which we laid in Abuja, Nigeria, in July 2006, and with God's help, AFREG will become a veritable platform for the transformation of Africa into a First World continent with Christian values. In conclusion, I believe that AFREG is an idea whose time has come. To buttress this point, I will quote from the book, *The Purpose Driven Church* by Rick Warren (1995:20):

> ...I also believe that pastors are the most strategic change agents to deal with the problems society faces. Even many politicians are coming to the conclusion that spiritual revival is our only solution...The most serious problems afflicting our society today are manifestly moral, behavioral and spiritual, and therefore are remarkably resistant to government cures. Doesn't it seem ironic to you that at a time when politicians are saying we need a spiritual solution, many Christians are acting like politics is the solution?

We are grateful for what AFREG has been able to do and this should be sustained. Therefore, like David of old, let us make ourselves available to serve the purpose of God in our generation.

National Transforming Leadership Award

PART 1

Family, Gender and Youth

Dr. **Bertha Kaimenyi** holds a bachelor's degree from UEA (Baraton), a master's and doctorate in Educational Administration from Andrews University in Michigan (USA). She initiated a master's program in Entrepreneurship at Jomo Kenyatta University of Agriculture and Technology (JKUAT) between 1992 and 1997. She joined Kenya Methodist University (KEMU) for two years. In 1999, she joined Daystar University. Dr. Kaimenyi is married with two children.

Currently, Dr. Kaimenyi is involved in educating society on how to achieve balance in the four areas of the human life: heart, soul, mind and body.

Healthy Family as Foundation for Societal Transformation

Dr. Bertha Kaimenyi

Introduction

In Mark 12:30, the Bible commands, "And you must love the Lord your God with all your heart, all your soul, all your mind, and all your strength." This is a command we must take seriously if we are to live within God's noble intentions for us.

The heart, soul, mind, and body (the holistic person) are comparable to the four wheels of a car. What happens when one wheel is punctured? The car is no longer able to continue in motion. We need to realize that when one area of life is not working, the whole body is affected adversely. For example, if the body is not functioning well, the resultant effect is fatigue, disorientated personality and loss of purpose in life. The essence of a holistic person is a balanced lifestyle, which has to be pursued as a primary goal in life.

We are living in a rat-race generation. Almost everybody is in the fast lane. We need to ask ourselves these fundamental questions: Where are we going? With whom are we competing? Some of us do not even have the time to eat a healthy meal. The food we eat is helping us dig our graves with our teeth and run there at an early age!

The Gateway to Healthy Living

To illustrate the power of balance, I want to share an experience I had when I was a lecturer at Jomo Kenyatta University of Agriculture and Technology in the mid-1990s. I was driving with some colleagues down Thika Road to Nairobi City. When we came near Kenyatta University, one colleague suggested that something was wrong with the car. I did not pay attention and continued driving. After driving for a short distance the car just stopped and when we got out to check, we realized that I had been driving on a flat tire; both the tire and tube were badly damaged.

The same applies in our personal lives. Some of us do not realize our parenting gaps until a school principal calls us to pick a dysfunctional child. Then we wonder when things got that far. Maybe it is your marriage; one morning your spouse says he or she is leaving. You might have seen the signs that things were not right, but you took them for granted. Some of us do not go for medical check-ups until we have a severe pain, and have no choice but to go and see the doctor. Then the doctor diagnoses you with a cancerous tumor, which by then has progressed seriously—a situation that could have been prevented.

Some of us go to church every Sunday, but we do not hear God anymore because we have crowded our lives with so much junk. We have replaced intimacy with God with other things, and it is not working anymore. Early in the morning when we wake up, or late at night, we hear an inner voice that tells us when things are not going well in the four mentioned areas. It is not that we do not want the balanced life; it is because we are too busy with other things to really care. Some of those "other things" that keep us busy from taking care of our health and families are rated high in the world. That is why it is important to make sure that your ladder of success is standing on the right course. Thus, before you gather steam to move fast, make sure your priorities are right. The words of Mahatma Gandhi capture well this dysfunctional state of things:

> One man cannot do right in one department of life whilst he is occupied in doing wrong in any other department; life is one indivisible whole.

How to Create Balance in Life
What do we need concerning holistic living? This paper is to caution those of us who are in the fast lane. The problems in the four areas require simple answers. For every blessing that God gives us, there is

a condition. The problem is, we do not like to obey God's commands. Instead, we like to pray for miracles and take shortcuts to our responsibility. Let us analyze some of the simple answers we need to heed.

The analogy is simple: the world is 75 percent or ¾ water; our body is ¾ or 75 percent water. We can see that water is life. So, what happens when we eat three meals a day and snacks in between but no water?

Let us illustrate this with an example. Imagine that you have visitors in your house for a birthday or a graduation party. All the dishes in your house are oily and dirty. You instruct your house-help to wash all those dishes with just a glass of water. Is that possible? That is the same with our bodies. We fill our body with all kinds of food in the course of the day—sometimes oily foods—and tell the body to digest all that with just a glass of water or no water at all. Medical science tells us that sometimes the fatigue or lethargy that we feel is because our body lacks water.

People argue about whether water can be substituted with tea or soft drinks. Let us illustrate it with a car. When you take your car to a petrol station, the attendant opens your bonnet and checks the oil, the brake fluid and the water. If you realize that you have no money for petrol, can you tell the attendant to put water instead of petrol? The paradox is we take better care of our cars than our bodies. It is in this generation that our bodies are refusing to take the mistreatment and are stopping in the prime of their time.

We need to realize that our bodies are the temple of the Holy Spirit and take care of them. What is one thing God made sure the children of Israel did not miss when crossing the desert? Water! There are no excuses in this regard. Water is life.

On the spiritual front, there is a similar "disconnect" in our churches. When people experience the Holy Spirit, they feel high, but when they go home, things become different; they feel low, dejected and helpless. It is not that the Holy Spirit has gone, but our bodies are not well. Some of us spend so much time in church because of the good feeling while we worship. From Monday to Friday, we are there for the morning glory and in the evenings too. For example, some of us women can spend every evening of the week in church. On Monday, we are there for a prayer meeting, Tuesday for Bible study, Wednesday for a miracle service, Thursday there is a visiting preacher, Friday there are overnight prayer vigils, Saturday women's fellowship and definitely on Sunday. What happens is that you leave work early, maybe before five p.m. to be in church. You leave church late and by the time you are home, the children are already in bed.

Someone told me that two kinds of people are untamable: your children and a husband. You cannot tell them what to do while you enjoy yourself in church. The pastor may not get concerned about you neglecting your family and spending too much time in church. Incidentally, spending time in church with people does not make you grow in the Lord. One lady who is so busy in church told me, "I have no devotional life on my own." She is either in a Bible study or a prayer meeting with people, but never alone with God. We grow when we are alone with God, seeking Him. Remember that success in your spiritual life cannot compensate for failure in your health.

The saying, "an apple a day keeps the doctor away" is true. The vitamins and minerals in fruits and vegetables can help reduce the risk of cancer, heart disease and high blood pressure. People whose diet is rich in fresh produce have more energy and are less likely to gain excessive weight. In the Garden of Eden before the Fall of man, Adam and Eve had only fruits and vegetables for their food before God allowed them to eat meat. Remember also that the Israelites ate meat only three times a year during the festivals and not as often as we are doing today. Their meat was boiled for so long until it started separating from the bone. Much of our traditional food that we now discard in the name of progress is what is good for us. We have to go back to that old time religion of eating arrowroots, sweet potatoes and yams.

How does our health relate to our marriage? The point is that if you are not feeling well, you cannot make someone else feel good. That is why eating the right kind of food and getting enough exercise is important for marriages. If you are not feeling well enough to meet the needs of your partner, your partner may try to meet those needs elsewhere. That is the truth of the matter. We are in a world of competition everywhere and we have to be relevant in our marriages too. Even professional men are going out with tea girls or cleaners from the office. The reason can simply be that the wife cannot smile and therefore cannot provide the fun and excitement for the partner.

The partner seeks the company of other men or women to have their needs met. This explains the increase of mistresses in our society. Why do women fail to obey Genesis 2:18: "…man should not be alone," by failing to provide companionship for their husbands? When David sinned, he was alone. That is when he looked through the window in the balcony and saw Bathsheba. If we become so busy at work that we sometimes have to carry extra work home in our lap tops, what does that mean for our children and spouse? We really have to understand that when we let our children loose during their free time, that is when they experiment with drugs. When we are so busy that we fail to fit in free time with our spouses, that is when we expose them to infidelity.

We find this exhortation in the book of Titus: women should love their children and husband and be busy at home. Some women leave their home earlier than their husbands do. Actually, Billy Graham, the famous evangelist, advocates that women should work before marriage and after children leave home. If the woman must work when the kids are young, she should do it in a less demanding career. However, even if a woman has to work full-time, she should use wisdom to keep her spouse fulfilled. Margaret Thatcher served as Prime Minister of Great Britain, yet was able to keep her marriage and still manage to carry out her premiership duties well. We never heard of any scandals in her marriage. It takes commitment, discipline and wisdom to have a successful marriage and a career.

Current research by Dr. Timothy Sharp (2009) states that success in your career and all the financial factors contribute to only ten percent of your happiness. This means that we spend 90 percent of our time on what gives ten percent of happiness. He states that 90 percent of our happiness comes from factors such as attitude, health and family. Can you see the paradox that we are spending ten percent of our time on what gives us 90 percent of happiness? We concentrate on the icing instead of spending more time on baking the cake. The cake is the holistic person that we talked about and need to build upon. The cake is the intimate relationship with God, our purpose, our relationships and our health. When these areas are working in harmony and balance, then the cake is well baked and sweet. In the process of fulfilling your purpose, you gain power, money and prestige, which is the icing on the cake.

I will use the following story to illustrate how the four areas form the foundation. One day a physics professor came and informed the class that there was going to be a practical assignment. He called the most intelligent student to come forward and try the following: Aim to fill a container with all the materials that were provided. There was a container, big rock particles, medium-sized particles and sand. Among the things provided were leaves. He explained that the leaves were distracters and should not be included in the container.

The student started filling the container by first putting the sand particles in the container, then the medium sizes and finally the rocks. This order did not achieve the intended objective, as some of the rocks could not fit in the container. Along the way, the student also included some leaves.

Another student came and tried but failed, and so did many others. Finally, the professor decided to do it himself. He told everyone to watch how the container could best be filled. He first placed the bigger rock particles at the bottom, followed by the medium-sized ones and finally poured the sand particles on top without any leaves. The container was well occupied and the arrangement was apparently intact.

The four rocks are the four areas of our lives. When they are in place and intact, you are able to be more productive in society. When you are intimate with God, carrying out your purpose, in a fulfilling marriage and having a healthy body, there is balance in your life. When the four areas are in balance they become the fire within that excites us and gives us passion, vision, and a spirit of adventure. If any of the four needs are unmet, the dominant factor takes all the energy and attention. If you are doing well in your career, but your marriage is not working, then all your focus and attention shifts to the area of weakness. If you are doing well spiritually, but your body is not well, then your health demands all your attention.

The sand particles and leaves are activities such as unnecessary meetings, and friends who prevent you from living a creative balanced life. Good things like excessive parties need to be evaluated and reduced. This is where discipline comes in. You have to deliberately discipline yourself and make the right choices. It is not about prioritizing your priorities, but about scheduling your priorities.

We need to understand that when the four areas are balanced and in harmony, we are able to give more to society. We are able to do more without stress. The four rocks in the story are our intimacy with God, purpose, relationships and healthy lifestyle. The sand and the leaves are things we do that are not important, and if they are worth doing at all, they are important to somebody else. These are number-less meetings at work, working overtime, church fellowships, pre-weddings, funeral meetings, and excessive celebrations. We need to learn to say "no" to good, but unnecessary things. We cannot be everything and be everywhere. We need to learn to turn off our mo-biles. We cannot be on call to the whole world.

A Healthy Attitude
Factors Influencing Healthy Habits
The choices we make influence how healthy our lifestyle is. We have to be conscious of many factors that influence our eating habits. We have to learn how to say "no" to wrong eating habits, "no" to the red meats and sugars, and "yes" to 6-8 glasses of water a day, and some exercise of 30 minutes 3-4 days a week. We have the power within us to cultivate the discipline that we need for a healthy lifestyle.

There is a common belief that there is a constant improvement in diverse areas of human endeavor. There is improvement in the ar-eas of education and technology. However, the quality of food is not improving, especially in developing countries. Even in our country Kenya, it is not any better. We have some unethical farmers who, for reasons of profit, use excess fertilizers and chemicals in farm produc-tion so when these foods reach our tables they are unhealthy.

Health has been affected by the removal of essential nutrients from the food supply. We have refined and processed food that is not good for our bodies. In many other areas of life, things are improving. For instance, in the area of technology, we use the latest mobile or computer. However, when it comes to food, we should be advised not to eat what our grandmothers would not eat. This means we need to eat food in its natural state as much as possible.

Research and science are calling heart attacks and strokes dis-eases of choice. Researchers show that 80 percent of heart diseases and 90 percent of diabetes may be linked to unhealthy diets and lifestyle habits. Cancer and heart diseases, previously considered more of a Western problem, are now on the rise in Kenya. The rate of incidence is so high that the government is urging Kenyans to go for regular medical checkups to ascertain their status. The leading cases involve breast, cervix, throat, prostate gland and stomach cancers.

The Ministry of Health is now recognizing cancer as a major cause of morbidity and mortality.

> Your health is your first wealth.
> – Ralph Waldo Emerson

Keeping on the Healthy Pathway
The life expectancy of Kenyans is now 55 years (World Bank). Cancer and other preventable diseases are causing death to two out of every ten Kenyans. Changes in eating habits are evident because more Kenyans who are affluent are abandoning traditional diets for Western foods. Many people, especially in Nairobi, prefer junk food or fast food to natural traditional foods. We are not only borrowing Western technology and ways of dressing, but also their food. Today, we find that many people, especially the youth, do not cherish traditional foods, which are low in cholesterol and much healthier than modern ones.

A major concern is that cancer is striking the young population in Kenya, unlike in the developed countries where most of the sufferers are older. We are bringing up an undisciplined generation. We are not teaching our children to make right choices when it comes to food.

Obesity has increased in Kenya, mostly among women and children. What is interesting is that women professionals in the urban areas, with higher levels of education and wealth, are more likely to be overweight. This shows us that the educational system is seriously lacking in teaching character, self-discipline and general life skills. I did physical education (P. E.) in primary school, but my teachers never told me why I was doing it. They never emphasized it as a healthy lifestyle that I should continue doing.

With this in mind, clearly the education system caters for only 20 percent of a person's success, while 80 percent lies in the ability to manage our personality (character development). We find that educators are not stressing a healthy lifestyle. They have turned P. E. and sports in schools into competition. The emphasis is on how to compete and win. Parents are also not modeling a life of exercise. Therefore, we have an unaddressed gap of critical issues in our lives. No matter how wealthy and educated we are, we need to cultivate discipline in our lives.

Why is the Church not making an impact on society? Could it be because we have emphasized the spiritual so much and left out issues of family and health? We have so many people in the Church who are out of shape. Some of the most educated and affluent can be the most ignorant when it comes to life skills like personal management. Being spiritual is not an excuse for lack of physical fitness. Praying to God for victory when you have symptoms of fatigue and tiredness is but for the grace of God a waste of time. Medical science tells us that a lack of water in the body causes fatigue and tiredness. Drink water! Does it make sense to you that the world is ¾ water and your body ¾ water, and we are told to drink six to eight glasses of water every day? Some of life's areas where we spend time and money in research require very simple answers.

A friend of mine once told me that if her food does not include meat every day, it is not serious food. There is nothing wrong with eating meat for as long as you maintain a lifestyle of exercise. My students once asked why I put such an emphasis on exercise and yet Jesus never exercised. I told them that Jesus never needed to exercise because all He did was walk. Some of the solutions are so simple. Just ask the *matatu* (public transport) driver to drop you 30 minutes from your house and take a brisk walk to complete your journey.

The main problem with Christians is complacency in relation to God's laws, and the tendency to choose what to obey and not to obey. Why are we Christians choosing a shorter life span when God gives us a long life? The Bible gives us 70 years, but life spans in Kenya have reduced to 45 years. In fact, in the book of Isaiah, people lived to 100 years. Even if you live for only 40 years, let it be without trouble.

The Old Testament is the dietary section of the Bible. Leviticus 7:22-27 talks of not taking fat even for generations to come. The fact that modernization and progress have come does not change God's Word at all. The fact that there is so much junk food on the super-market shelves does not mean we buy it. The fact that we can afford it does not mean that we need it. The kingdom of God is within us, and this means we have the power to make right choices.

Paul Zane Pilzer (2007:79) says that today, "most religious people begin with prayers thanking God for providing them with food, as opposed to thanking God for giving them the knowledge of what to eat to be healthy." We need to have zealous commitment when it comes to making choices about our health. John Wesley (1771) said that few of us Christians manage to make a complete turn from sin and so we are neither hot nor cold. We need to have zealous commitment like Peter in our obedience to God's instructions regarding our diet. Each time Peter was asked to do something like allowing Jesus to wash his feet, he went overboard (Jn 13:9).

The best things in life are free, like watching a sunset, worship, and exercise. Some of the solutions to fatigue and tiredness require simple answers like laughter. Laugh alone and find time to laugh with others. We are caught up in the busyness, worries and troubles of life, and forget to watch the sunset, the beauty and miracles around us. We need to learn from children who are normally happy and have no worries. Put laughter on your "to do" list and look for occasions in the day to laugh. Research immunologists have discovered that a moment of happiness will boost your immune system up to a period of 4-8 hours, whereas a moment of depression will bring it down for a period longer than 4-8 hours.

Abraham Lincoln once said, "With the fearful strain that is on me night and day, if I did not laugh I should die." The strain of the presidency and any other demanding calling is borne best by those who are able to laugh. Laughter strengthens the immune system, reduces stress, lowers blood pressure, and eases pain. It improves complexion and makes you feel good about yourself. When you smile with the muscles on your face, the result is an increased blood flow to your face, and this makes your face radiant.

When you come from class or work in the evening, you have the following choices. One, is to sit down and watch television because you are tired. Two, is to sit down, read your Bible, and pray. Three, to change your clothes and do some exercise such as brisk walking or even jogging. Alternatively, you can play ball with your kids. When we choose options that involve exercise, the brain produces endorphins, which make us feel good. Set a routine in your house that is difficult to break. One of the most popular excuses for lack of exercise is lack of time. However, as we exercise, we glow with wellbeing, which is inner-centered.

We need to work on our character and how we feel about ourselves. We need to know that inner power is equal to outer beauty.

I believe that marriages would improve if women took the message of healthy exercise more seriously. Some of us are tired, ill, and out of shape most of the time. When we say we do not have time for physical fitness, what are our priorities? We need to pause and consider what we define as success. Is it to have a healthy body or quality shoes or designer clothes?

We need to check constantly how we feel, in the same way we might check the temperature or petrol gauge of the car. Do I feel good or upset? Am I joyful or irritated? Is it something to do with my health or my spirit? The Bible commends a gentle and quiet spirit, and that is what we should be checking all the time.

There was a day when I passed by a salon at 7:00 a.m. and found married women. What sort of preparation did they make in their home for them to make it to the salon that early? Did they prepare a good breakfast to give them enough energy for the day? Did they have time for prayer with their family? When we feel good inside spiritually because we spend time with God, enjoy breakfast and cater for our physical wellbeing, then nothing can defeat us.

If a woman does not reflect and pray, how can she really be beautiful? Beauty is hardly a matter of cozy dressing and make-up. The nice designer clothes we wear and the make-up we put on are merely the icing on the cake. The real cake lies in being healthy spiritually and physically.

A simple solution to our health problem is to eat breakfast like a king, eat lunch like a prince, and eat supper like a beggar. However, we mostly do the opposite. We miss breakfast which we need for energy during the day, and eat so much supper, which we do not need, sometimes late at night.

The Bible says in 3 John 2, "Beloved, I pray that you may prosper in all things and be in health, just as your soul prospers." Our health is so important and we actually do not realize it until we lose it. We are living in a society where people are getting sick and tired more than before. Do all you can to invest in your health. Decide to make a commitment and make progress. Expect and demand results from yourself.

Understanding Killer Diseases

We need to learn how to stay healthy, but we also need to be aware of disease symptoms, so that we can take necessary action and become our own doctors. We need to be aware of the voices calling us to change our lifestyle.

Dr. Robert Mathenge, of Equatorial Heart and Blood Vessel Clinic at the Nairobi Hospital, gave us a warning in an exclusive article in the *Daily Nation* (July 8, 2007) under the headline, "Dying Young." Dr. Mathenge reckons that AIDS is no longer the deadliest silent killer on the scene. Bad food, alcohol and lack of exercise are killing thousands of Kenyans in their prime. Over the span of 15 years, health-related illnesses will kill more people under 40 than AIDS and all infectious diseases combined. In that same article, Dr. Mathenge, one of the country's leading heart disease experts, warns:

> The incidence of cardiovascular diseases among the young Kenyans is fast approaching epidemic proportions. If we do not do anything about it, we will, in the next 15 years, be losing more young people to lifestyle diseases than to all infections such as malaria and HIV/AIDS combined.

Dr. Mathenge remembers that during his five years of medical school he saw only two or three patients who had experienced a heart attack. Today, at his clinic, he sees at least one new patient daily, suffering from cardiovascular disease (Mathenge, July 2007). Most of these patients are in their 30s or early 40s. This is in contrast to his experience in the United States, where most of his patients were elderly people.

A chilling warning issued by the World Health Organization (WHO) is also not far-fetched. Today, hospitals are treating hundreds of young patients suffering from diseases that for a long time have only really afflicted the elderly. Many as young as 25 years or less, and a significant number will die. These diseases include coronary heart disease, diabetes, stroke, hypertension and alcohol-induced liver cirrhosis. According to the medical experts, with the wide distribution of antiretroviral treatments (ARVs), these lifestyle diseases are now on the verge of edging out AIDS as the leading killers of young Kenyans. "The fact is, we have a crisis on our hands," says Dr. Peter Gathirimu, a Registrar at the Department of Internal Medicine at the University of Nairobi, and a consultant physician. "The impact of cardiovascular disease is now more than the impact of HIV/AIDS." We can do something about these lifestyle diseases by observing the danger signs and how we can fight them.[2]

There are many challenges facing us as far as living healthy lifestyles are concerned, especially concerning our children. We live in environments crowded with houses and flats with nothing more than a parking lot for the children to play. Then with the rising insecurity, the parents will not let their children go out on the streets.

So then, how do we deal with the situation? We give our children the television, DVDs and PlayStations©; and, add to this a diet of soda, crisps, sausages and other junk foods. We then have children who are restless and sometimes obese. Did you know that if you gave your child a sausage five days in a week for seven years, that child would have leukemia? An emerging trend is the increase in the numbers of children, as young as three years, with diabetes (a disease traditionally associated with the elderly). Kenyatta National Hospital is already handling 300 cases.

One solution to this problem is to get children involved in as many sports programs as possible in school. Sports have a big social and mental development impact because they will help to keep them active, healthy and bright and, in the process, promote intelligence.

Another problem that the unhealthy lifestyle brings is that we become a burden to our children and spouses early in life. When you get a preventable disease at age 60, it means that your children, who are probably in their 40s and in the prime of life, will have the burden of taking care of you. This does not even take into account the financial responsibility. In our sunset years, we spend all the savings to pay hospital bills. We also put a heavy burden on our spouses.

Mary Ruth Swope in her book *Lifelong Health* (1997:139) gives the following moving story:

> I remember a touching story told by my former employer about his wife. She began to have severe pains in her back. She was about sixty at the time. The pains grew worse until she went to a physician for help. She was diagnosed with arthritis but with treatment, she could improve.
>
> Although she followed his advice, she became so ill, that she was bedridden and immobile. Finally, the family decided to take her in an ambulance to her son's home in another state. Her son, a medical doctor, examined her and found that her back was broken in two places. The bones of her spine had literally deteriorated and crumbled. She was diagnosed as having osteoporosis (porous bones). Soft drinks, red meat, and sugar are directly related to this condition.

I will never forget what her husband told me. "You're a nutrition teacher," he said. "Tell your students about my wife's case. We have been married for nearly forty years, and I have never seen her eat calcium-rich foods. For years, I have been telling her that she would have brittle bones when she got older, but she could not listen. Now she'll be in a cast for several months, and unless there is a miracle, she may never be able to put the weight of her body on her feet again without crutches or a walker."

This man probably wonders why he has to suffer the consequences of his wife's habits. She will never again be able to live a normal happy life doing all the things she had contributed to their home and marriage. This story has far-reaching lessons for those of us who live lives without balance, specifically in the area of health.

Personal Management Initiatives

When we look at progressive and successful organizations, they all have a vision, mission statement, objectives and goals that guide their activities. Their mission statement is visible everywhere for people to see—on notice boards, in boardrooms, corridors, etc. Everybody is expected to know and adhere to it. There are deadlines and activities planned to help meet the targets on time, profit or whatever it is. What happens to people who fail to meet the target or who slow down the organization? They are retrenched or fired. We cannot afford to do less in our personal lives.

We need to make the right choices every moment of the day. Our future may be judged by the choices we are making today as we leave behind a legacy. We need a vision and a personal mission statement. Our personal mission statement becomes the DNA for every decision we make. The personal mission statement guides us, so that our compass faces the true north. An internal compass that follows the right principles, and not just urgent matters or the clock, then drives us. The clock, goals, commitments, or other people's deadlines do not enslave us. We learn that we cannot put God on a "to do" list. To make the most of your time on earth, you must maintain an eternal perspective. This will keep you from majoring on minor issues and help you distinguish between what is urgent and what is ultimate. So much of what we waste our energy on will not matter even a year from now, much less in eternity.

When our children write our history maybe 50 years from now, they will be asking why we did not manage our personal lives and make the right choices. Specifically, they will be asking why mum or dad died early. Why did dad or mum die of a preventable disease? Why did they not make the right choices regarding what to eat? Why did mum and dad divorce? Why did we allow negative circumstances of the day like unemployment and poverty to grow? They will not be looking at the technological advancements. History will judge us for not balancing our lives.

What choices are we making everyday? When your company tells you to advance your training, and it offers to take you overseas for three years and you have a one-year-old child, what choice do you make? No doubt, your prayer group will make that a thanksgiving item. As a mother or even a father with a young family, what choice would you make? What consequences will your choice have on your family?

A Call to Repentance
The final word is the call to repentance. John the Baptist's message, as he prepared the way for Jesus, was a call to repentance. This is also my call today as we come to the end of this paper. The reason many people struggle to live a creative and balanced life is a failure to make choices that reflect obedience to God. For most Christians who have Jesus as Lord it is the failure to turn away completely from sin. In Isaiah 1:16-17 we read: "Take your evil deeds out of my sight! Stop doing wrong, learn to do right!" Whilst in Ezekiel 18:30, we read, "Repent! Turn away from all your offenses; then sin will not be your downfall." John Wesley (1771) says the average Christian never makes a complete turn from sin. We see this big problem among many Christians today.

We Christians need to see the evils of society as failures on our part. When we do nothing, evil increases. We should repent for doing nothing about our neighbors. Yes! You may not have done it, but you did not prevent it from happening. When we repent and desire to live rightly, God will give us ideas regarding how to make positive contributions in our country.

Repentance Precedes Revival
After repentance comes the in-filling of the Holy Spirit and the power to obey the first commandment and live a balanced life. We have to

be friends with the Holy Spirit; otherwise, we will be going round in circles. Whatever God asks us to do; He gives His power to do it. It is impossible to say "no" to all the opportunities around for having a good time, and all the unhealthy food around us without the power of God that raised Jesus from the dead. To have this power we must be one with Christ. According to Kathryn Kuhlman (1973 sermon), if you find God's power, you have heaven's full treasure.

Jesus came preaching the kingdom of God. Jesus came to make the kingdom of God real. He came saying: The kingdom of God is within you. We are kings and priests; royal blood flows within us. God's purpose is for man to take dominion. God meant that we should rule with Him. We Christians should be at the forefront in leadership, economics, politics, science, education, entrepreneurship, and every sector of the society. When you see the underdevelopment, the poverty, disease, the gap between the rich and poor increasing, and the unemployment crises especially among the youth, then you know something is wrong. If, as we understand, 80 percent of Kenyans are Christians, then something is missing in our Christianity. This is what we have been trying to address in this paper. We will not have the power to bring the kingdom of God to Kenya if we are living in disobedience to the Word of God.

Our development achievements should stand out because of the many Christians in this country and in Africa. Christians need to lead in every area of society. I believe we will lead with the power of the Holy Spirit. Jesus is Lord.

Healthy Family as Foundation for Societal Transformation

Victor Manyim has a master's degree in Mechanical Engineering and has worked with Campus Crusade for Christ since 1997. After founding a Campus Crusade ministry at the University of Dschang, Cameroon, he was later appointed as Director of Athletes in Action, a ministry for people involved in sports. This responsibility gave him the opportunity to serve men and women in sports at the highest level throughout the world. Manyim was an official Chaplain at the Athens Olympics in 2004.

Presently, he is Director of the Young Leaders League, an International Leadership Foundation initiative focusing on the development and training of young leaders. Victor and his wife Florence live in Yaoundé, Cameroon, and have four young children.

Equipping and Empowering Youth for Leadership and Development in Africa

Victor M. Manyim

Introduction

Leadership is the key factor in determining the justice, development and wellbeing of society. The teachings of our Lord Jesus Christ contain the essential and eternal principles of efficient servant leadership that could save our nations and Africa in particular. The Church should therefore, be committed to a mission of restoring effective leadership in order to transform our societies.

The younger generation is a key element in this mission of transformation; indeed, it would be absurd to allow our young people to grow up with the same leadership paradigms that have led Africa to where she is today. Young people are ambitious and enthusiastic. They can easily discard ready-made ideas and creatively develop their own ideas. The ambition and faith of our youth make them a particularly important mission field in any efforts towards transformation. Young people are the future; they comprise the largest population group in Africa and are teachable.

Another factor that makes the training of youth in leadership so important is the void currently existing in training and preparing young people for life. Modern ideas do not seem compatible with our traditional systems of educating young people for life. As a result, youth receive only intellectual training, without the depth of a value system or a well-defined identity. It is therefore extremely urgent to put in place systems that will equip and empower our youth for transformational leadership. However, how can we carry out such a mission?

First, we need authentically African curricula based on three fundamental sources: The Word of God, African culture and tradition, and modern leadership principles. These curricula should be complementary and have the ultimate aim of giving glory to God by restoring leadership practices in Africa that will honor Him. These curricula will be taught to young people, both within the formal framework of school and within a more informal framework, where they will be able to learn transformational leadership principles through experimental training methods and actual field experience.

An important part of this equipping of young people will be to instill in them a strong sense of positive self-identity. They will need to see and hear a positive and more authentic description of Africa. Practical transformational leadership training, combined with a clear spiritual and cultural identity, will no doubt produce the new generation of leaders that Africa needs.

The message of Jesus Christ is a light that, as it penetrates the life of an individual, a village or a nation, brings deliverance. The Lord Jesus said at the beginning of His earthly ministry, after the devil had tempted Him for 40 days and 40 nights in the desert:

> The Spirit of the Lord is on me, because he has anointed me to preach good news to the poor. He has sent me to proclaim freedom for the prisoners and recovery of sight for the blind, to release the oppressed. (Lk 4:18, NIV 1984)

Having read this passage and declared that this Word of scripture was being accomplished at the very moment He was reading it, the Lord Jesus demonstrated that it was indeed being accomplished: He fed the hungry, healed the sick, and freed the oppressed. The good news of the gospel should therefore, not only deliver Africans, among others, from spiritual ignorance, but this spiritual deliverance should radiate throughout the whole intellectual, social and physical being of the individuals who experience it. As a result, the families, villages and even nations comprised of this new breed of men and women, will experience healing and deliverance from all the infirmities undermining our cities and our society.

There is, however, an astonishing contrast found on this wonderful continent of Africa. The Church is growing exponentially. At the beginning of the 20th century, ten million people on the continent of Africa claimed to be followers of Christ. A century later, nearly 400 million claim to be Christians. Paradoxically, the number of social problems is growing at the same rate as the number of Christians. The multi-sided crises faced by Africa today are growing simultaneously, along with the growth of the Church of Jesus Christ on the continent. The rapid growth of the Church in Africa does not seem to have an impact on the moral qualities of the leaders of our fine continent. Delanyo Adadevoh says: "No culture can rise above the character of its leaders, and no culture can rise above the leadership capacities of its leaders."

If it is true that the character and quality of the leaders are a determining factor in limiting the development and wellbeing of a society, then the Church needs to urgently develop a strategy for building up leaders of integrity capable of leading transformation in Africa. We then need to ask two questions: Why do we need to equip young people in particular in transformational leadership? How can the Church go about accomplishing such a huge task?

Why Youth?

There are several reasons why we believe that any initiative aiming to restore effective leadership in Africa, which does not include a plan for youth, is doomed, if not to actual failure, at least to having minimal impact.

Young People are Blank Pages Ready to be Written Upon

How can we even imagine breaking the cycle of selfish leadership in Africa without including the younger generation? Indeed, it would be madness to let our youth grow up with the same paradigms that are handicapping African leadership today. We therefore need to train and prepare new generations of leaders of integrity, capable of leading transformation in Africa. It is our urgent duty to not allow the gangrene of selfish leadership to corrupt our young people. If the youth of today grow up with the same leadership paradigms that have led Africa to where she is at present, we may have sacrificed another whole generation of Africans. In addition to this, many of our present leaders no longer believe that things can change, which would not necessarily be the case with young leaders.

One does not need to spend much time with the men and women who are leading Africa today before realizing to what extent they have lost hope that Africans will ever be able to close the gap in development that separates us from other countries. This anesthetizing of creative thinking comes, no doubt, from the present leaders being very conscious of the accumulation of so many past failures.

To explain this phenomenon, we can make an analogy with a popular game among children in many African villages. The game consists of standing a chicken on the ground and stopping it from moving by putting some big stones on its feet. The children then run after the chicken until it loses the reflex to try to run away. They then take the stones away and the chicken is physically free. The children continue to chase it but the chicken does not move, it stays rooted to the ground, in an imaginary prison created by the many unsuccessful attempts to escape.

Like the chicken in the game, our present leaders may already be conditioned by so many negative practices and experiences, that they dare not believe they can make ambitious plans for the continent without the endorsement of past leaders. They only seem able to put in place projects endorsed and supported by former leaders.

The younger generation is in the process of forming its convictions and practices. If the Church is absent from leadership training among this generation, then these young people will be obliged to fall back on the same convictions, and therefore, the same leadership practices as their fathers, and for which we are suffering today. It is therefore a strategic necessity that the younger generation be included as a priority in any initiative that aims to break the paradigms of ineffective leadership in Africa.

Young People have a Strategic Place in Society
Many say that youth are the spearhead of the nation. If you want to know what the society of tomorrow will be like, look at what our youth of today are becoming. If you want our society to be better tomorrow, guide the youth of today in the right direction and prepare them to be better than the adults of the past. Young people are ambitious, creative and full of energy. They want to try new things and they are capable of acquiring and developing new attitudes and practices, naturally, and apparently without effort. They are in what many would consider the most exciting phase of life.

Youth constitute the largest population sector in Africa. More than ever before, those in government, the Church, and leaders of opinion, have the responsibility to equip this young generation who really desire to make a difference. It is time to mobilize every positive force, and it is time for the Church to really act. The Church can give these young people the tools that will prepare them to manage the cities of tomorrow, with a force of character and moral fiber hitherto unknown in Africa. This approach is indispensable for the transformation of Africa—leading to a better future for our rich continent.

Young People are Creative and Full of Ambition
The young are creative and bold. Unaware of their limits, they often try things that adults would not attempt. This is certainly risky, and in Africa, we are very conscious of risk. We are probably too conscious of it to realize the potential, in this way of thinking, for original, and hitherto unthought-of, solutions to some of the numerous evils undermining our continent. Young leaders have much to offer Africa, provided they receive the necessary encouragement, training and supervision.

It is easy to build up a younger generation that has faith in its own capacities. It is easy to develop a younger generation that is fully aware of the importance of its role in resolving the problems of Africa. The Church can be on the front line, teaching young people how to participate in the construction of Africa, rather than continuing to remind them of what they cannot or should not do.

Formal Structures No Longer Exist for Training and Preparing Youth for Life
In traditional societies, there existed formal structures for the training and preparation of young people for adult life. Even if there were no printed books or school curriculum on the subject, there were practical schools, in the oral tradition, for preparing future men and women in our traditional societies. A young boy, coached by the men who would prepare him for manhood, would be able to contribute to the stability and social equilibrium of the family and the village. In the same way, the women would prepare a young girl to become a woman so that she would be ready to take on the responsibilities of a wife and mother within the family and the village.

Western influence has certainly contributed the necessary tools for formal intellectual education, but it has also contributed to the loss of the preparation for life that African girls and boys received in traditional society. In African society today, going to school to receive an intellectual education seems to totally exclude any kind of preparation for life. Often, parents have not received adequate life preparation and have been obliged to develop certain survival reflexes in order to cope with whatever life brings.

As a result, we have a large majority of young people who are intellectually equipped, but who have not received any kind of training for life, or their African or spiritual identity. Because of their academic qualifications, these young people will certainly have more opportunities for career-track employment, but they will be ill-equipped for life as it relates to their character and identity (both traditional and spiritual).

How many young people can really say, "I prefer suffering with my people to the delights of being an adopted son in the royal family," as Moses did in Egypt? How many young people experience a relationship with the living God that would allow them to say, like David, "Who is this uncircumcised Philistine that he should defy the armies of the living God?" (1 Sm 17:26, NIV 1984). How many young Africans have been initiated to their African identity to the point of refusing fashions from elsewhere that are constantly inventing new ways of transforming the bodies of adolescent girls and boys into sexual objects? Daniel and his friends considered the dishes of King Nebuchadnezzar as being unclean. They politely, but firmly, begged the chief eunuch not to force them to defile themselves (Dn 1:1-21, NIV 1984). The Lord said that we, His disciples, are the salt of the earth and the light of the world. This salt and light can give back a sense of cultural and spiritual identity to the young people who have been uprooted at every level.

The necessity of including youth in the strategy of the Church for social transformation is therefore clear. The obvious question is: "How do we go about equipping young people in new leadership paradigms?"

How to Equip Our Youth for Transformation in Africa
In the same way that theoretical knowledge, combined with practical abilities, is needed to build a house, the development and involvement of youth in transformational leadership need both theoretical knowledge and practical abilities that are acquired through experi-

ence. Theoretical knowledge leads to strong convictions and creates a desire for action. A structure is therefore needed which will give the opportunity for action that is inspired by the above mentioned convictions and which will bear visible fruit that will glorify God and build up the community.

Specifically African, Original and Complementary Curricula
In Africa, we are blessed to have a younger generation willing to listen and accept guidance from their parents and elders, especially regarding their options and choices in life. Our experience with young people has taught us that many young Africans are looking for a new way to approach life—an approach with the right values. Many young Africans want to do things in different, and of course better, ways than their elders, parents, teachers, pastors, leaders, etc. This fortunate state of affairs should lead us, as partners with governments in the building of our nations, to develop leadership curricula based on three fundamental sources:

- The Word of God
- African tradition and its specific conception of leadership
- Modern leadership principles, as developed in both theory and practice by leadership specialists

Different creative thinkers can develop all sorts of curricula, but they must be in constant communication with each other. Maintaining this permanent contact ensures that the courses are complementary and in harmony and ensures that individuals work together in the same spirit and pursue the same aim—in this case, the development and transformation of the African nation. The final objective is of course to glorify God by helping to reveal the beautiful face of this continent created by God, but which has been hidden for so long by the sores of human greed, selfishness and irresponsibility.

A curriculum is only a tool. It can stay unused and therefore dead, or it can be badly used and therefore harmful. It can also be well used and bear fruit. So, how should we use a curriculum of leadership development for young people?

Training Within a Formal Structure
Most young people in secondary education do not receive teachings on leadership. Even if introduced, it would probably be from a curriculum developed by educators from the West. If some courageous

Africans set out to develop such materials in Africa, it is likely that today's decision-makers in the world of education would first seek approval for their ideas from the leaders of yesterday, before allowing them to be taught in schools. Such is the simplistic paradigm of the African mentality today. The notion of faith in God is rarely debated among Africans (whether Christians, Muslims or Animists, etc.), and is not taught in our education system apart from religious schools.

We are not attempting here to preach a doctrine advocating total self-sufficiency or the superiority of African ideas. However, it is important for us to believe in ourselves and to rid ourselves of the tendency to seek ratification of our projects elsewhere before they can be implemented in Africa. Theophile Obenga (2007) says: "Africa is destined for greatness—greatness that will be specifically her own. But first we need to rid ourselves of our inferiority complex."

We do not want to underestimate the importance of talking with others, listening to their ideas and comparing them with our own. It is therefore important that our young people receive African-specific teaching on leadership within the formal secondary education system.

Training Within an Informal Structure, Outside School and Within the Community

The training of our young people cannot be limited to theoretical ideas taught in school. Youth need opportunities for open discussion, where they can express their ideas and learn to apply the notions of leadership they have learned through extracurricular activities. It would be a great challenge to get young people to enroll in and commit to such activities that by definition are not obligatory.

The quality of the programs and activities proposed in these extracurricular meetings will not be the determining factor in the degree of participation of the young people. The main factor that will persuade them to attend these activities regularly is if the program leaders manage to consistently demonstrate that future success depends on reliable participation (Little and Lauver, 2005).

We need to give our youth the opportunity of experiencing new leadership paradigms in ways other than formal teaching. We also need to give them the opportunity to participate in leading the transformation of Africa; stimulating their awareness of the problems surrounding them and helping them find workable solutions.

The approach is experimental. Yet, it enables the young people to put into practice what they have learned.

Another advantage in helping youth carry out transformation projects is that it helps increase their confidence in their own capacity to be change agents. It allows them to fulfill their potential, as they become convinced that the key to change is already in their hands. An approach that involves young people in action by giving them responsibilities also helps to increase their participation in major development activities (Walker and Arbreton, 2005).

Sport can be another important element in the training of young people. One can experience all the complexities of life in society through sport. Sport can effectively communicate ideas such as the surpassing of oneself, determination, hard work, discipline and creativity.

Restoring a Positive Identity
A sense of identity is the base on which to build up our African youth. Without a clear, strong identity, attempts at development will yield minimal results. In our interaction with others, if we lack a sound sense of identity, we will be swallowed up in theirs. In order to develop a strong sense of identity, we need to go back to Africa's history, and the great men and women that she has contributed to the rest of humanity. This history can be studied through the traditional African wisdom stories handed down to us since time immemorial.

We can also study the great African historical figures. Beginning with Imhotep, who at the age of 27, around 2650 B.C., designed the first carved stone monument in the history of humanity. The young Berber theologian, Saint Augustine (354–430 A.D.), whose writings are an integral part of the foundation of Christian doctrine (Obenga, 2007) is another African figure that may inspire young people. The most recent hero to come out of Africa is Barack Obama, who, against all odds, managed to conquer the White House, the very symbol of economic and military power. These, and many other well-known and influential African leaders, can serve to reveal a strong tradition of leadership and help today's young people discover a positive self-identity from their heritage.

For centuries, young Africans have grown up knowing nothing about Africa apart from what non-Africans say. Almost exclusively, the images they conjure up send implicit but clear messages to young Africans: "You are an inferior race; you are not good enough." A new image of Africa, and of the great and glorious historical figures produced, should replace this doctrine.

In fact, we can say that religion should become a key factor in the transformation of Africa. The light shed by God's people on this continent should shine through a younger generation, trained and equipped to lead the transformation. In our efforts to heal Africa, we must remember youth as an important element in this transformation. Their willingness to listen and receive training, their creativity and energy, and the strategic place they occupy in our African countries, are all good reasons for the strategic investment today towards their preparation and development as the next generation of African leadership.

However, we need to bear in mind that any such initiatives on the part of African believers must bear the original stamp of fine, authentic African values. It is time for Africa to enrich herself, and the world, with her own values and the style of servant leadership, following the model taught by Jesus Christ. If we do not save today's youth, they will certainly grow up with the same foibles that have been undermining leadership and development in Africa for these many years.

Professor Leah Marangu holds a Ph.D. in Education, two master's degrees, and the following firsts for a parastatal in Kenya: female full professor, vice-chancellor and chair.

Prof. Marangu has received two Head of State commendations and has received 20 international and national awards for her outstanding leadership qualities and character. A member of 27 international bodies, Prof. Marangu has written 20 international publications and 46 feature articles.

She is currently the Vice-Chancellor of Africa Nazarene University, Nairobi, Kenya. Prof. Marangu has been a member of the Commission for Higher Education in Kenya since its inception.

An Overview: The Current Contribution of Women to Development in Africa

Professor Leah T. Marangu, Ph.D.

Introduction

Women, by nature—having been given a natural right by the Supreme to bring up new lives—play a key role in the society. With the increased access to education, health, credit, formal legal rights and employment opportunities, their social economic role has improved in the developing countries, Africa inclusive. Former United Nations Secretary General, Kofi Annan (2005) said, "There is no tool for development more effective than the empowerment of women." Undoubtedly when women thrive, all the society benefits and succeeding generations have a better start in life (Karongo, 2007:24-25). While women may be participating in family decision-making, the impact will be more significant if this participation sustains and extends to other sectors of the economy. The empowerment of women is fundamental in addressing gender issues such as discrimination and subordination.

According to Kenya's development plan, *Vision 2030* (Republic of Kenya, October 2007:133-137), one crucial goal is to increase opportunities all round among women, youth and all disadvantaged groups. Specific strategies will involve:

• Increasing the participation of women in all economic, social and political decision-making processes (e.g. through higher representation in Parliament).

- Improving access of all disadvantaged groups (e.g. business opportunities, health and education services, housing and justice).
- Minimizing vulnerabilities through prohibition of retrogressive practices (e.g. female genital mutilation, child labor) and by up-scaling training for people with disabilities and special needs.

Current Level of Involvement

Women provide the backbone of the rural economy in much of sub-Saharan Africa. About 80 percent of the economically active female labor force is employed in agriculture. Food production is the major activity of rural women and their responsibilities and labor inputs often exceed those of men in most areas in Africa.

Women are responsible for ten percent of food production, 50 percent of domestic food storage, 100 percent of food processing, 50 percent of animal husbandry and 60 percent of agricultural marketing (Manuh, 1998). Women's role in food production continues to increase as urbanization and economic difficulties drive men to the cities, leaving women to compensate for their absence (Saito, Mekonnen and Spurling, 1994).

Overall, in sub-Saharan Africa, women hold an average 16.8 percent of parliamentary seats, close to the global average of 17.1 percent, according to the Inter-Parliamentary Union (IPU), an international forum for dialogue among legislators. Ellen Johnson-Sirleaf, a former World Bank official and grandmother of six, is Liberia's President. Often referred to as the "Iron Lady," Johnson-Sirleaf is Africa's first elected female Head of State. Yet, she is hardly alone on the continent. Across Africa, voters are increasingly putting their hope in women as capable and upstanding saviors—partly in a "throw the male bums out" reaction to continued corruption. Looking at Kenya, women are represented in several ministries. Currently, there are six women ministers, five assistant ministers and five permanent secretaries.

The status of women in many countries is improving. Women are making it clear they will not put up with the situation anymore and governments are creating opportunities for women to contribute skills and talent to national development. In September 2000, 189 countries, including Kenya, adopted the Millennium Declaration. The main objective of this declaration was to define a common vision for development by 2015. With this endorsement, Kenya set a limited number of attainable Millennium Development Goals (MDGs) for the year 2015. Goal number three is to promote gender equality and empower women (MDG, 2008).

More women are joining the formal sector of the economy (especially the public sector), more girls are continuing to higher education and taking technical courses. More women can also be found in the management hierarchy whilst others are moving into professions so far dominated by men, and many more are becoming self-employed (Omar, 2004:360-373).

They are also involved in small businesses like trading, fashion design, and business management, while at the same time, managing their homes; hence, women are playing an increasingly greater complementary role in national development. In Nigeria, according to the World Bank census of 2001, the population of Nigerian women was 50.7 percent, which was slightly above half, and therefore, their productivity in the formal or informal sector was formidable and could not be underestimated (Iwe, 2005:319-322).

Changes in the attitudes of society toward women have led to the enhancement of the status of women. They have moved forward from times when they could not view the four walls of a classroom, let alone stay in it to university level. They have moved from the situation where society dictated their ultimate ambitions; that is to marry quickly and procreate. Now women have shifted from a lifetime of drudgery into impressive public policy-making bodies. The population of women in Kenya's universities was 40 percent in 2007. The leadership of both public and private universities in Kenya consists of five women vice chancellors, and several deputy-vice chancellors.

In Kenya, the *Kenya National Gender and Development Policy* (2000:8) explicitly notes the importance of women's roles related to the environment. The government recognizes that environmental degradation is a major cause of poverty. In this regard, we note that women play a major role in the management of natural resources such as water, soil, food, and forests. Their dominant roles within the household and in agriculture make them the daily managers of the living environment.

Due to their roles and experiences, women have profound knowledge of the local environment including the food crops, livestock, plants, and ecological processes around them. The success of ongoing and any new efforts to halt the alarming rate of environmental degradation and destruction demands deliberate awareness creation to bring about fundamental changes in attitudes and practices. This is because the proper management of resources relates intimately to sociocultural attitudes and practices. Consequently, it is important to recognize women's contribution to environmental management all over Africa and their potential usefulness as a major force for sustainable development.

This is important since women are normally the first victims of environmental degradation. Professor Wangari Maathai, a Kenyan scholar, activist and politician, in 2004 became the first woman from Africa, and the first environmentalist, to join the ranks of Nobel Peace Prize laureates due to her contributions to sustainable development, democracy and peace. She is the first African woman to receive this prestigious award.

Another prominent figure is Graca Machel, who has been very active internationally and is world-renowned for her commitment to children's and women's rights, education, and development. She has facilitated greater community access to knowledge, technology and patterns of sustainable human development. She is a major force in increasing literacy and schooling in Mozambique and is outspoken on the needs and rights of children and families from platforms all over the world. Machel is recognized for her leadership in organizations devoted to the children of her war-torn country.

Significance
Africa and the international community increasingly acknowledge African women's contributions to food production systems and national economies (Morgan, 2008). Women are the backbone of Africa's rural economy, accounting for 70 percent of food production.

Things are starting to change for women in Africa and women themselves are behind the move. At both the grass roots and national levels, women's associations are forming and taking advantage of the new political openings to assert their leadership. By improving their own positions, women are simultaneously strengthening the African society as a whole, as well as enhancing the continent's broader development prospects.

Observed Trends

In trade and industry, women are usually confined to small-scale operations in the informal sector; however vibrant these operations are, and despite the trading empires built up by the most successful female entrepreneurs, women's average incomes are relatively low.

There are low participation levels of women entrepreneurs in value-adding business opportunities. Some of the chief barriers to promoting women in business include cultural and societal problems, psychological impact of cultural norms, employment legislation and policies. Others include lack of information, training, finance, markets, technology and business infrastructure, the absence of vehicles for skill development and capacity building, fragmented approaches to identifying issues and developing strategies to influence policies affecting business and government interventions.

Despite economic success for some, both women and men face difficulties in achieving economic security. More than half of the population lives below the poverty line. While recognizing that many are poor, there are legal, institutional, and cultural constraints that have a disproportionate, negative impact on women. Some key statistics reflected these constraints. One estimate reveals that women own less than ten percent of titled land (one report estimates the figure is one percent of agricultural land).

Women also tend to be over-concentrated in informal employment and in lower-paying professions, including within the Export Processing Zones (EPZs). Although the overall women's literacy rate is rising, it is still lower than that of men (79 percent versus 90 percent in 2003).

Shifts in economic structure have a profound impact on the differing positions of women and men in the labor market. Because of structural constraints (e.g. less access to education and skill development), women adapt less easily to changing demands in the labor market. Consequently, they tend to be crowded into agriculture in developing countries; into manufacturing in fast-growing countries; and into services in industrialized countries.

With respect to agriculture, trade liberalization tends to favor medium and large producers. Women, mainly holders of small plots of land, experience losses when their farming land is taken to produce export-oriented agricultural goods. Constraints in women's access to credit, transport and storage facilities further limit their ability to increase their production and gain from trade.

Access to information is another priority issue; women typically have less formal education, lower literacy rates, and less familiarity with market information than men do. Women worldwide still hold secondary positions; they are under-utilized in the labor market and are still a wasted resource.

A majority of women employees still fill the lowest ranks of organizations, find it difficult to rise to senior and executive management levels and are not benefiting from government policies and legislation to advance their careers. The business world, for various reasons, is still male-dominated. Clearly, social biases and stereotypes still exist in organizational environments, which work against women, thus undermining governments' affirmative action and employment equity policies. This brings in the challenges of gender equality to senior positions and shattering the glass ceiling for professional women to reach the top positions.

Several organizations in Africa, including FAWE (Forum for African Women Educators), bring together female ministers in charge of education, university chancellors, vice-chancellors, permanent secretaries and other influential women to work towards increasing girls' access to education in Africa.

What Needs to be Improved?
Several things need to improve to bring about sustainable development in Africa. The following are some of the areas needing improvement:

Women in Leadership
Africa is overflowing with women leaders, but some lack the training and the means to bloom. This highlights the next big step needed for advancing the position of women in Africa: strengthening their capacity and skills and expanding the opportunities for women to more fully develop their leadership roles (Manuh, 1998).

Women's leadership skills in their communities, groups and associations, need harnessing and formalizing to give them political and decision-making powers. The reasons why many women do not assume top political, military and managerial positions are obviously compounded by their triple roles (reproductive, productive and community) (Fonjong, 2001:223-234). However, the few women leaders in these institutions are beginning to make a notable leadership impact.

As noted earlier, in Kenya there are six female cabinet ministers, five assistant ministers and five permanent secretaries, some of them heading key ministries. Several women have secured appointments as chief executive officers or board chairs of parastatal corporations. In the judicial and legal services, the number of women judges and magistrates has increased from 196 in 2003 to 215 in 2007. In legal service, the number of women lawyers has increased from 1,645 in 2003 to 1,763 in 2008. However, even with the above statistics, a lot more still needs to happen to promote women in leadership at all levels.

Women's Welfare and Health Concerns
A healthy population is a better labor force. Women are the most affected because of their particular health needs (maternity, childcare, sexually transmitted diseases). Inadequate provision of health needs increases women's absenteeism from work and consequently reduces their participation in the formal sector.

Women and Economy
Food security in Africa is uncertain without improving the situation of women producers. Given women's key role in food production, the simple raising of the productivity of women to the same level as that of men would increase the total production by ten to 15 percent, eliminating a key constraint to food security.

When women achieve the same levels of education and experience, and gain access to the same farm inputs that currently benefit the average male farmer, they increase their yields by 22 percent. Consequently, poverty reduction strategies (PRS) are linked to women's access to productive inputs. Longer-term strategies should aim at addressing the underlying problems of gender inequality in agricultural development and support women's crucial contributions to agricultural production.

Women's Employment and Income
Women face greater vulnerabilities in the labor market because of their relative lack of education and training, the tendency to channel women into certain occupations, and the continuous heavy burdens of unpaid domestic work, childbearing and childcare, which restrict the time and energy for income generating activities (Manuh, 1998). Despite high economic participation rates, women are mostly con-

centrated in casual, low skilled, poorly remunerated and irregular forms of informal sector employment.

Sex-stereotyping on the part of parents, educators, religion, the media and society encourage the impression that certain jobs are exclusively for men. Women's "double shift" at home and at work affects their professional progress. In Africa, the home shift includes caring for parents, in-laws and younger siblings. In addition, women have to work twice as hard to prove to men that they are capable of doing their jobs well. There is often a conflict among the three roles of mother, wife and employee, and many feel a sense of guilt and give up employment.

Access to Credit
Government and the local authorities must be committed to removing legal impediments and sociocultural obstacles against women, especially in the rural areas where the majority of women live and are economically active. Women's access to land, credit and extension services, inputs, and new technologies should be free from constraints and opportunities created.

Women should have access to credit at affordable rates, with the private sector assisting government efforts to secure credits for women (Manuh, 1998). Micro-financing, small loans given to the poor generally at slightly elevated interest rates, could play a role in empowering women with no other economic lifeline. Micro-finance is really their one glimmer of hope, their one way out of poverty. It is a potential bridge for the gender gap (Reuters, 2008).

Women in Politics
Women are under-represented in parliament, cabinet-level positions, councils and ambassadorial roles, and in international organizations. Women are also absent from the formal positions of decision-making and power. Even in countries like Zimbabwe and Guinea Bissau, where women participated in armed struggle for national liberation, they still tend to experience marginalization and few attain formal positions of power or gain rights to land and resources in their own names.

Groups such as Emang Basadi in Botswana, the Forum for Women and Democracy in Uganda, the National Women's Lobby Group in Zambia, and the Women's National Coalition in South Africa, have all forced changes in political participation and the rights of women in their countries. In Kenya, the number of women elected members of parliament has grown from one in 1998 to 19 in 2007. However, improvements must extend even further in Kenya and the rest of Africa.

Technologies to Reduce Labor Time
Appropriate technologies for household chores and food processing should be available to women. The provision of portable water and cheap, reliable energy resources will help reduce the long hours that women work.

Women's Rights
Women's empowerment requires that the population in general, as well as the women themselves, know the extent of their problems. Women should understand that girls have equal rights to education as boys and, in the case of a divorce, a full-time housewife is entitled to one third of the family property or 50 percent of the property for any contribution made to an investment during marriage.

What Needs to Change?
Women's Education
In many African countries, parents still prefer to send boys to school and see no need for girls' education. Existing sociocultural norms have so far restricted girls'/women's access to education, training and employment. In addition, factors like adolescent pregnancy, early marriages and girls' greater burden of household labor, act as obstacles to their schooling.

Studies have shown that a woman's education beyond primary school is a reliable route to economic empowerment and long-term change in the *status quo*, as well as being a determinant of a family's nutrition and health. Education beyond ten or more years of school is a reliable predictor to improved infant survival, reduced maternal mortality and an enhanced level of infant development and educational attainment.

There is need for more education and training opportunities for girls and women in Africa, both for overall national development and to improve their individual quality of life. Gender biases in the education system, training and employment must change to give women opportunities for achievement.

Under Representation of Women in Various Sectors
Professional women are under-represented in the ranks of public and private agricultural development services (Saito and Weidemann,

1990). In the economic sector, they are mainly found in the informal sector, where they operate small enterprises (e.g. selling food stuffs and other articles on the streets, and they operate small restaurants). In terms of waged employment, women are mostly found in the teaching and nursing professions, which are generally looked upon as an extension of their caring roles (Fonjong, 2001:223-234).

Gender Stereotyping
The most insidious barrier to women's equal participation in decision-making and leadership is the persistent stereotypical attitudes towards the respective gender roles of women and men. Without a voice in decision-making, women have no access to resources. Without access to resources, women will continue to be sidelined (Razaana, 2004:40-41).

The prevailing firm belief that women do not show leadership potential, and that they behave differently from traditional male leaders in ways that could be detrimental to them, and to the organization (Mathur-Helm, 2005:56-71), could create obstacles to women's promotional chances.

Labor Laws
Women produce more than half the food grown in Africa. However, despite this dominant role, both modern laws and traditional customs make it difficult for women to own land or obtain credit. NEPAD's 2003 Comprehensive Africa Agriculture Development Program states that special attention must be given to the vital food-producing and entrepreneurial roles of women in rural and urban African communities.

Credit and Inputs
In addition to land and labor, women face problems of access to other inputs, including credit, technology, extension services, agricultural training, and marketing. Some credit associations and export-crop marketing cooperatives limit membership to household heads in many countries, thereby excluding most married and unmarried women. Banks demand collateral in the form of landed property and male approval before making loans to women, while men often have been reluctant to support women's applications.

Men growing export crops, with improved seeds and tools going to larger commercial farmers, who are almost invariably men, receive the most resources and technical assistance. Only five percent of the resources provided through extension services in Africa are available to women.

Women and Employment Benefits
When in formal employment, women are disadvantaged in terms of security, remuneration and other benefits such as paid annual leave, paid maternity leave, access to further training and promotion prospects. Low wages are a major source of job dissatisfaction and most women workers supplement their income with income from other activities.

The UN Deputy Secretary General Asha–Rose Migiro said, "Gender equality cannot be a women's business alone, but should concern everyone. We must all work together purposely and vigorously." She expressed concern that, while many African countries have, in the past few years, experienced positive economic growth; sadly, there remains disparities between women and men, boys and girls (Malanda, 2009:14-15).

Ida Odinga, wife of Kenya's Prime Minister asserts, "Women are trapped in a cycle of poverty despite being responsible for 70 to 80 percent of household production." Graca Machel, wife of Nelson Mandela says, "We need people in Africa to realize there is strength in a woman." Women are the backbone of the nations and can help to change them. Quoting Mahatma Gandhi, Graca Machel says, "If the future should be peaceful, then it should be with women." A woman in Kibera, Kenya remarked, "Every day I live, I win. Winning means another day of difficult choices, even the healthy suffer for the sick, staying alive is a full time job" (Fortunate, March 2008).

Vision
Africans are confident that the future of the continent, and its entire people, will be secure when Africans enjoy full gender equality and women are fully empowered and are free from all forms of violence. This dream can and is being achieved (Malanda, 2009:14-15).

Women have a significant role in Africa's socioeconomic development. The New Partnership for African Development (NEPAD) is committed to the cause of strengthening and encouraging women entrepreneurs. Women need to acquire the right skills, and mentoring to harness their abilities as they contribute to Africa's development. Africa's sustainable growth and development are assured if women are enabled to participate actively in the economy (Morgan, 2008).

Training programs are needed to help women develop their technical competence, to enable them to be better informed, better equipped to gain access to political and economic structures, and achieve maximum competence and means. It is critically important for policy-makers to listen and work with women to improve their positions and accelerate Africa's development. African governments should develop laws, policies, procedures and practices that ensure equal rights and opportunities in all sectors.

Governments, in conjunction with development agencies and women, can use a comprehensive approach to remove social, economic and legal constraints on women. Women's institutions in the community, marketplaces and trades, must be recognized and utilized to increase women's participation in decision-making in society. To develop Africa, you must develop the leadership of African women.

Women are called upon to embrace formal and vocational education, learn and practice family planning, and work towards economic empowerment (Muraya, 2008:31). Muraya paints a picture for women entrepreneurship in Africa and predicts that with generation change, more women will take up entrepreneurship in areas less explored, such as Information and Communications Technologies (ICT). If all challenges facing African women entrepreneurs are handled well, the contribution of women to the GDP would be at a growth rate of 3.4 percent. Women need to build their businesses around three key areas: profitability, environmental management and visionary leadership. This will eventually help to accelerate social transformation.

Now is the time to reverse the once tolerated injustices. Now is the time for women, who produce most of Africa's food and cash crops, and undertake the vast majority of care giving, to enjoy their rightful access to ownership and control over land, food, housing and property. It is time for women and girls, many of whom are deprived of the right to literacy and education, to be able to fulfill their capabilities.

If we want to develop Africa, we must develop the leadership of African women.

Policy Recommendations
This paper highlights several issues affecting women's involvement in development. However, each government needs to arise and implement favorable policies in all sectors of the economy. The policies should eliminate discrimination in traditions, laws which violate women's rights, and ease the burden on women of social problems emanating from poverty, unemployment, poor health, childbearing and childcare roles, illiteracy, physical violence and negative cultural practices.

ENDNOTES FOR
Family, Gender and Youth

1 Discussion with Dr. Peter Gathirimu, who is a consultant physician and Registrar at the Department of Internal Medicine, University of Nairobi.

PART 2

Government

Chief Ojo Maduekwe was formerly Minister of Foreign Affairs for the Federal Republic of Nigeria from July 2007-March 2010. He was National Secretary of the ruling political party, the People's Democratic Party (PDP) from 2004-2007.

In previous years, Maduekwe served as Culture and Tourism Minister, and Minister of Transport. He studied law at the University of Nigeria, is the son of an ordained Minister, and is an elder of the Presbyterian Church of Nigeria.

Chief Maduekwe has a rich Christian background with his legal training. He has over 20 years of leadership experience while serving the government of Nigeria. Hon. Maduekwe is married to Ucha and blessed with four children and several grandchildren.

Towards the Theology of the Christian State

Honorable Minister Chief Ojo Maduekwe

Introduction

My charge today is to talk about the theology of the Christian State. The problem is that I am not a professional theologian; I am at best an elder of the Presbyterian Church, and a professing Christian who takes seriously the doctrinal basis of my faith and, therefore, could be engaging, even philosophically, about the faith that animates my worldview. So how am I to speak theologically about the Christian State? Perhaps, the only way I can speak theologically is to speak as a layman who thinks about his religion. My second challenge is how to talk about the Christian State when I am a top government official of a secular State with people of different, and at times, opposing faiths? In other words, should we be talking of a Christian State?

I will proceed in the manner of a reflective churchman and public official who believes that the scripture speaks to the reality of the modern State and can provide effective guidance as to how the State can be responsible for, and responsive to, the needs of its citizens. I will also attempt to define the doctrine and a scripturally justified and theologically mandated theory of the State. Ultimately, I would like to use the scripture and its theological groundings to challenge us, as African leaders, as to the practice of statecraft that will redeem the promise of freedom and prosperity in Africa.

In what sense can we speak about a "theology of the State"? Is it in the sense of how the scriptures define the existing State, or is it in the sense of how scripture defines the ideal State—that is, what the State should be? In other words, are we concerned about the descriptive or prescriptive vision of the State in the scriptures? I will speak of the State in the language of the scripture both from descriptive and prescriptive perspectives. It can be said that the Bible speaks more about "nation" than "State." The Bible begins its story of Creation with individuals mandated to have children. From these individuals and their children the idea of a Nation, of a people, began to take shape. The history of Creation, the Fall, and Redemption in the Bible hinges on the concept of "a nation."

After the Fall of man in Chapter 2 of Genesis, God bestowed His grace upon Abraham, who was to become the source of a nation that would be used to realize the promise of redemption. Genesis, Chapter 12, verses 1-2 underline the centrality of the concept of "the nation" in the divine agenda: the Lord said to Abraham, "Leave your country, your people and your father's household and go to the land where I will show you. I will make you into a great nation and I will bless you; I will make your name great, and you will be a blessing" (NIV 1984).

Max Weber (2000) provides the most authoritative and accepted definition of the State in his book, *Politics as a Vocation*. He says that a State is, "a sovereign entity within a defined territory that holds a monopoly of the legitimate use of violence in the enforcement of its orders." The *Wikipedia* online reference (2009) defines "the nation" as a "body of people who share a real or imagined common history, culture, language or ethnic origin, who typically inhabits a particular country or territory." It is clear from the definitions that the nation is of more ancient origin than the State. Most modern States consist of multiple nations, and have real or imagined common histories, cultures, languages, etc. It is appropriate that the Bible begins its account with a nation formed from an individual and his immediate family. Much later in the New Testament, we begin to encounter the State, especially the Roman Empire, which was an imperial state. The difference between the State and the nation, and their relationship, will become a useful analytical tool when we consider how the Christian community should view the State.

The State is primarily a legal concept. From Weber's definition of the State, we can derive some formal characteristics of the State. Weber (2000) defines the State in terms of sovereignty; the State is sovereign within its territory. This means that the State dominates through the expression of its will. Weber also says that the violence the State exercises is legitimate; it is made legal by law. The idea of the State is tied to the legal relationship between people in a given territory. The exercise of violence by the State is in pursuance of its judicial and administrative orders. We encounter the legal basis of the State in Paul's challenge of his ill treatment by zealous soldiers. He reminded them that he was a Roman citizen. Quoting this passage in full is well deserved:

> And they listened to him until this word, and then they raised their voices and said, 'Away with such a *fellow* from the earth, for he is not fit to live!'
>
> Then, as they cried out and tore off their clothes and threw dust into the air, the commander ordered him to be brought into the barracks, and said that he should be examined under scourging, so that he might know why they shouted so against him. And as they bound him with thongs, Paul said to the centurion, who stood by, 'is it lawful for you to scourge a man who is a Roman, and uncondemned?'
>
> When the centurion heard that, he went and told the commander, saying, 'Take care what you do, for this man is a Roman.'
>
> Then the commander came and said to him, 'Tell me, are you a Roman?' He said, 'Yes.'
>
> And the commander answered, 'with a large sum I obtained this citizenship.'
>
> And Paul said, 'But I was born a citizen.'
>
> Then immediately those who were about to examine him withdrew from him; and the commander was also afraid after he found out that he was a Roman, and because he had bound him [italics added]. (Acts 22:22-29, New King James Version NKJV)

This encounter between St. Paul and his attackers dramatizes the proposition that at the heart of the State is the idea of the legitimate exercise of violence. The State must exercise violence legitimately because of the idea of citizenship. Citizenship is a bundle of rights, which further constrains the exercise of violence in a designated territory. This experience of the power of the State to protect citizens from undignified treatment and to secure for them the social space for the exercise of religious consciousness is at the heart of the Pauline theology of the State. This theology has become the cornerstone of liberal theories of the State as of Thomas Hobbes and John Locke. It is important to pursue this concept of the State, as a guarantor of social peace and social space for a flourishing life of dignity and faith, which God has mandated and is working out in human history. However, we must proceed in this inquiry by underlining the fact that a State is that entity which exercises a legitimate monopoly of violence in a given territory.

The State in the Biblical Mirror

The Bible is a book of the story of man and his relationship with God. The relationship between God and man necessarily casts a shadow on the relationship between human beings. As we observed, the story of human relationship in the Bible begins with a bilateral relationship between God and a man. It then includes the man's wife and his children. Soon it expands to include a nation. Abraham is the anchor of the making of the nation that carried the message of redemption to the people of the world. When God spoke to Abraham about his descendants possessing the land of Canaan, He had in mind the birth of a nation that would reflect the divine agenda on earth. That idea of a holy nation took greater shape after the Exodus and the formation of a putative State in the wilderness.

It is important to bear in mind that by the time God began to put together the model of the holy nation—Israel—nations and nation-states already existed in the territories that bounded Palestine. These were States built on conquest; these were heathen nations and nation-states. Their practices were outrageous and constituted the moral background for the exceptionalism of the nation of Israel. After God delivered Israel from the house of bondage, He made it a nation under the leadership of Moses.

The book of Deuteronomy narrates how Israel became a nation-state. The new nation God was constructing on the soil of Canaan would be a different nation. The holy nation had to eliminate the religious and social symbolisms of the pagan nations that inhabited

Canaan, and it had to establish a new society founded on a new theology and anthropology. Israel is a "…people holy to the Lord your God. The Lord your God has chosen you out of all the peoples on the face of the earth to be his people, his treasured possession" (Dt 7:6, NIV 1984). The nation of Israel was to be different from the nations existing in the Old Testament world, in terms of their exclusive devotion to God and in their obedience to His ordinances. The need to preserve the nation from the syncretism and idolatry of its neighbors necessitated the enactment of the Ten Commandments and other regulations comprised in the Torah. Little wonder the Torah has become an enduring icon of the Western world.

From a scriptural point of view, the State is an instrument in the hands of God. It is an instrument, a vehicle for the redemption of the world. States existed before the formation of the State of Israel. These States were pagan states in as much as they never had a direct and sustained relationship with Jehovah. However, they remained instruments in the hands of God. As occasions demanded, pagan states assisted in the birth of Israel and to punish Israel when it failed to live by divine covenant. God's dealing with Israel as a nation shows that states serve utilitarian purposes. The prophets commended or denounced every state according to how it fulfilled the divine agenda of world redemption. The State does not have an essential value; its value is instrumental. If it helps to proclaim the glory of God on earth, then it fulfills its purpose. Theologically, the purpose of the State must relate to its redemption on earth. The State is to teach and model righteousness. The State is to become the oracle of God. The State is an instrument for the maintenance of social justice.

Israel's failure to live up to the high ideals of the founding covenant with God led to the belief amongst early Christians that the Church superseded Israel as the nation of God. St. Peter also compared the Church to the new Israel nation when he argued that the early Christians have become, "…a chosen people, a royal priesthood, a holy nation, a people belonging to God, that you may declare the praises of him who called you out of darkness into his marvelous light" (1 Pt 2:9, NIV 1984). The Church is the new holy nation inaugurated to proclaim the praise of God. Later in his missionary work, the Apostle Paul had cause to review the nature of the State and its theological justification. In his letter to the Romans, Paul focused on laying down the theological explanation of the role of the State in the sinful world; that is, to be recreated through the redemption in Christ Jesus. By the time of the apostles, there was a transition from viewing the State as an instrument of divine mandate to being an indirect instrument of divine justice. In fact, the condemnation of the world in the gospel of Christ meant that the State was deeply mired in sustained rebellion against God. The State was no longer relied upon to promote righteousness. Its responsibility had moved more towards creating an environment that allowed the elect (the people of God) to worship God and fulfill His redemptive purpose. Paul now lays out the purpose of the State as simply to punish evil and promote justice. This is now the new minimum condition of the State: to exercise its monopoly of violence, to deter evil and encourage good. The State is now a schoolmaster leading us to virtuous behavior and not necessarily glorifying God. This is captured in the long paragraph of Romans 13:1-6 (NIV 1984):

> Everyone must submit himself to the governing authorities, for there is no authority except that which God has established. The authorities that exist have been established by God.
>
> Consequently, he who rebels against the authority is rebelling against what God has instituted, and those who do so will bring judgment on themselves.
>
> For rulers hold no terror for those who do right, but for those who do wrong. Do you want to be free from fear of the one in authority? Then do what is right and he will commend you.
>
> For he is God's servant to do you good. But if you do wrong, be afraid, for he does not bear the sword for nothing. He is God's servant, an agent of wrath to bring punishment on the wrongdoer.
>
> Therefore, it is necessary to submit to the authorities, not only because of possible punishment but also because of conscience.
>
> This is also why you pay taxes, for the authorities are God's servants, who give their full time to governing.

The Church and State in Modern Politics

One trend of thought unites the Old and New Testament. It is the commitment to justice and righteousness. The Bible is unrelenting in its commitment that every human institution should promote justice and righteousness. Righteousness is defined more from the perspectives of human dignity and freedom. The prophet Isaiah insists that we, "Stop doing wrong, learn to do right! Seek justice, encourage the oppressed. Defend the cause of the fatherless, plead the case of the widow" (Is 1:16b-17, NIV 1984). The prophet Amos summarizes the obligation of justice and righteousness as "Hate evil, love good; maintain justice in the courts" (Am 5:15a, NIV 1984). Righteousness is a broad concept closely related to mercy, goodness of heart, love of neighbor, compassion for the poor and the weak, gentleness, the capacity for giving joy, forbearance, justice, especially towards the needy, and many other virtues.

On the negative side, the State stood for "the absence of avarice, bloodshed, destructiveness, bribery, violence, envy, oppression, and tyranny" (Gingerich, 1968:158). These qualities were not handed down through a kingly edict or a democratic legislation, but because of the covenant relationship of the holy nation. They are the very nature of God and constitute the essence of the claim to a special relationship to God.

> As they understood it, God's purpose in history was to build community, that is, to call to Himself a people, who were reconciled to Him and to each other. They recognized that injustice, oppression, hatred, and the lack of mercy and compassion always militate against the ideals of a people of God. (Gingerich, 1968:158-9)

Since the Enlightenment, the relationship between Christianity and the State has been controversial. It is the general thinking today that the Church should leave the State alone. The separation between Christianity, as represented by the organized Church, and the State is somewhat now complete. Two dominant characteristics of this separation are the retreat of the State as an enabler of Christian belief and the devaluation of religious insights in the governance of the modern State. This dominant liberal order emerged because of the struggle for power and ended up changing the philosophical and political landscape of Europe. In fact, the history of liberal democracy is an offshoot of this struggle. Pierre Manent, French philosopher and liberal theorist, argues (1995:4) insightfully that modern liberalism was built on what he calls the "theo-political crisis" at the root of Western philosophy.

The relationship between the Church and the State is now more a matter of deference than of interference and subordination as in the early days of organized Church. We still observe occasional flashpoints of interference and interventions by organized Christianity in the affairs of the State, especially in the United States where the Christian Right continues to wage a battle to define the character of the State. The defining aspect of this relationship is the loss of faith in the potential of the modern State to play a significant role in the redemption of the world. St. Augustine in his magisterial work, *The City of God*, ably captures the loss of faith in the State as an instrument of righteousness. Augustine argues that the secular State is trapped in sin and therefore, cannot be obedient or submissive to God. As he puts it (Powell, 2001:79), "A secular society is unjust both in that it denies to God the sacrifice that is his due, and because in so doing it leaves its members 'alienated from God' and by that fact 'wretched.'" St. Augustine has become a decisive influence in Western philosophy and his legacy has defined the uneasy relationship between Christianity and the State.

St. Augustine and his followers settled on the promotion of peace and justice as the theological value of the State. Sam Amadi (2004a) has argued that the interpreters of St. Augustine have emphasized the twin principles of sin and human goodness as indicative of the character of the modern State. The first makes justice necessary and the latter makes it possible. Powell (2001:81) argues that "freed from any need to posit the fundamental goodness of any society other than *The City of God*, Augustine is also free of the temptation either to idolize or demonize society and the State. He can see them for what they are in truth, the site of the ongoing, universal human search for temporary peace that is God's greatest gift suitable for this world." Augustinians, therefore, engage in social justice from the point of view of securing peace such that we may do the will of God. They do not share such high hopes of human social redemption through "a secularized righteous order" (Amadi, 2004b). The Augustinian uncertainty about the theological character of the modern State has created ambivalence in commitment to human rights for, as Powell (2001:86) puts it,

> The Augustinian, then, has good theological reasons to support the enforcement of certain individual rights as a strategy for protecting and promoting the temporary peace of American society. At the same time, it would be a mistake to ignore the negative impact, which cultural rights have on the members of the American society, including the society's Christian members.

St. Thomas Aquinas, the intellectual godfather of Catholic social teaching, differed significantly from St. Augustine in the theological grounding of the State. St. Aquinas (*circa* 1270), the synthesizer, placed more emphasis on human goodness and the power of right reason. His commitment to justice goes beyond revelation and is equally grounded in right reason, even though right reason is enlightened by revelation. These conceptions of justice, human goodness and the nature of the State suggest greater concern about the State and more faith in its potential to facilitate the godly life. Catholics, who are custodians of Thomas Aquinas' theological grounding of the State, have proved to be resistant to the radical separation of Church and State that the Enlightenment brought in its wake.

It is difficult to talk about the Christian State whether in terms of a State inhabited by Christians alone, or a State that is committed to what is generally referred to as Judeo-Christian values. The fact of religious and philosophical pluralism and the dominance of the civic ethic of tolerance have made it almost passé to talk of the Christian State, whether in Europe, North America or Africa. The world has come of age. This coming of age is characterized by the denial of exclusive privilege to the Christian faith. The ideal of tolerance, which has almost become the religion of the secularized world, now forbids the appropriation of the public space for the proclamation of any faith, even the Christian faith. Political philosophers are now struggling to discover an overlapping consensus within which we can sense a public reason that provides secular morality for the modern State. John Rawls (1996), Harvard political philosopher, tried to sketch a political liberalism that can provide ethical justification for the secular State.

Two factors have led to the world coming of age and the decline of the influence of organized Christianity in politics in the post-Enlightenment world. The first is internal to the Christian faith and the other is external to the faith. The internal and external factors worked together to undermine the privilege of organized Christianity. The internal factor is the tendency amongst some believers to resent the authority of the Church and resort to internalizing belief. In this sense, the essence of religious belief was reformatted to focus less on the performance and more on the conscience and belief. The persecuted minority Christians did not want the State to interfere in religious affairs because the State has become the handmaid of organized Church. This led to the privatization of religious experience. William James (1982:504) captured this new dimension of religious experience in his classic work, *The Varieties of Religious Experience*. The true religious experience is the inward experience of the religious person. He argues that:

> The theories, which Religion generates, being thus variable, are secondary; and if you wish to grasp her essence, you must look to the feelings and the conduct as being the more constant elements. It is between these two elements that the short circuit exists on which she carries on her principal business, while the ideas and symbols and other institutions form loop-lines which may be perfections and improvements, and may even some day all be united into one harmonious system, but which are not to be regarded as organs with an indispensable function, necessary at all times for religion to go on.

Reflecting on the way the organized Church has corrupted itself through engagement with the State, and how this necessitated the internalization of religious experience, William James (1982:334-335) argues that:

> A survey of history shows us that, as a rule, religious geniuses attract disciples, and produce groups of sympathizers. When these groups get strong enough to 'organize' themselves, they become ecclesiastical institutions with corporate ambitions of their own. The spirit of politics and the lust of dogmatic rule are then apt to enter and contaminate the originally innocent thing.

Dorothee Soelle (1974) supports this view and argues that, under imperial Rome, the ecclesiastical Church turned Christianity into a political religion and intermingled with the imperial State to the extent that the State itself became an object of religious worship.

Professor Charles Taylor (2003:11), one of this century's most versatile philosophers, revisited the William James thesis and concluded that the result of this internal protest at religious conformism and ecclesiastical hegemony is the belief that to take religion seriously "is to take it personally, more devotionally, inwardly, more committedly. Just taking part in external rituals, those that do not require the kind of personal engagement, which, say, with its self-examination and promise of amendment entails, is devalued on this understanding.

This isn't what religion is all about." The result of this internal protest at ecclesiastical religion is to value personal devotion as opposed to external rituals as being the essence of religion. The privatization of religion has implications for the theological concept of the place of the State in the divine order. It works together with the external dynamic—secularization—to make a theological conception of the State difficult.

Secularization as a force of history seems to be running down with the resurgence of religious extremism, especially in the form of political Islam in many parts of the Middle East. There is a sense in which we can say that the world is witnessing some form of de-secularization. Nevertheless, the imprints of secularization are still visible and definitive to constitute a background for the theology of the State today. One can describe the medieval period as an age of enchantment; God was the center of physics and metaphysics. The invariableness of the Holy Scripture predicated moral realism. The Roman Church proclaimed its authority even over science. The overthrow of the Platonian world and its replacement with the Newtonian world meant a breach with the tutelage of the ecclesiastical institution.

Charles Taylor (2003:66) describes the disenchantment of the world in the wake of the Enlightenment as:

> A shift from the enchanted world to a cosmos conceived in conformity with post-Newtonian science, in which there is absolutely no possibility of higher meanings being expressed in the universe around us. But, there is still, with someone like Newton himself, for instance, a strong sense that the universe declares the glory of God.

The privatization of religion in the wake of the Enlightenment goes a long way to displace religious values and ideals as the legitimacy of the modern State. Instead of grounding the modern State in the ideal of the divine order, we construct values and ideals that share the same commitments to human dignity and freedom as the divine order. The key point is that these constructed values do not find their justification in God and His divine purpose. Charles Taylor (2003:70) argues that the rift with the past comes:

> From the fact that what makes this order the right one is, for many, though not by all means for all, no longer God's providence; the order is grounded in nature alone, or in some con-

cept of civilization, or even in supposedly unchallengeable a priori principles, often inspired by Kant.

Therefore, where do we stand today with respect to the theological explanation of the modern State? Well, it is definitely obvious that we cannot speak about the State as an instrument of righteousness as the Old Testament prophets are wont to assert. We also cannot argue, as the Roman Catholic fathers argued, against the imperial State in the mediaeval era that the social order is under the control, direction and guardianship of the ecclesiastic Church. But, we can still speak about the moral character and moral obligation of the State. The truly modern State is religiously neutral, but that does not make it amoral. The modern State is still moral in as much as it pursues the promotion of some ideals that are somewhat related, though indirectly, to religious doctrines. In this way, the modern State still pursues the functions of promoting peace and justice, which St. Paul assigned to it in his epistle. We can, therefore, argue that though the State is not our father, as Yale Law School Professor, Stephen Carter (1994), would say, "the State enables us to worship God as we choose."

What is left theologically, after the debris of secularization, is a State that commits itself to protecting an environment that enables men and women to worship God as their inner light. This is the resolution of the 'theo-political crisis' at the root of Western liberalism. All the major theologians from John Locke to Jurgen Habermas have announced the triumph of liberalism and the enthronement of liberal tolerance as the ethic of civic State. All the divergent theories of liberalism converge in reflecting the "trend of intellectual debate about God, human nature, truth and freedom. Even as the correlation between moral and theological skepticism and tolerance is not linear, one can safely say that a certain intellectual atmosphere characterized by critical biblical scholarship, disapproval of religious authority, empiricism, and rationalism provided the intellectual persuasion for the idea of tolerance and the right of conscience" (Amadi, 2004a). The challenge is to speak about the State theologically in an overlapping consensus such that the exclusivities of God are either concealed or conflated into a Kantian universalism.

I think the post-Enlightenment theology of the State can be sketched along Pauline lines. Going by the devastating critique of St. Augustine and the disenchantment, which the post-Newtonian world has experienced, the State may no longer be conceived in the prophetic tradition of the instrument of divine righteousness. In the world that has rejected the reign of God, either through His prophets or the ecclesiastical institution, the State will pursue a minimum agenda. The responsibility of the State will be to secure the social environment for the people of God to freely worship God. The State will not be a schoolmaster to lead people to righteousness in the sense of living like the covenant people of God. However, it should be a schoolmaster to punish evil and reward good. The question remains as to how the State could discern between evil and good when it has banished the prophetic voice. After sidelining God, how do we still speak coherently about evil and good?

The world seems to have found its own way in the midst of the debris of the collapse of the enchanted word by secularizing Christian virtues into what today stands as the eternal edifice of the Universal Declaration of Human Rights and its many legalistic progenies. The secular State has now transmuted its theocratic essence into the assertion that God created all human beings, endowing them with dignity and freedom. The pursuit of freedom, life and happiness, in the language of the United States' *Declaration of Independence*, now defines the essence and purpose of the State. The legitimacy of the modern State is defined by its commitment to monopolize violence in the society to achieve for its citizens human dignity, freedom and happiness. This reformulation of the theocratic nature of the State has attained universal acceptance at least to the extent that nations that do not comply with the requirement of protecting human rights try to explain away their failure.

Cast into scriptural terms, a commitment to promoting dignity, freedom and happiness of the people will fall into the Pauline model of the responsible State. The modern State should be strong and humanized so that it can protect social peace in order to enable the people of God to live peaceful lives. Such a State should also inhabit a moral universe that will constrain it to recognize and punish evil and reward good behavior, so that there will be little disincentive for those who want to live the righteous life. St. Augustine's ambivalent conception of the State best exemplifies the Pauline thesis. The secular State, like the natural man, is a fallen entity. It does not know God and cannot submit to the will of God. Yet, it retains some mark of the divine nature as long as we continue to inarticulately seek God, even in the guise of our narcissism. The theocratic State is replaced with a technocratic State, with a Kantian commitment to universalize the good in the secular terms of life, freedom and happiness.

The New Theology of the State and the African Predicament
I call this Augustinian concept of the State a new "theology" of the State. What does this new theology say about the State in Africa and state (nation) building in Africa? First, we should see in the Augustine and Pauline theology of the State an understanding of power and violence. Neither St. Augustine nor St. Paul is sentimental about the fact and reality of the use of force in human community. They prefigured the realism of Max Weber; the State is the master of violence. Nevertheless, the State must ensure that its monopoly of violence produces the minimum violence for the social good, order and peace. Straight away, we recognize that the precarious state of some African countries wracked by civil wars and internal insurrection compromises a core component of the responsible State. State failure negates the Pauline theology of the State. Every State should retain humanized control of violence within its territory. Failure of a State to maintain legitimate control of violence in its territory places it inside the column of an irresponsible State. State failure is a negation of the divine mandate for the modern State. It does not glorify God if States become the playfields of insurgents and warlords. It is important to note the caveat that such a monopoly on violence must be legitimate.

Illegitimate monopoly on violence does not make a State responsible. The State fails mainly from a chronic crisis of illegitimacy. State failure may be denoted by many interesting features including, the inability of the State to control the use of violence within its territory, failure to provide good enough social services, and the capture of State apparatus by a small minority who seek to enforce their will on the excluded majority. Harvard University Professor Rotberg, one of the leading authorities on State failures, offers an interesting analysis of the manifestation of State failure (2004; quoted in Maduekwe, 2006). In his view:

> A collapsed State exhibits a vacuum of authority. It is a mere geographical expression, a black hole, into which a failed polity has fallen. Sub-state actors take over. These warlords or sub-

state actors gain control over regions and sub-regions of what has been a nation-state, build up their own local security apparatuses and mechanisms, sanction markets, and other trading arrangements, and even establish an attenuated form of international relations.

Underlying the crisis of legitimacy at the root of State failure, Rotberg (2004; quoted in Maduekwe, 2005:208) argues that:

> Once the State's capacity to secure itself or to perform in an expected manner recedes, and once what little capacity remains is devoted exclusively to the fortunes of a few or to a favored ethnicity or community, then there is every reason to expect less and less loyalty to the State on the part of the excluded and disenfranchised. When the rulers are perceived to be working for themselves and their kin, and not the State, their legitimacy, and the State's legitimacy, plummet. The State increasingly comes to be perceived as being owned by an exclusive group, with all others pushed aside.

This criterion of legitimacy in the management of violence underlines the importance of the institution of "the rule of law." A responsible State is one whose monopoly of violence in a designated territory is legitimate. Legitimacy is a legal and political concept. As a legal concept, it means that the exercise of power (which is the same as the monopoly of violence) should be underwritten by an appeal to higher authority. This higher authority could be the constitution, a basic law or established convention. This is what St. Paul articulates as submission to the higher authority. Politically, legitimacy relates to the approval, which the State receives from the body polity, concerning its management of violence. If the majority of the people have withdrawn support for the State, maybe in the quest for self-determination, the State ceases to exercise monopoly of violence in a politically legitimate manner, even if it still sources its power from the constitution or basic law.

Today, the idea of legitimacy is most relevant to the African predicament in terms of commitment to free and fair elections and promotion of rule-based behavior. Free and fair elections should not be seen as a Western imposition or as theologically problematic for the Christian. In the secular world, the voices of the prophets and the priests have become the voice of "We the People." We can see the intimation of this transformation in the early history of the people of God when they asked for a king in order to be like the other nations and God asked Samuel to oblige the people of their request. We also behold this oracular voice of, "We the People" much later, when the people, elders, and captains of Israel came together and agreed to make David king, even though he had been anointed king by Samuel years before.

The new theology of the State must proclaim first that a responsible State must entrench free and fair elections at the core of its definitive character. In an age where political authorities have discarded the gospel and are, therefore, not privy to prophetic inspiration, the people become the new priests and prophets to inaugurate the higher authority that can legitimately monopolize the exercise of violence. As Leszek Kolakowski (1990:179) rightly observed, although the politics had dispensed with religious justification and neither the priest nor the Pope can control the emperor or the king anymore, the prince must still seek divine authorization. There is no other divinity beyond the people themselves. The voice of the people is the voice of God in statecraft.

Free and fair elections have another important value in the new theology of the State. They help to preserve the legitimacy of power in a manner that stabilizes society. We may never have the sort of social peace that St. Paul thinks necessary for effective worship of God, if we do not secure the foundation of free and fair elections. In today's secularized world, social peace is only sustainable through a political succession system benchmarked by free and fair elections. One clear implication of the sequestration of politics from ecclesiastical control is the phenomenon of inter-subjectivity, which means that after the deluge of modernity and enlightenment, we now speak different voices. Each voice represents a worldview, a moral belief system, what John Rawls (1996:159) calls a "comprehensive doctrine." It is difficult to harmonize these voices except through proceduralized neutrality, which allows people to communicate inter-subjectively; that is, to provide justification to other people who do not share their basic premises. The implication of secularism in the matter of statecraft is that we can no longer justify political authority by reference to any scriptural or priestly tradition. Political authority must proceed from within us. The fiction for this general will is electoral democracy.

Thomas Hobbes (1651) and John Locke (1689) grasped this vital truth; hence, they resorted to securing political legitimacy after the Enlightenment through a contrivance called *The Social Contract*. *The Social Contract* is another way of explaining the need for procedural-ized neutrality in which the citizens of a secular State act both stra-tegically and communicatively. While maintaining their competing worldviews and strategic interests, they still find a way of forming a government to protect their common need for security and free-dom. In Africa, the need for convergence is even more pronounced as many fault-lines have emerged, the fault-lines of religious dif-ferences and the fault-lines of ethnic or sub-ethnic identities. With the added breakdown of authoritarian regimes that had the look of pseudo-ecclesiastical establishments, divergence has become a constitutive order in Africa. Only the institution of free and fair elec-tions can convert these divergences into an overlapping consensus for the promotion of the theological goods of social peace and free-dom in Africa.

Apart from the institution of free and fair elections, African states will do well to accept the establishment of a culture of "rule of law" in private and public transactions. This is another aspect of the legiti-macy question. Without the rule of law, there can be no justice. As St. Augustine (415, Chapter IV) wisely observed, "without justice na-tions are like bands of robbers." The political stability and economic prosperity of a nation is guaranteed only when the rule of law is fully established and protected in its systems. Rule of law is central to any effort to rebuild the African States.

I have argued elsewhere (Maduekwe, 2005:214) that a failed State is the ultimate proof of the failure of the rule of law. The State is the muscular expression of the law in its ultimate form.

> In modern times, it has come to represent the supreme expression of the will of the people. When it collapses, the entire legal liga-ments are torn into shreds and in their place is a no-man's land that celebrates arbitrariness and brute force. The prevention of State failure and indeed the reconstruction of a failed State must look closely in the direction of restoring the rule of law.

The rule of law challenge is not just about making the judiciary work independently and impartially; it is also about laying new mo-rality of public life. The essence of the rule of law is, as Susan Rose Ackerman (quoted in Maduekwe, 2005:217) puts it, "not just the ability to assert power over others, but also the ability to justify the exercise of power to those who feel its weight." The idea of the rule of law is incompatible with the culture of impunity and unaccountable management of human and natural resources in Africa. Not just dictatorial governments daily breach the requirement of transparency and accountability. Business and community leaders are not significantly different in placing themselves at the judgment of those they lead. The churches in Africa may be the biggest victims of the so-called, "African Big-man" syndrome. Christian leaders in Africa have appropriated the divine right of kingship to constitute themselves into the new ecclesiastical hegemony. You can imagine the tragic effects of unaccountable priestly power in a culture of authoritarian politics.

Just as African leaders must establish and strengthen where strong foundations for a State of the rule of law exist, they must also enhance the capacity for effective social service delivery. This includes effective administration of justice. A State is not a proper State if it fails to provide the good life for its citizens. One feature of State failure is a chronic incapacity to deliver basic social services. The vision of the Kantian universalism that has replaced the theocratic justification of the State includes the commitment to provide social and economic structure of the life of dignity. The Universal Declaration of Human Rights (UN, 1948) and its legal progenies have included economic and social rights as core fundamental objectives and directive principles of good governance. Any State that fails to demonstrate a real commitment to secure the economic and social foundations for the protection of life, liberty and freedom for its citizens fails both the theocratic and secular conceptions of the purposes of the State.

The challenge of building a critical infrastructure in Africa should be linked to the need to avoid the fate of State failure and the commitment to building a State that truly answers to both the Pauline and Weberian descriptions. A State that cannot maintain basic infrastructures cannot deliver basic social services and will very soon run out of legitimacy. It will even compromise its theological justification as it fails to guarantee peace and encourage the virtuous and righteous life. Christian leaders, while engaged in building the State, should bear in mind that no matter how secularized the city of man, it remains the only real grooming site for those who will be heirs of the throne of glory.

The Responsibility of Christian Politicians in the Secular State
The Christian State does not exist. But, the State still exists and its relevance to godly life on earth is not diminished. Therefore, how do we deal with the State? What should be the commitment to the State of the politician who is also a Christian? First, the Christian politician must understand the character of the State. The Pauline thesis remains true. The secular State, just like the carnal mind, does not understand the things of God and cannot submit to God. This is simply a theological statement of fact. Our Lord has declared to us forthrightly that the whole world lies in wickedness, as if it were in the grip of the evil one. No secular idealism or revolutionary commitment should obscure the fallen nature of the secular world.

What is the essence of this fallen nature; this separation from God? In the language of the New Testament, it is rebellion; the spirit of independence from God. The world's coming of age is also its rejection of divine guidance and abidance in grace. Just like the Children of Israel rejected theocracy and asked for a king to lead them like other nations and God unveiled for them a world of capricious and self-serving monarchs, so also the world that has eaten the fruit of the knowledge of good and evil, has to contend with diabolic manifestations. Leszek Kolakowski (1997:175) has described politics (and by extension the State) as the "realm of the devil." He argues that to the extent that politics is a struggle for power, it is "bound to be the realm of the devil by definition; it then simply releases out *libido dominandi* as a drive that expands, as it were, for the sake of its own expansion and has no objective beyond itself." The reason why the realm of politics easily becomes the realm of the devil is because:

> Once political goods acquire autonomy and become ends in themselves, they are at the service of the devil. (*ibid*:176)

One should expect, as Kolakowski states (1997:177), in conformance to Christian and, in particular, Augustinian teachings, that:

> Any area of life, if it achieves independence and issues for itself all verdicts about what is good, valid, excellent, or proper in it, falls under the sway of the devil. Those verdicts, one can argue, then become a matter of free human choice, and human choice—not informed by grace—naturally opts for evil; whether in making those choices we surrender to an actual diabolic

temptation or to our own rotten nature, the result will inevitably invigorate the infernal forces.

These are crushing words. They seem to place politics in a "no win" situation. Kolakowski (*ibid*:181) continues his depreciation of politics in a secular State by likening it to a "hunting ground of the devil as it is directly responsible for wars, persecutions, and all imaginable and unimaginable atrocities which the struggle for power brings about."

It is a misreading of Kolakowski's insights to simply shrug our shoulders and sign off from politics. He does not argue that politics, as a realm of human endeavor, is uniquely diabolical. What makes the realm of politics the realm of the devil is not politicking per se, but that the sin nature will—without the grace of God—lead to *libido dominandi*. In fact, the *libido dominandi* may be more devastating on private spheres where the struggle for power and choice remains visible. In the same passage where he argued that politics seems to be the hunting ground for devils, Kolakowski argues (*ibid*:181-182) that:

> The demons from the department of politics can be simpletons or debutantes, whereas those who operate in art, philosophy, and science must be much wiser, subtler, and more farsighted. The evil produced by tyrants and conquerors is intentional, easily identifiable, and in part even calculable, but who can identify and calculate the evil that resulted (unintentionally) over the centuries from the mindsets of great philosophers and artists, from the creative toil of Plato, Copernicus, Descartes, Rousseau, or Wagner.

The sinfulness of the vocation of politics should not de-motivate the Christian politician from politics. The understanding of the inherent diabolism of "the pursuit of power" should rather support the seeking of grace and commitment to seek true transformation. It should also serve as enlightenment for those who have swallowed the revolutionary rhetoric of secular ideologies without locating the deceptive chalices in which their brews are served. An understanding of the heinous nature of the secular State should free us from any easy victory and false optimism. It should steel us to fight the good fight of faith even in the cesspit of political struggle for power.

The responsibility of the Christian politician, therefore, is to first acknowledge that the world lies in wickedness and any realm that sequesters itself from the influences of the grace of Christ easily becomes the "hunting ground of devils." He or she has to affirm that evil is bigger than him or her, but resolve that evil should not occur by his or her hand. We cannot just wring our hands and say, "the whole world lies in wickedness and continues to support the diabolism of politics." We must be like the Pergamum Christian of whom the Lord testified that:

> I know where you live—where Satan has his throne. Yet you remain true to my name. You did not renounce your faith in me, even in the days of Antipas, my faithful witness, who was put to death in your city—where Satan lives. (Rev 2:13, NIV 1984)

The Christian politician must be an agent of light and transformation. Even as the secular State is no longer the instrument of redemption, the Christian politician must work hard to ensure that the State continues to maintain its legitimacy without which it cannot be an instrument of peace and social justice in today's world. Whatever the State lacks in theological grace, it must make up for in technocratic capacity and liberal disposition. The African State should realign to the creative Augustinian ambivalence and experience freedom from the theocratic leftovers of a dead age.

The African Christian politician should work hard to entrench in the culture of statecraft the passionate commitment to an overlapping consensus that is based on the inter-subjective communication of persons who have become autonomous. Any statecraft that continues to pretend that there is an Archimedean perspective for overcoming the crisis of the State is misplaced. The solution may well rest in finding a constructive platform for engagement between the *Moral Man and Immoral Society* of Reinhold Niebuhr's universe.

H. E. Stephen Kalonzo Musyoka has served Kenya in several different government positions, including: Assistant Minister for Works and Physical Planning, Minister for Foreign Affairs and International Co-operation, Minister for Education, Information, Tourism and the Environment and Vice President.

Traveling widely, Musyoka has represented the country during major global meetings and events such as the United Nations General Assembly.

In 2008, amid a tumultuous and sadly, violent presidential election bid, Stephen Kalonzo Musyoka was appointed Vice President of the Republic of Kenya and Minister of Home Affairs. He is married to Mrs. Pauline Kalonzo Musyoka and they have four children.

Christianity and the Pursuit of Good Governance

H. E. Dr. Stephen Kalonzo Musyoka
Vice President and Minister of Home Affairs
Republic of Kenya

Introduction

The relationship between religion and government is a recurrent subject of discussion and debate in many parts of the world. One of the most topical themes in this regard is about whether religion should be separate from the State. The theme often attracts mixed opinions that lie on a continuum. On one end, we have opinions that favor the complete separation of the religious domain from the domain of the State—that is, separation between the sacred and the secular. On the other end of the continuum is an opinion that favors a fusion of State and religion to produce a theocracy. Many variants of the two opinions exist along this continuum. The debate on this subject becomes especially active in periods of social strife and political stress, as societies seek ways to overcome collective challenges and attain political stability, as well as social and economic progress.

The consensus is that democratic governance offers the most promising solution to the problems and challenges that face human society. Indeed, other forms of organizing society have created or exacerbated these problems rather than help to solve them. Theocracies also fall in the latter category, regardless of the particular religion that they may be based upon.

Here in Africa, an attempt at theocracy was made in Sudan under the government of President Gaffaar Numeiry; this endeavor, unfortunately, contributed to the outbreak of a protracted civil war. Indeed, the Comprehensive Peace Agreement (CPA) signed in Kenya in 2005, lifted the application of a particular set of religious doctrine upon people with other religious beliefs in the course of governance of the State. The CPA was in some way, therefore, an effort to move away from theocracy in favor of democracy. Lately, an attempt to introduce sharia law in some states in Nigeria has resulted in violent resistance in which many lives have been lost, property destroyed, and pre-existing peace and social harmony disturbed.

Theocracy is, therefore, an inappropriate framework for governance, because society is characterized by religious diversity and each one of the diverse religious groups expects and deserves respect. Furthermore, other bases of diversity also exist and each category similarly expects and deserves respect. From the standpoint of the plurality of religions and other interests in society, one can quickly appreciate the appropriateness of democracy and, for that matter, the separation of State and religion.

While the merit for separation of religion and statecraft cannot be gainsaid, an understanding of such separation in its absolutist sense, whereby religious conscience is out of bounds in the governance—in the management of the State—can only be absurd. Indeed, the core of my presentation is that Christianity is a body of knowledge with teachings—that is, values, norms, and principles that can aid good democratic governance, and which do not compromise or infringe upon the secular character of government. I believe the same reality is evident from the point of view of other religions as well.

I will now discuss briefly the functions and responsibility of the government in modern society. This will help pave the way for a subsequent discussion and illustration of the ways in which Christian teachings can inform political leadership, produce good governance, and enhance the capacity to overcome present social problems and challenges.

For What do Governments Exist?
One of the most cited classics on the role of government in society is the writing of Thomas Hobbes (1660) in *The Leviathan*. Hobbes employed a powerful metaphor of a state of nature on the one hand, and

a civil society on the other. He postulated that government—that is, the Leviathan—was created as a means that could enable human society to move away from a state of nature, where life was brutish and short, into a civil society where life was orderly and pleasant. The transition occurs when people agree to surrender their individual discretion for unilateral action to the Leviathan. The Leviathan, therefore, undertakes responsibility for order and the safety of every individual.

The role of government, even in modern society, is therefore, to maintain law and order, and thereby create conditions that can enable citizens to safely pursue their goals in life; protect individual rights against undue infringement; ensure justice in the management of conflicts; and protect the State and the population against external aggression.

However, this traditional and restricted role of government has been expanded beyond original limits, following new ideas about the welfare state. Today, governments are expected to also undertake responsibility for improvement in the material condition of the population; that is, alleviate poverty, diseases and ill health, hunger, starvation, illiteracy and ignorance. Simply put, to promote development. The State is expected to undertake these responsibilities in the public interest, and this is where the concept of good governance comes in—to safeguard the interests and wellbeing of the governed.

However, the enunciation of the functions and duties of government, including an exposition of the operation and merits of democracy, is more easily discussed than put into practice. Many countries in Africa are familiar with all of these ideals, yet many have faltered in the actual pursuit and realization of democracy and good governance. Conflict, social strife, poverty and political instability abound in many parts of Africa and the world. This suggests that beyond knowledge of the functions and operations of good governance, one has to be familiar with the principles and values that make it possible for us to translate aspirations into reality, theory into practice, and pronouncements into action for tangible and positive results. Some of these values and principles include responsibility, accountability, honesty, integrity, meritocracy, and trustworthiness. In the next section, an explanation shows that these principles and values are scriptural attributes, clearly illustrated in the Bible.

The Scriptures and Good Governance
The hallmark of good governance is in leadership. What are the characteristics of good leadership that can produce good governance?

Appreciation of the Functions of Government and Formulation of a Vision
Vision refers to foresight. Visionaries are people, who are not satisfied with what is happening, but who are interested in what is going to happen and how they can make it happen. Without a vision, people perish. A visionary leader can help people prepare for difficulties so as to help them escape trouble when the problems are close (Prv 17:24). Martin Luther King, Jr.'s, "I Have a Dream" vision helped African Americans realize civil liberties in the United States of America. In Genesis 41:47-49 and 47:13-25, we see how visionary planning, as well as fairness and social responsibility, played out through Joseph and how he rescued his people from perennial famine by collecting all the food produced in the seven years of abundance. The food Joseph stored in the cities also provided seed for planting in the fields. The reverse is familiar in Africa where, for example, the El Niño flood waters go down the drain when they could be dammed to irrigate dry lands to produce food all year round and save the continent from dependence on food aid.

Integrity and Honesty
The population entrusts leaders who have responsibility, with enormous resources and political power to apply for the good of their people. The abuse of office, and of the resources bestowed in such office, is a real temptation. This places a tremendous demand for integrity and honesty on the part of political leadership. The story of Joseph in Genesis, Chapters 37–50, gives hindsight as to what God expects of us under different circumstances. Joseph was put in charge of Potiphar's household because he demonstrated integrity, honesty, consistency, and tenacity in resisting the temptation to take advantage of what had been entrusted in his care. He paid the price of his persistent refusal to give in to sexual advances of Potiphar's wife; he was imprisoned on false accusations of attempted rape (Gen 39). The story is different in many of our countries, as few would choose to protect their integrity and honesty by resisting the temptation to exploit situations under their charge.

Honesty is also about the willingness to accept weaknesses. In present terminology, we could call it transparency. The Bible tells us that David, despite his greatness, was humble enough to admit his failures, confess and repent accordingly (Ps 51). Many leaders do not accept when they fail the people, neither do they repent of their sins, yet this is what we are expected to do for God to restore us.

God-Fearing
The functions and responsibilities of government could be treated from a rational, scientific point of view. Yet, because science and rationality can also fail, it has to be augmented by belief in God. That is, leadership must be God-centered. Leadership is a gift of God to humanity. A Christian leader is obliged to provide God-centered leadership to God's people. Being God-centered is most important for successful leaders who desire to lead their people in God's direction. Moses looked upon God to lead the Israelites out of the Egyptian bondage and they crossed the sea on dry land in-between the waters. Pharaoh trusted in the might of his army and they drowned in the Red Sea (Ex 14:26-31). David, another God-centered leader, transformed Israel from a tiny state into a successful superpower in the ancient Middle East and planned to build a temple for God. Many African political leaders fail because, instead of being God-centered, they become ethnic-centered, Western European-centered, power-centered, material-centered, witchcraft-centered and self-centered—all of which lead to destruction, not construction.

Servant Leadership
A leader is without value outside the context of the people that he or she leads. Therefore, good leadership puts the people first. Good leadership is servant-leadership; committed to the service of the population. A Christian leader must understand himself as a servant of the Lord Jesus Christ, who is serving others on behalf of Christ. Jesus said that He did not come to be served, but to serve humanity and demonstrated this by washing His disciples' feet (Jn 13:1-17) as an example to them. Paul taught Christians the importance of providing selfless service to others (Phil 2:3-4; Rom 12:9-13; and 2 Cor 5:14-15).

The characteristics of servanthood leadership are shown in Matthew 5:7-12:

> Blessed are the merciful...
> Blessed are the pure in heart...
> Blessed are the peacemakers...

Blessed are the persecuted...
Blessed are the reviled/despised...

Mercy is the concern of people in need. Being pure in heart ensures a good motive for service. The persecuted are those who accept to suffer innocently for the sake of serving others.

Furthermore, leadership must value people. Christian leadership values people because people are more valuable than anything, including wealth. John 17:12 shows that Jesus also valued people more than anything. John 17:6 demonstrates that Jesus saw His followers as gifts from God. People are attracted to places where they are valued, but run away from areas where they are not valued. A nation that attacks its leaders will be void of leaders, for no leader worth his salt will want to lead such a State. A nation that attacks its wealthy citizens will be poor when the rich run away and new investments stop coming. A nation that undervalues its professionals and youth can suffer "brain-drain" and a bleak future. A nation that does not value its citizens is in danger of civil strife and becoming a failed State.

Rule of Law
The rule of law is the foundation of order and justice in the society. The Bible firmly expresses this fundamental constitutional principle in modern government through the Ten Commandments.

The Ten Commandments, part of the Torah, are universal and relevant to Africa's social, political and economic life today. The Bible also recognized the importance of structures of delegation. For example, Moses' father-in-law, Jethro, advised Moses to delegate authority to the elders to help him govern the Israelites (Ex 18:17-23). The Apostles delegated authority to deacons (Acts 6:1-4).

The Bible and Christianity do not condone a situation where leaders undermine structures by pretending to know it all, whereby one person holds many important positions of responsibility. The Bible can help African leaders recognize the importance of delegating to others some of their many responsibilities.

Justice is a fundamental aspect of the rule of law; leadership must promote justice to all. In the Bible, every Hebrew king had a prophet who catered to his excesses of power. As such, the prophets of God rebuked Hebrew leaders who abused their political powers by practicing and condoning injustices. Elijah rebuked King Ahab for taking

Naboth's farmland after executing him (1 Kgs 21:17-29). The Prophet Nathan rebuked King David for his adulterous relationship with Uriah's wife and for executing him on a war front (2 Sm 12). In the New Testament, Jesus was also deeply concerned with issues of justice. In His first sermon, Jesus said He came to set the captives free (Lk 4:14-19). Unfortunately, in many African states, there are cases of denied justice through the deliberate delay of cases, bribery, corruption, and exclusion based on ethnicity and cultural differences.

Rev. Dr. Japhet Ndhlovu is a former General Secretary for the Council of Churches in Zambia and former Executive Staff at the All Africa Conference of Churches (AACC). He holds two master's degrees: Missiology from the University of South Africa and Ecumenical Theology from the University of Dublin. His doctoral degree is in Practical Theology from Stellenbosch University in South Africa.

Japhet is married to Caroline and together they are blessed with three children. He now serves with the Christian Organization, Research and Advisory Trust (CORAT—Africa) as an Associate Consultant.

Theology of a Christian Nation: The Case of Zambia's Declaration as a Christian Nation

Rev. Dr. Japhet Ndhlovu

Introduction

The Republic of Zambia is a Christian nation located in sub-Saharan Africa. By 2011, its estimated population will be 13.8 million, with 42 percent of the population living in its cities. According to the 2000 Zambian census, approximately 87 percent of the population is Christian; one percent is Muslim (of late there has been a rapid increase in the population of Muslim communities) or Hindu; seven percent adhere to other faiths, including indigenous faiths; and five percent did not report their religion. More than 70 percent of the population comprises Bantu-speaking ethnic groups (US Department of State, 2006).

On December 29, 1991, Zambia's newly elected President, H. E. Frederick Titus Jacob Chiluba, a former trade unionist and Chairman General of the Zambia Congress of Trade Unions, surprised many, including the Church, by declaring Zambia a Christian nation. He was at the height of popularity, enjoying the solidarity of the trade unions, the Church and the general populace. Chiluba served two terms in office (1991-2002), with his declaration remaining controversial to the end.

This declaration of Zambia as a Christian nation ignited a nationwide debate, such that it divided into two opposing sides—those in favor of and those against the declaration. Since then, a plethora of divergent views and questions has crossed the Zambian religious and political platform. Perhaps the most important question is: "Is it right to declare a nation Christian?"

This paper seeks to contribute to this debate and suggest the need for clarity and coherence as to a theological basis and the legal implications of the said declaration; and then demonstrate that religion and politics can never be separated practically. It is also important, from the onset of this dialogue, to point out that this paper is not intended to criticize or find fault in the former President Chiluba or other presidents, but it is about the meaning, implication and development of the declaration of Zambia as a Christian nation. Analysis comes from a Christian perspective. Let me observe that people have a general tendency to discuss personalities rather than issues. I have made an effort to postpone my personal judgments in an attempt at objectivity in my approach.

When Christianity came to Zambia, it introduced a new faith and culture. It brought a Western form of education, modern medicine and missionary-Western culture. Christianity not only converted souls, but also condemned much of the African way of life as primitive, pagan, diabolical and animistic. In spite of the missionaries' condemnation of religious and cultural beliefs and their views that the practices of the people were diabolical, the African traditional beliefs and practices somehow survived. Later, after independence, Zambians began to reclaim the good within their culture and practices. Nevertheless, Zambia still faces the challenge of the contextualization of the gospel of Jesus Christ—that is, putting the gospel in the cultural wrapping of the local context within which preachers are called to proclaim the gospel. To a certain extent, Christianity is a composite of Zambian traditional religions and "Western White Christianity." This leads to a conclusion that an attempt to separate the Church and the State in Zambia is practically a daunting task in light of the fact that Africans (Zambians in this case) are deeply religious in every way. They take religion wherever they go, whether they go to work or they go out hunting. John S. Mbiti (1999:15) holds that:

> ...the individual is immersed in a religious participation which starts before birth and continues after his death. For him therefore, and for the larger community for which he is part, to live is

to be caught up in a religious drama. This is fundamental, for it means that man lives in a religious universe.

Mbiti demonstrates that people in Africa have a completely different worldview from those in the Western world. This singular fact is important in the analysis and understanding of the declaration of Zambia as a Christian nation. It may come as a surprise to some that have Western mindsets to see a Head of State who makes religious pronouncements openly for, and on behalf of a nation, but it may not be so to many Zambians. It can rightly be stated that in traditional Zambia, religion and government are an "indissoluble marriage." Traditional chiefs are both political and spiritual leaders.

President Chiluba was determined to use biblical principles as part of his reform strategy. The majority of indigenous persons in Zambia belong to several different Christian Churches, which cover Roman Catholic, Reformation Churches and several Pentecostal and Evangelical Churches. There are several hundred churches in Zambia, and four major Christian church bodies: namely, the Zambia Episcopal Conference for the Catholic Church (ZEC, a body for the Roman Catholic dioceses), the Evangelical Fellowship of Zambia (EFZ, for evangelicals), the Independent Churches and other Ministries of Zambia (ICMZ), and the Council of Churches in Zambia (CCZ, for historical protestant churches). Not long ago these church organizations, with the exception of the Independent Churches and other Ministries, formed an alliance known as the Oasis Forum to address certain constitutional issues. Apart from being the "conscience" of the nation, this forum held the government accountable for the failure of its organs to perform their duties as mandated by the Zambian people.

Since the rise of churches to the defense of the poor in Zambia and their subsequent involvement in political debates, many clergy and laity are getting involved in politics. This affirms that religion cannot be privatized; it cannot be removed from public life. Metaphorically speaking, religion and politics are like the body and the blood—the two are inseparable while the body still lives.

As for the term "Christian," it is used in reference to believers and followers of Christ Jesus. Although not everyone in Zambia is a Christian, a common attitude among the modern public is that anyone who goes to church is a Christian. Many Zambians ascribe to the Christian faith and that is the very fact that prompted President Chiluba to declare Zambia a Christian nation.

It is not just a political thing either—more than 80 percent of the country's nine million residents are professing Christians—and the numbers are growing. By 2025, predicts *The World Christian Encyclopedia* (cited in Olsen 2002), 87.8 percent of the country will be Christian; by 2050, it should top 92 percent.

From the outset, this paper seeks to underpin that, although colonialism attempted to destroy and disturb the indigenous Zambian cultures, negate the historicity and humanity of the indigenous people, and impose its own institutional structures, routines and governance, religiosity remains intact at the core of existence of the people of Zambia. The call to erect a "wall of separation of Church and State" is one bred and rooted in an American cultural environment. It is a foreign ideology, which is inconsistent with the indigenous Zambian religiosity.

In this paper, the Roman Catholic Church is critically analyzed because of its attempt to superimpose a foreign ideology of separation of Church and State on the development of the Zambian political system. The Zambian political system should remain rooted in its own specific cultural context and should address the needs and aspirations of its own people in order for it to remain relevant. Catholics and their collaborators petitioned the constitutional review commission to exclude the declaration of Zambia as a Christian nation from the preamble of the Zambian Constitution, without taking into account the adverse consequences of such acts as exemplified in the United States of America.

We shall attempt to demonstrate how the declaration could be applied. It also shows the importance of developing institutions that would support the implementation of the "marriage of Church and State" in Zambia through the declaration. With the previously mentioned in mind, it is not an easy task to build a Christian nation, as it shall not end at declarations and constitutions.

The Historical Perspective of the Declaration
Northern Rhodesia, a former British colony, was renamed Zambia after independence in 1964; it was on October 24th that Zambia became independent of British rule. Thereafter, Zambia adopted a multi-party system of government. President Kaunda banned all other political

parties except for the United National Independence Party (UNIP), which was his own party; this marked the beginning of one-party rule. UNIP and its government enjoyed the support of the Zambian people. During 27 years in power, former President Kaunda, who was a charismatic leader, made some remarkable achievements. His government succeeded in the integration of black and white children in schools, the rapid expansion of education and the establishment of the University of Zambia. The country unified numerous ethnic groups, which included some 72 dialects, under the slogan "One Zambia, One Nation." Additionally, the song *Tiyende Pamodzi Ndi Mtima Umo* (Let Us Walk Together in One Spirit) helped communicate a message of unification to all parts of Zambia and the country became a haven of peace. Christianity played a significant role in making Zambia a peaceful nation. Since then, Zambia has enjoyed peace in the region apart from the economic turbulence it has undergone, especially in the mid-1970s and thereafter.

The concentration of power in one party became a source of oppression and caused discontentment among many Zambians. President Kaunda became so powerful that many of his followers almost deified and worshipped him. The party carders coined slogans that ascribed to him divine attributes such as omnipotence and omnipresence. Slogans chanted at political rallies and wherever President Kaunda went, included: *Ku mulu! Lesa. Panshi apa! Kaunda ne nchito ne fyuma*—"Heaven is God's habitation, but the earth is for Kaunda, work and wealth." *Konse konse, Kaunda*—"Everywhere Kaunda." Although President Kaunda neither sanctioned nor solicited such praises, his followers attributed to him that which is due to God only. Indeed Kaunda's presence was felt everywhere (through his vigilantes and party carders) in the nation making him appear to be omnipresent. Another slogan warned that, *Kaunda Mulilo uwaikatoko apya, Uwaiketeko alipile, Uukekatako akapya*—"Kaunda is fire, whoever touches him is burnt, whoever touched him was burnt and whosoever will touch him will be burnt." Nevertheless, it was not until the early 1980s that the economy of Zambia began to decline and the ruling party and its government lost popularity and its powers faded away. The decline of the economy brought untold misery among the people of Zambia, which resulted in political instability.

Political, Economic and Theological Solutions
The political solution to the plight of Zambia lay in the change of government and its system of governance. Zambians demanded a change of government and the adoption of a multi-party democracy as opposed to one party system. This move intentionally promoted checks and balances, which is why people demanded that Zambia become a democracy, and in 1991 democratic elections took place.

Economists saw the solution being in the change of the economic system from a command system (a system in which the government runs the economy) to a liberalized market economy (an economy in which prices of commodities are determined by supply and demand). Private investors run the economy and market forces determine the prices of commodities, unlike the economic system where government-owned businesses (known as parastatal organizations) controlled prices of commodities. Therefore, the economists' solutions lay in privatization and in a liberalized market economy.

Another solution, advanced by one segment of the Church in Zambia, was a theological one. Some churches and individual Christians saw the droughts, poverty, corruption and other evils afflicting Zambians as punishments from God. Their view was that Zambia had sinned against God by falling away from Him and turning to the worship of other gods. Christians became apprehensive when the Kaunda government turned to socialist countries. Zambia saw an influx of religions from India and other parts of Asia claiming that they would establish heaven on earth.

The call by Zambians for a reformation of the entire nation and its system gained momentum. The Movement for Multi-party Democracy (MMD) grew like wildfire around Zambia, with the support of the Church (including Catholics), non-governmental organizations and the majority of the people in Zambia. Frederick Chiluba, a Chairman General of the Zambia Congress of Trade Unions, led this political party. The churches in Zambia played a major and significant role in a combined effort to remove the UNIP government from power and ushered in the MMD government in 1991. Zambia witnessed a peaceful transfer of power, which is unique on the continent of Africa.

President Chiluba and his government adopted the Structural Adjustment Programs prescribed by the International Monetary Fund (IMF) as part of Zambia's economic solution. The IMF and the World Bank demanded that private investors run Zambia's economy, and that the agricultural sector should produce for export rather than local consumption only. Under the reign of Chiluba's government, Zambia saw a rapid privatization of mines and many other government-owned estates, but there was no corresponding improvement in the quality of life of the people of Zambia. That caused a serious problem to Chiluba's government, given that the majority of the population lived below the poverty datum line. Soon, there were serious corruption allegations against senior government officials.

Consequently, on Tuesday, October 26, 1997, there was an attempted *coup d'etat* (a taking over of government by military force) led by Captain Stephen Lungu who, during the *coup*, used the pen name of Captain Solo. At 6:39 GMT, British Broadcasting Services (1997) aired the announcement of the *coup*:

> …the people of Zambia were woken to that statement on the radio that was made by Captain Solo who claimed to be a member of the National Redemption Council that has allegedly claimed to have overthrown the government of Frederick Chiluba…. On the line, 'This morning we have toppled the MMD government of Mr. F.T.J. Chiluba. Because of his criminal means and corrupt means the country was going to ruins. It was collapsing completely and there is only one institution, one organized institution which can put an end to such criminal activities, and that is the military. Otherwise the Bible could not have done anything…

Ironically, after the *coup* was crushed, Captain Solo was found hiding in a container and had in his possession a New Testament Bible. Thereafter, President Chiluba addressed the nation at 10:00 a.m. on Zambia National Broadcasting Corporation Radio 2 (1997). Despite surviving a *coup*, Chiluba still continued his reform program based on biblical principles. Chiluba reaffirmed the declaration of Zambia as a Christian nation. He encouraged the people of Zambia with these words:

> In the name of our Lord Jesus Christ, I want to repeat that no weapon formed against our government, no weapons surely formed against us shall ever prosper. Yes, they surely gathered together, but not by the Lord and those who have gathered together have fallen…every inch of our soil is Christian. The Lord Jesus is in full control. Be not afraid, don't be intimidated, there shall be no power greater than that of our Lord Jesus. For He

who is inside us is greater than the enemy outside and those with us are more than those against us. Be not afraid, the Lord is keeping His hand on our nation…We shall continue with the Lord's program, we shall continue with the political program, we shall continue also with the economical program…

The Declaration of Zambia as a Christian Nation
It was on December 29, 1991, that Chiluba, standing on the steps of a state government building, declared Zambia as a Christian nation. This is what he said:

On behalf of the nation, I have now entered into a covenant with the living God and therefore, I want to make the following declaration. I say here today that I submit myself as President to the Lordship of Jesus Christ. I likewise submit the government and the entire nation of Zambia to the Lordship of Jesus Christ. I further declare that Zambia is a Christian nation that will seek to be governed by the righteous principles of the Word of God. Righteousness and justice must prevail in all levels of authority and we shall see the righteousness of God exalting Zambia. My fellow Zambians let this message reach all civil servants in all government departments. The time of corruption and bribery is over. For too long these wicked practices have been destroying and tearing down the nation. Now the hour has come for our building up. The hour has come for our stability. Proverbs 29:4 declares, "He who is greedy for bribes tears down a nation, but by justice a king gives the country stability." ("'Christian' Zambia: Heaven on Earth?"2000)

Furthermore, President Chiluba (1997) made a confession and a renunciation of the sins of Zambia. In his prayer he said,

Dear God, we humble ourselves and admit our guilt…We repent from our wicked ways of idolatry, witchcraft, the occult, immorality, injustice, and corruption, and all other sins that have violated your righteous laws. We turn away from all these and renounce it all in Jesus' name.

Although the declaration of Zambia as a Christian nation was made in good faith, yet it is not without shortcomings. Chiluba entered the Office of President with the understanding that the crisis Zambia found herself in was a punishment from God for sins committed in the past. The original intent of the declaration was to bring divine benediction on Zambia.

Therefore, the acknowledgement of God and the Lordship of Christ was meant to be a source of spiritual and material blessings. In a world of moral confusion, people needed to understand and appreciate that Christianity offers a love ethic in which, faith, hope, peace, justice, prudence, temperance, loyalty, honesty in all dealings and transactions, morality, hard work, accountability, responsibility, forgiveness, reconciliation, obedience to authority, respect and discipline do exist. Besides calling people to repentance and salvation in Christ, Christianity also offers abundant life on earth and in heaven. It develops strong and moral leadership, which the world so desperately needs. Therefore, in order for the Zambians to benefit and prosper, they must embrace and apply the declaration to their daily lives. Christianity must be judged by the content of its faith.

The declaration, understood in covenant terms, is imbedded in the preamble of the Constitution of Zambia (1991), which reads thus:

WE, THE PEOPLE OF ZAMBIA by our representatives, assembled in our Parliament, having solemnly resolved to maintain Zambia as a Sovereign Democratic Republic;

DETERMINED to uphold and exercise our inherent and inviolable right as a people to decide, appoint, and proclaim the means and style to govern ourselves;

RECOGNISE the equal worth, of men and women in their right to participate, and freely determine and build a political, economic and social system of their own free choice;

PLEDGE to ourselves that we shall ensure that the State shall respect the rights and dignity of the human family, uphold the laws of the State and conduct the affairs of the State in such manner as to preserve, develop, and utilise its resources for this and future generations;

DECLARE the Republic a Christian nation while upholding the right of every person to enjoy that person's freedom of conscience or religion;

RESOLVE to uphold the values of democracy, transparency, accountability and good governance;

AND FURTHER RESOLVE that Zambia shall forever remain a unitary, indivisible, multi-party and democratic sovereign State;

DO HEREBY ENACT AND GIVE TO OURSELVES THIS CONSTITUTION.

A preamble is designed to serve as the introduction to the constitution. It sheds light on the resolve, determination, spirit, and purpose for which a constitution is established. While it is true that a preamble does not create (and is not a source of) power, yet it serves the purpose of establishing the nature, extent, and application of power. It calls the government to be mindful and respectful of the purpose for which a constitution is established. Although a preamble may not be a source of power, judges can refer to it as evidence of the origin, scope and purpose of the constitution. Therefore, a preamble can be said to have bearing on the constitution.

In this Christian nation, anyone, regardless of his religious, social or political affiliation or persuasion, can hold any office in government and become President of Zambia as long as he or she qualifies according to the requirements of the Constitution of Zambia. In 1996, Zambians voted for Mr. Dipak Patel, a Hindu, in the Parliamentary elections even when he stood as an Independent against the MMD Christian candidate. It was a testimony not only to Mr. Patel's political caliber, but also to the maturity of the Zambian voters in his constituency who obviously did not let religious considerations influence their voting decisions (Seshamani, 2009).

Some have argued that the declaration infringes on the rights and freedoms of people of other religious persuasions, however, contrary to such claims, the rights of religious minorities are protected under this declaration. The declaration is not a call for a Church-run State in which non-Christians would go into hiding and not play a part in the running of the government. Instead, it is an inclusive declaration, understood in covenant terms. Zambians freely chose to invoke God's blessing through the declaration. There is sufficient evidence to prove that the rights of such religious groups are protected. For instance, people in Zambia are free to attend educational institutions of their choice, including those that may not be of their faith. Several religions in Zambia have their own schools and have various publications available through their places of worship, libraries and other distribution points. All religions coexist and are in harmony with one another. Zambia has never experienced religious intolerance (International Covenant on Civil and Political Rights, 1998). That means the declaration falls within the parameters of international human rights obligations. The declaration simply augments that Zambia has always been, a "Christian nation."

This declaration has its fruits within the Constitution, for instance, the said declaration clearly spells out in the preamble that, the people of Zambia have resolved to "declare the Republic as a Christian nation while upholding the right of every person to enjoy the person's freedom of conscience or religion." This is in reference to article 19 of the republican constitution (Constitution of Zambia, Part III, 1996):

> Everyone shall have the right to freedom of thought, conscience and religion. This right shall include freedom to have or to adopt a religion or belief of his choice, and freedom, either individually or in community with others, and in public or private, to manifest his religion or belief in worship, observance, practice and teaching. No one shall be subject to coercion, which would impair his freedom to have or to adopt a religion or belief of his choice. Freedom to manifest one's religion or beliefs may be subject only to such limitations as are prescribed by law and are necessary to protect public safety, order, health, or morals, or the fundamental rights and freedoms of others.

Religion is very much at the core of the Zambian culture such that to separate, for example, the Church from the State is a denial of historical evidence and of the Christian identity of the Zambian peoples. This singular act is like cutting off the roots from which the Zambians have grown; especially since Zambia is a deeply religious community that is permeated by Christian values and practices. To the contrary, there have been incidents of violence committed by extremists in the name of Christianity, yet this faith is not about violence; it is a religion of peace, love, justice, redemption and reconciliation.

The distinctions proposed between the Church and the State are artificial and inconsistent with the Zambian traditional religious beliefs. Religions permeate all spheres of Zambian life such as: culture, kinship, health and disease, fertility of crops, animals, leadership, business and human beings. In African traditional religions, there is no distinction between the sacred and the secular, the two are interwoven. A completely secular world does not exist in sub-Saharan

Africa. Most Zambians eat, drink, sleep, work and do, practically, everything religiously (Isizoh, 2009).

The Declaration Controversy
This declaration excited a plethora of responses in both Zambia and abroad, leading to a nationwide and international debate. People from all walks of life joined the debate: Christians and pagans, the rich and the poor, academics and philosophers, sociologists, Anglicans and Catholics, Evangelicals and Pentecostals, lawyers and politicians, journalists and non-governmental organizations including traditionalists and people from other religions. The nation was divided into two blocks, those in favor of the declaration, led by some Evangelicals and Pentecostals on the one side, and those against it, led by mainline churches such as the Zambia Episcopal Conference, Council of Churches in Zambia, the Evangelical Fellowship of Zambia, on the opposite side of the debate. Since then, an abundance of divergent views and questions crossed the Zambian political arena. The issue of Church and politics in Zambia has been a very controversial one. Politicians on several occasions have made public calls for the Church and the clergy to leave politics to politicians and to concentrate on Church matters only. However, Church leaders have refused to heed such calls; they hold that politics is too important to leave to politicians only. Since the coming of the missionary, the Church has all along taught that Church and politics do not mix. The mindset of demonizing politics emanates from early missionaries who instructed their converts not to get involved in advocating or opposing contentious political views or solutions. There are some denominations in Zambia, which still hold that politics is a dirty game and as such, Christians should not get involved in it. This doctrine was taught for a long time to the extent that many people, including professionals, have shunned politics. One thing they do not understand is that to claim to be a Christian is a political statement in itself. That is to say, "I pledge allegiance to Christ first, before I do anything to the government." The Roman Empire understood very well that the claim of allegiance to Christ is a political statement. That is why Nero persecuted the Church.

A Biblical Perspective of the Declaration

The analysis of the biblical perspective of the declaration of Zambia as a Christian nation looks at various passages used by President Chiluba in his speeches and conversation. He further applies his biblically-based values to the national reform program. Chiluba ascended to the presidency with the understanding that Zambia had sinned against God and that the economic woes she was in was a consequence of the sins of the former leadership and the people of Zambia. He, together with many other Evangelicals and Pentecostals, held that repentance and a return to God would save Zambia.

President Chiluba was convinced that Christian values and principles were the best remedy to the malady of corruption, poverty, witchcraft, immorality, oppression and exploitation that destroyed Zambia. He was convinced that the evils perpetrated by the former leadership against the people of Zambia grieved God. Following this line of thought, President Chiluba is of the view that this resulted in droughts, disasters and mass poverty in Zambia. Apart from the social and political solutions, President Chiluba resolved that a national repentance, prayer, and a biblically-based reform program would suffice.

Immediately following his ascension to the apex of power, President Chiluba (1997), on Zambia National Television, led the nation in a prayer of confession. He shouted, as the people cheered triumphantly, "Jesus is the Lord of my life, Jesus is Lord in the government, and Jesus is Lord over Zambia." Chiluba then embarked on a reform that was after the pattern of Josiah's reform. Having studied King Josiah's reform, he gave himself to leading a radical cleansing of Zambia from the worship of false gods, witchcraft and every other occult practice.

President Chiluba presupposes that the condition Zambia is in, and has been going through, is a consequence of sins committed by the people of Zambia and their leaders. He then sees Zambia's hope in the promise that God will forgive the sins that brought the judgment of drought, mass poverty, various incurable diseases and disgrace, and heal the land. That means if Zambia recovered from her economic, social and political ills, and the breakdown of social order, then sin, which is the obstacle to social, economic and political progress in Zambia, would no longer exist. It is with the previously mentioned in mind that President Chiluba embarked on a vigorous, biblically-based national reform program.

President Chiluba cited 2 Chronicles 7:14 during the funeral service at Independence Stadium in Lusaka for the Zambia national football team, which perished in a plane crash off the coast of Gabon. He resubmitted and rededicated Zambia to the Lordship of Jesus Christ and reaffirmed Zambia as a Christian nation. By so doing, he renewed Zambia's covenant relationship with God. Given the context within which he cited 2 Chronicles 7:14, it is suggested that the death of the national team was a punishment from God on Zambia because His wrath was not yet appeased. This theology falls short of the teaching by the psalmist that God does not treat us as our sins deserve or repay us according to our iniquities. For as high as the heavens are above the earth, so great is His love for those who fear Him (Ps 103:10-11).

A Theological Perspective of the Declaration
The declaration is perhaps one of the most misunderstood, misrepresented and maligned concepts in today's Zambian political, legal, and religious debates. It is accurate to observe that everyone has an opinion, but unfortunately, many of the opinions are seriously misinformed. The Jesuit Centre for Theological Reflection, in their publication on the declaration of Zambia as a Christian nation (Henriot, 1998), stated that,

> ...this declaration is very unclear both theologically and constitutionally. *Theologically*, what does it mean to say that a political entity such as a nation is declared to be Christian? Certainly, you can't *baptize* a nation—or even all ten million of the inhabitants of a nation! You can't expect the profession of the Apostle's Creed to be made by a nation. Nor can a nation, as such, perform a liturgical act of Christian worship. These are the hard theological questions that, unfortunately, neither the State nor the Churches have thought about in a way that would bring clarity and understanding.

This statement reveals the perspective from which the Catholics analyzed the declaration of Zambia as a Christian nation. The Roman Catholic Church finds it hard to reconcile how a nation, a political entity, can be Christian. The opinions expressed by the Catholics are representative of most of the people and groups that are opposed to the declaration.

The declaration of Zambia as a Christian nation still stands today and is found in the National Constitution in spite of all the debates as to what it means. Zambia lacks an agreed common position as to the meaning and implications of being a Christian nation. President Chiluba tried his best, but the churches never reached a consensus on the issue. Meanwhile the Church continues to have a huge influence on the life and living of the Zambian people.

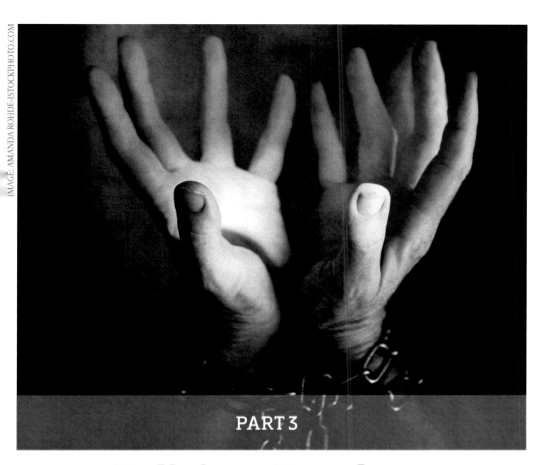

PART 3

Religious Freedom

Rev. **Dr**. **Andrea Z. Stephanous** holds a Ph.D. from the University of Manchester and a M.A. in Theological Studies from Eastern University in Pennsylvania. Currently he serves as the General Director of the Coptic Evangelical Organization for Social Services and, since 2007, has served as Vice President of the Protestant Community of Egypt. He is also President of the Fellowship of Middle East Evangelical Churches and a part-time lecturer on Political Religions and the Theological Foundation for Social Change at the Evangelical Theological Seminary in Cairo, Egypt.

Having written more than 40 articles in Arabic, his publications are in both Christian magazines and national newspapers, like *Al Ahram*. As author of two books, Rev. Dr. Stephanous' most recent title (published in both Arabic and English in 2006) is, *Political Islam, Citizenship and Minorities: The Future of Arab Christians in the Middle East.*

Religious Freedom in a Pluralistic Society

Rev. Dr. Andrea Z. Stephanous

Human Rights

The latter part of the 20th century witnessed significant development in the arena of human rights. The Universal Declaration of Human Rights, issued by the United Nations in 1948, expressed an overwhelming international concern for the upholding of these rights. Many international charters following the declaration discussed the complex concept of human freedom (Welch, 2001:167-168). There was international conviction that the driving force behind those charters was the human desire to seek respect for humankind and appreciation for human dignity. Humans possess dignity and self-worth; these concepts are not extraneous to the human experience (Weingartner, 1999:484).

Despite this growing interest in human rights, the established Church approached this issue with some reserve for many years. After World War II, however, some theological trends emerged which were supportive of human rights and of religious freedoms (Weingartner, 1999:485-486). Although Christianity is characterized by denominational pluralism and numerous variations in worship styles, there remains an underlying agreement that all humans are endowed with certain rights. Nevertheless, it is undeniable that there are varying attitudes among Christians about the source and nature of these rights.

Issues, such as abortion, euthanasia and homosexual marriage, trigger sharp disputes among Christians regarding the concept of human rights (Moltmann, 1984:7).

Numerous theological approaches attempt to define a Christian concept of human rights. One example is the theological trend that believes in a God-given natural law, which controls patterns of human behavior. According to this doctrine, God-given mental faculties determine whether human behavior is compatible with natural law (Mouw, 2005).

Another theological trend, which emphasizes the basic theological concepts of Creation, the Fall, Redemption, and Consummation, finds Christianity compatible with support for human rights. This understanding of Christian doctrine focuses on liberation as a theological basis for human rights. Christ is the Liberator, in the universal sense of the word. The object of liberation is to restore God's image in humans, since humans were created in God's image, but this image was marred through sin. This liberation is also a futuristic work, since it will be consummated in the final fulfillment of the kingdom of God.

Toward an Arab Perspective on Human Rights
As an Arab Christian, I base my view of human rights on theological principles from the Creation narrative and from Christ's description of the kingdom of God. The Creation story states plainly that humans are created in the image of God. This image is reflected through equality between men and women, and emphasizes creativity and responsibility. The fact that God is the Creator makes Him the source of life; consequently, Creation is the product of God's handiwork. This product has God as its source, and therefore, should not be belittled, as it possesses intrinsic dignity. The second aspect of this image is a reflection of God's creative nature. Humankind's mental and emotional faculties are divine expressions. The incident related in Genesis, when God entrusts Adam to name the animals of the earth, may be a genuine expression of creativity. To give a name in Hebrew means to give identity and future. There are many Old Testament examples to support this idea. Humans also participated in the Creation process, because God gave Adam the authority to define the future vision and condition of the Creation surrounding him.

This responsibility extended to the administration of Creation, where the third dimension of this image comes into play, i.e. responsibility. Responsibility here reflects three dimensions: responsibility before God, before man and before nature. This image of God in humans presents a clear commitment to human rights; no Christian should ignore human rights when dealing with other people or with the earth.

The second dimension of this question is the concept of the "kingdom of heaven." Most scholars, in their interpretation of the kingdom, fall into one of two major camps: the eschatological interpretation or the non-eschatological interpretation. The eschatological interpretation advocates for strong focus on spirituality. Supporters of this view believe that the Lord Jesus' teachings on the kingdom were entirely eschatological. These scholars believe that viewing the kingdom as a present day reality was not Christ's intent; rather, this is a human addition. The kingdom, they believe, has always been an apocalyptic reality, capable of fulfillment through the miraculous intervention of God.

As for the non-eschatological interpretation, Albert Ritschl is considered one of the most important contemporary theologians to present views on the social dimension of the kingdom. According to Ritschl (1900:12), the kingdom of God is, "the organization of mankind through a labor of love." It is "the ethical unification of mankind, through an act of comprehensive love for the neighbor," or "the gathering of people in a mutual and general act of love" (*ibid*). Rauschenbusch, who is called the "prophet of social justice," is another theologian in the "non-eschatological" camp. He believes that the kingdom of God will come to earth in the realm of human history. In his opinion, "Jesus never transferred the hope of the kingdom from earth to heaven. The kingdom belongs all the more to this earth, so much so, that the Lord Jesus promised to return to the earth from heaven in order to establish it" (Rauschenbusch, 1912:49 and 66). The kingdom is present today, and will continue to be in the future. This affects the present day and calls for individual involvement. Each human can participate with God in the ushering in of the kingdom. The kingdom is humanity organized according to God's will. It is a noble social order that can fill the gap between the religious and the social (*ibid*).

There is another theological trend which understands the kingdom as the dominion of the redeeming God, who is actively consolidating His authority with people. According to this trend, the kingdom, which will be completed as an eschatological act at the end days, has already come into human history in the person and message of Jesus Christ. Jesus conquered sin and freed people from its power, bringing people the blessings of God's dominion on earth. The kingdom of God involves two great phases: the ushering in of the kingdom, which is within the realm of history, and the moment of its consummation at the end of history (Ladd, 1974:218). This idea is confirmed in Matthew 12:28, "But if it is by the Spirit of God that I drive out demons, then the kingdom of God has come upon you." Thus, we see that God's active dominion has invaded the present day without turning it into the age that is to come. The kingdom is entirely God initiated. It is not utopian, inevitable progress, or merely God's work in history; rather, it is God's breakthrough into history, through the person of Jesus Christ—the coming of the kingdom into the world is God's miraculous work (Ladd, 1974:188-189).

In view of the above, one can say that the kingdom of God is a tangible reality. Especially with regard to values and principles, this kingdom does not belong solely to this age; it is also related to the age to come. Through the kingdom, the Lord Jesus invades human history and our hearts to tell us what the coming age will be like.

In the Gospel of Mark (Mk 1:14-15), we can see Jesus speaking of the kingdom. "After John was put in prison, Jesus went into Galilee, proclaiming the good news of God. 'The time has come,' He said. 'The kingdom of God is near. Repent and believe the good news!'" With these words, Jesus alluded to the prophetic hope of the coming Messiah. The prophets had prophesied of a day when the Messiah would come to pour out the Spirit in a new way (Jl 2:28-29) and restore *Shalom*: God's people as a visible community, living in right relationship with God, their neighbors, and the earth.

The kingdom of God is both a tangible reality and a future hope at the same time. It is God's supernatural work, as much as it is also humankind's work. In his book, *The Mind of Christ*, William Barclay (1960:60) analyzes the Lord's Prayer and concludes his analysis with this definition of the kingdom: "The kingdom is the state of affairs on earth when God's perfect will is fulfilled as it is in heaven." Hence, the kingdom is fulfilled through the liberation of the oppressed, the feeding of the hungry, loving the unlovable, and the sinner's reception of Christ as Savior and Lord.

The Christian concept of human rights is based on these two pillars: humans are created in God's image, and they are called to be active in the fulfillment of the kingdom. God's image, represented in humans through equality, creativity and responsibility, makes it possible for humans to achieve a society of justice and equality.

Arab Christians and Human Rights: Current Challenges
There are many challenges currently facing Arab Christians in the area of human rights. I am certain that there is much development in Egypt striving to promote respect for human rights in general and the rights of minorities in particular. To effectively promote human rights, there must be a revision of the challenges that prevent a human rights culture from taking root.

The Right to National Belonging
Many human rights challenges facing Arab Christians are associated with Islamism. Among them is the emphasis on religious identity, regarding it as the only necessary identity for political participation. This has led to a restructuring of identity and resulted in cultural and political disturbance. National loyalty and a sense of national belonging were replaced by religious loyalty and a sense of religious belonging. This shift from a primarily national to a primarily religious identity has created a unique situation for Christians, where, as a religious minority, their national loyalty and sense of national belonging are called into question. Religious affiliation has become stronger than national affiliation. In this context, the Christians' relation to the "Christian West" has been discussed and their patriotism has been undermined.

None can deny the significance of religious ties: Both Christianity and Islam emphasize brotherhood among their followers, reinforcing these internal ties. Yet, the reduction of all other identities to the religious identity has contributed to the curtailment of plurality and the creation of a monistic concept of loyalty. This has played a major role in undermining patriotism and reducing national ties, which are the foundation of social, political and cultural cohesion.

The Right of Doctrinal Conviction
No doubt the long history shared by Christianity and Islam involves points of convergence and points of conflict and mistrust, but coexisting religious groups that do not learn from history, do not progress effectively toward the future. Thus, one side casting doubts on the doctrines of the other creates bitterness and leads to marginalization, violence and/or withdrawal. Although I believe that both parties are

guilty of mistrusting one another, the media space given to those who cast doubts on Christian doctrines is much greater than the reverse and is of substantial proportions. Television interviews, newspaper articles and cassette tapes, casting either direct or indirect doubts on the doctrines of Christians, have contributed to the formation of the recently exacerbated social schism.

It is easy for a member of one religion to cast doubts on the doctrines of another religion, but the scars that these doubts create cannot be easily removed; rather, they linger for several generations. In some cases, contempt for doctrine swells and develops into the rejection of individuals, and sadly, this may evolve into hatred.

Freedom of Belief
Freedom of religious belief is a thorny issue in Egypt. No doubt, there are attempts from both Muslims and Christians to convert one another. Though I am not interested in addressing the issue of *Da'wa*, or evangelization here, the political factors accompanying this process contribute to a culture of fanaticism. For example, it is normal for a Christian to declare his or her adoption of Islam, yet the conversion of a Muslim to Christianity is accompanied by security threats and complex problems. Many accounts are given of the seduction of Christian girls and the encouragement of Christians to embrace Islam. These factors create a sense of frustration with Egypt's Coptic Orthodox Christians (the Copts) and lead them to emphasize themes of persecution and marginalization. Thus, the question of freedom of belief is an important issue that must be handled delicately. The recent events Egypt has witnessed, such as the announcement of the conversion of a Coptic priest's wife to Islam and the corresponding Coptic demonstrations outside the Coptic Cathedral, are the best example of this mental image. Granting every individual the freedom to believe, without exercising any pressure, is necessary. Yet, the matter does not stop here; freedom of belief must include freedom of religious education and practice, as well as the individual's right to choose what to believe. Pressures related to changing one's religion contribute to the creation of fanatical attitudes toward "the other."

Selective Treatment of History
Historical emphases on Muslim-Christian relations are selective and subject to current feelings. When tolerance is the *status quo*, Qur'anic texts and historical situations, which call for friendliness with and

respect toward "the People of the Book," are remembered and quoted. When the *status quo* is intolerant, historical situations of marginalizing "the other" and charging "the other" with unbelief are recounted. This eclectic treatment of history and tradition forms unstable mental images and contributes to making coexistence a relative experience. Thus, the retelling of history and tradition must follow methodological principles and must be based on scientific analysis, the encouragement of new interpretive judgments (*Ijtihad*), and the re-reading of texts in their cultural and circumstantial context. If made, these changes can create new respect for tradition and history, and will contribute to the establishment of a more stable future.

Social and Cultural Alienation
The feeling of alienation among Egyptian Christians is a factor resulting from long-term marginalization and exclusion. I am certain that Egyptian laws call for equality among citizens; yet, there are no clauses in the constitution or the numerous laws calling for discrimination between citizens on religious or racial basis. The problem lies in the practices of some leaders and officials—the author would like to emphasize the word "some," because generalization in such matters is untruthful and inadmissible.

Discrimination, when committed by persons of responsibility, creates a sense of persecution and leads to negative images, which can contribute to an atmosphere of alienation. Thus, individual fanaticism plays a significant role in creating collective stereotypes when the individual is a person of power. This type of alienation represents a social dysfunction and contributes to collective strife. Although social alienation is dangerous, cultural alienation is even more dangerous because it can create collective strife. The issue of cultural alienation is complex and needs a more comprehensive study. Some factors that help create this type of cultural alienation include: limited space allotted to Christians for religious expression in the media; the exclusion of the Coptic family from sitcoms; the artistic portrayals of Copts as disfigured and suspicious; and limited portrayals of Coptic history. All of these factors have contributed to the formation of cultural alienation.

In presenting some of the challenges that Christians face in the area of human rights, this author does not claim to have covered all of the related factors. What I have included is based on personal interpretation, which may be right or wrong. I have tried to analyze some of the negative stereotypes about Christians, but this does not mean that Christians themselves have not contributed to the creation of negative stereotypes about Muslims. Certainly, when all factors are studied, we will find that all have contributed, in one way or another, to the creation of those negative stereotypes.

The author believes that the development of democracy, and the reinforcement of general principles of human rights, will contribute to the creation of positive images about "the other" and equality, as it relates to justice. Equality extends beyond political equality to the freedom of belief and doctrinal conviction; it regards plurality as the basis for political, social and cultural participation, and it recounts history and uses scientific methodologies so that the present may be supportive of the future.

Religious Freedom in a Pluralistic Society

PART 4

Societal Transformation

Dr. Delanyo Adadevoh is passionate about helping transform Africa into a responsible and respected member of the global community. He believes that discovering, developing and empowering leaders of integrity will usher the continent into a bright and promising future. To realize this dream, Dr. Adadevoh established the International Leadership Foundation (ILF) in 2004. He currently serves as President of ILF, the mission of which is, "building leaders of integrity to transform Africa and beyond."

Dr. Adadevoh earned a B.Sc. in Chemistry at the Kwame Nkrumah University of Science and Technology (KNUST) in Kumasi, Ghana, a M.A. in Leadership at Azusa Pacific University in California, and a Ph.D. in Theology at Leeds University, England.

A citizen of Ghana, he has also lived in Nigeria, Kenya and Zimbabwe. Dr. Adadevoh and his wife, Elizabeth, have a son and two daughters and currently reside in Orlando, Florida, USA.

The Whole Gospel to the Whole Person

Delanyo Adadevoh, Ph.D.

Introduction

The message of good news for all humanity is a unique characteristic of Christianity; it invites people to participate in a new life and community promised to all by God. This universal message is central to Christianity and shapes Christian missions worldwide. Yet, we may ask if Christians fully understand and appreciate the implications of the good news. Are they aware of their own specific roles in Christian missions? Do they understand God's call on their lives?

For Christians to wholly realize their roles and responsibilities here on earth, they must continually revisit the good news message so they can clearly understand and recognize the value of God's call on their lives. Revisiting the good news will enable Christians to engage in more biblical and effective missions.

The focus of this paper is to explore the common theme of the gospel or good news in the biblical story. By investigating the different words and concepts used to express what we have come to refer to as the gospel, we will enrich our understanding of the gospel, increase our awareness of our particular roles, and more fully grasp the gospel's broader significance for humanity.

The historical usage of the term gospel contributes to its world of meanings, particularly as it applies to Christianity. From the Greek word *euangelion*, the "gospel" literally means "good news." In ancient times, the *euangelion* would be proclaimed from city to city to celebrate the accession of the new king to the throne upon the death of the old ("Gospel" at biblestudyplanet.org).

> In the Greek New Testament, gospel is the translation of the Greek noun *euangelion* (occurring 76 times), "good news," and the verb *euangelizo* (occurring 54 times), meaning "to bring or announce good news." Both words are derived from the noun *angelos*, "messenger." In classical Greek, a *euangelos* was one who brought a message of victory or other political or personal news that caused joy. In addition, *euangelizomai* (the middle voice form of the verb) meant "to speak as a messenger of gladness, to proclaim good news." Further, the noun *euangelion* became a technical term for the message of victory, though it was also used for a political or private message that brought joy. (Keathley, 2000)

A careful reading of the Old Testament reveals that the concept of the gospel is not limited to Greek-Roman culture or New Testament Christianity. Therefore, we will look at the gospel based on the entire biblical disclosure of the good news of God's intended blessings for humanity. Christians need to understand the gospel as good news to humanity made possible by God's blessing intentions and God's unique acts in history, notably the life, death and resurrection of Jesus Christ as the Messiah of God.

Some of the concepts used for the gospel have to do with the heart of God (blessing intention for humanity), the act of God (the sending of Christ to die for the sins of humanity), and the appreciation of humanity for the goodness of God. The phrases expressing the gospel from different perspectives include, "blessing," "the kingdom of God," "the new covenant," "Christ and Him crucified as the atonement for sins," and the "risen Christ as the source and hope for abundant and eternal life."

As Christians, we should seek to recover the biblical breadth of the gospel in order to investigate more extensively its implications for missions. This paper will look at the gospel through the lenses of these four concepts: blessings, the kingdom of God, the New Covenant, and Jesus the Christ. Studying the different biblical concepts used to express the gospel will lead to a better appreciation of the message and a far-reaching biblical understanding of the good news. Ultimately, our enhanced insights and awareness of the gospel will yield a broader perspective on Christian missions.

Concepts of the Gospel in the Bible

The Concept of Blessing and the Gospel
At the time of Creation, humanity was blessed and commissioned by God to play a unique stewardship role. It is important to capture the pre-Fall situation of humanity in order to understand the import of the gospel. The reason is that the gospel is the good news of humanity being restored to the condition (and its associated responsibilities) she had before the Fall. The condition of humans at the time of Creation can be described in three parts: spiritual, social and physical/material. Spiritually, humans were very close to God. They enjoyed intimacy with God. They were totally transparent before Him, and were not ashamed in His presence. There was no need to be ashamed, because there was nothing ungodly in them. God could come to Adam and Eve and walk with them in the Garden of Eden. Socially, Adam and Eve were one flesh. There was peace and harmony in their relationship. They were each other's companion and keeper. There was no conflict in their relationship. They listened to God and walked with Him together. Materially, humans were given stewardship authority over all of God's Creation on the earth. The material Creation was to bring satisfaction to humanity. This was not only in terms of providing food, but the interaction with Creation was to bring deep satisfaction to humanity. The beauty of God's Creation was to bring a deep God-shaped satisfaction to humanity; this satisfaction is the whole concept of the Garden of Eden. The garden presented a unique purposeful beauty satisfying God and humans. Humans were also given the responsibility of ensuring that all of God's Creation served God's intended purposes. Humanity was invited to enjoy God's Creation. The invitation of Adam and Eve to name what God had created was meant to establish a connection with Creation. This connection was meant to provide joy to humanity. It was also meant to position humans as caretakers of everything God had created. Humans were, therefore, invited to be co-heirs with God over His material Creation. This was the nature of the blessings God bestowed on humans at the time of Creation. The blessings covered the intellectual, spiritual, emotional, social and material aspects of human life and existence.

What happened at the Fall was a successful effort (though temporal) on the part of Satan to interfere with the blessed state in which God had placed humanity. He worked through Eve, and then Adam using deception. He tempted Eve and Adam to doubt God's Word to them. He then invited them to believe a lie; that they will not surely die when they eat the forbidden fruit, but would become as wise as God. When Adam and Eve disobeyed God and ate the forbidden fruit, they immediately died spiritually, and later socially and physically. They fell from the blessed status of being children of God, and co-heirs with God over all that God had created.

God came into the situation to explain to Adam the consequences for their disobedience. They were hiding from God because they felt naked and ashamed before Him. They were distant from one another. Adam blamed Eve. They could no longer enjoy everything God had created because some of the beautiful plants in the garden had turned into thorns. They could no longer be trusted co-heirs of God's Creation because they did not work within the boundaries God had given to them. The consequences of the Fall included the man ruling over the woman. The man became a slave worker. The man found his satisfaction through sweaty labor and the woman through submission to the man.

As is characteristic with God, He provided hope in the announcement of this fallen state of humanity. The hope was for the seed of the woman to crush the head of Satan, the serpent (Gn 3:15). This destruction of the head of Satan means the end will come to this archenemy of God. This end of Satan will open the way for humanity to be restored to her original state of blessing. This *hope of restoration* is the launching of what we have come to call the gospel or the good news. It is indeed good news that God launched a redemption plan which will restore humanity to the condition of blessing she had before the Fall. The good news is about the reversal of what Satan had done to rob humanity of God's blessings. The plan of redemption itself carefully follows a reversal strategy.

Satan deceived Eve; therefore, the seed of Eve will crush the head of Satan. Because Satan used deception as his weapon, the seed of Eve will be truth; He will use truth as His weapon. The objective of the deception was to create doubt; this uncertainty led Adam and Eve to disobey God. The objective of the seed of the woman bringing truth will be to restore faith in God and His Word resulting in obedience to God and His Word. A major consequence of the Fall is death. A major consequence of the seed of the woman crushing the head of Satan and ushering humanity into a restored relationship with God is life eternal. Therefore, the seed of the woman will be both truth and life for humanity. The power of truth is to restore faith in God. Faith, therefore, replaces doubt in this restorative journey of humanity. It makes sense when Jesus, as the seed of the woman, introduces Himself as the way, the truth and the life. He also claims to be the light of the world, and through Him, humanity escapes the trap of groping hopelessly and helplessly in a dark world of lies and death, and enters a new world of truth and life.

The gospel is, therefore, a redemption and restoration story; it is a restoration to a blessed spiritual, intellectual, emotional, social and material state. By summarizing the concept of garden, we can partially capture the nature of this original condition of blessing. Certain characteristics of the Garden of Eden can help us appreciate God's original blessing intentions for humankind. First, *goodness* characterized the garden; God saw all that He had made and it was good. Goodness speaks to positive effect. *Beauty* was the second element; beauty brings a unique sense of pleasure and satisfaction to humans and it actually shapes what we would call sense. A unique pleasure comes from beauty, which is powerfully attractive to humans; one could say that humans exist for beauty. When we talk of a new utopia, or heaven, we usually refer to the spectacular and overwhelming beauty of this ideal future. We are excited about a future heaven with crystal blue oceans and streets of gold. The satisfaction humans derive from beauty is almost unexplainable. When we are in a place of beauty, and we take time to absorb the power of the beauty, we experience a re-centering and re-ordering within ourselves releasing incredible peace and a sense of having arrived at a destination for which we have been yearning. We simply come together. God made us for beauty.

Order is a third element of the concept of garden. The difference between a garden and the wild is not so much what is in them; it is the ordering of what is in the garden as opposed to the random nature of the elements in the wild. Order itself contributes to our concept of sensibility. *Purpose* is a fourth element; God created everything for a purpose. God gave the responsibility of the stewardship of Creation to humans; they must ensure that everything God made serves God's intended purpose.

Satisfaction is a fifth element of the concept of garden. Actually, we can extend this to the satisfaction of Creation because of the element of interdependence in God's Creation. There is a sense of balance in Creation where things that were created need one another. Coexistence and interdependence characterize God's Creation. The purpose is to satisfy the basic needs of everything that has been created. Humans are to find satisfaction for their human needs from God and His Creation.

Intimacy with God is the sixth element. God comes to walk with humans in the garden and takes pleasure in them. He visits His garden to take pleasure in all He has made. God created humans so they could share in His pleasure. Walking with God in the garden of life was supposed to be a source of pure joy for humans; it was meant to be a deeply satisfying intimacy. Through this intimacy, God would reveal His will to His people, share His nature with them, and work through them to ensure good stewardship over all He has made.

The net good effect of God's garden is intimacy, purpose, satisfaction, pleasure and gratitude. All of these came with the responsibility of *stewardship-leadership*. Even this responsibility is part of the blessing of God because it is actually an invitation to be co-heirs with the Son of God for whom God created all things.

God promised the restoration of the blessings of relational intimacy, purposeful living, satisfaction, pleasure and gratitude to Abraham and through him to all humanity. God declared Abraham righteous because he believed God. It is important to note the principle at work here. When the devil tempted Adam and Eve, he attacked their mental faculties and created doubt regarding the Word of God. Therefore, when Abraham believed God, he was exercising reversal faith. He trusted in God instead of doubting God. Faith is the key to reversing the interference of Satan in God's original plan to bless humanity. Abraham became the example of the new community of faith-filled people who would believe in God and, therefore, be declared righteous. As a result, he is the father of faith, and the father of all nations that will by faith enter into the blessings of God.

This was the promise of God to Abraham who was to become the father of faith. God said to him:

> I will make you into a great nation and I will *bless* you; I will make your name great and you will be a *blessing*. I will *bless* those who *bless* you, and whoever curses you I will curse; and all peoples

on earth will be *blessed* through you [italics added]. (Gn 12:2-3)

God repeated this promise:

> The angel of the LORD called to Abraham from heaven a second time and said, "I swear by myself, declares the LORD, that because you have done this and not withheld your son, your only son, I will surely *bless* you and make your descendants as numerous as the stars in the sky and as the sand on the seashore. Your descendants will take possession of the cities of their enemies, and through your offspring, all nations on earth will be *blessed*, because you have obeyed me [italics added]. (Gn 22:15-18)

God promised to do two things. First, He was going to make Abraham into a great nation. Second, He promised to bless other nations of the world through Abraham. A nation in this context simply refers to a "people," which is a community of people who have established a common identity binding them together and differentiating them from other people. Language and religion are two main distinguishing factors; the languages of a people and the deities they worship shape their culture and establish them with unique identities.

The Hebrew word for blessing is *barak*. What does this word mean in the context in which God uses it? What does it mean for a nation to be blessed? A nation or a people are blessed when they adopt the faith of Abraham: trusting in the God of Abraham and joining the family of Abraham. The blessings involve a relational reconnection with God. Blessings also include having minds that trust in God, instead of doubting God. This intimacy with God will lead to joy and the freedom to open up to God. This is the emotional blessing. God also works through such people to ensure proper stewardship of His Creation, which is the material aspect of the blessings. This promise of redemption and restoration to the original, God-intended blessings is good news. The Apostle Paul appropriately referred to this as the gospel.

> So also Abraham "believed God, and it was credited to him as righteousness." Understand, then, that those who have faith are children of Abraham. Scripture foresaw that God would justify the Gentiles by faith, and announced the *gospel* in advance to Abraham: "All nations will be blessed through you." So those who rely on faith are blessed along with Abraham, the man of faith [italics added]. (Gal 3:6-9)

God's intended blessing of all nations is the message to which the gospel points. In other words, the gospel is about ushering people into the promised blessings of God through Jesus Christ.

In Ephesians 1:3, the Apostle Paul testifies that God has given us all the spiritual blessings in the heavenly places through Jesus Christ. All the spiritual blessings God intends for humanity are available through Jesus. It is important to establish a link between Jesus Christ and Abraham. All nations are blessed through Abraham and all nations can actually enter into God's blessings through Christ. What is the link between Jesus Christ and Abraham?

Abraham provides the example of the kind of faith we need in God in order to be declared righteous. However, he (Abraham) cannot personally bring into human experience what he modeled so well. Even though he is in God's presence, he is not eternal, and does not have universal presence or power. Jesus Christ, however, as the eternal and omnipresent Son of God, has been given the authority to bring into human experience what God promised through Abraham. Jesus, in a sense, earned this right by becoming human and perfectly meeting the demands of the law on behalf of humanity. He became Son of Man and Son of God. He represents humanity before God and can bring into human experience all that is in God, which humans can appropriate.

Jesus entered the human world to become a part of human history and community, not only as Creator, but also as a fellow citizen. He identified fully with the human struggle with sin and its full implications. He fought sin, resisted all temptations, and tasted the ultimate penalty for sin: death. He tasted death on behalf of humanity. However, He faced death in order to overcome and overpower it. When He rose from the dead, He demonstrated His victory over death. This risen Jesus Christ invites all people to identify with Him, the same way He took the initiative to identify with humanity. Those who identify with Him share in His death and resurrection. They become victors over sin and its penalty, which is death. Humans are able to participate in God's blessings by identifying with the victorious Jesus. The reason is simple. On the day Adam and Eve sinned, humanity surely died; we became separated from God. Through the victory of Jesus Christ over death, we are reunited with God. This reunion brings us back to the blessings of God.

Jesus was able to win this victory over death because He is perfect and eternal. As He Himself declared to the Jewish religious leaders, "Before Abraham was born, I am" (Jn 8:58). The eternal "I am," Jesus Christ, entered into human history and satisfied the demands of the law, so we can share His life. Because He lives, we also live. It is written that the fullness of the Godhead dwells in Jesus Christ; when we have Jesus Christ, we have access to the fullness of God. It is for this reason that the Apostle Paul declared that all the spiritual blessings God intends for humanity are available to us through Jesus Christ. When we are in Him, we are in God's blessings.

He Himself was righteous from the beginning. His acts of righteousness, unlike those of Abraham, were not so that He would be declared righteous, but for humanity to have the possibility to be declared righteous.

The Concept of the New Covenant and the Gospel
Covenants are agreements between God and His chosen people. The Bible broadly speaks of two covenants: the old and the new. Therefore, the Bible is divided into the Old Covenant (Old Testament) and the New Covenant (New Testament). It is important for us to appreciate the covenants God made with His chosen people in biblical history. God made His first covenant with Adam and Eve:

> So God created man in his own image, in the image of God he created him; male and female he created them. God blessed them and said to them, "Be fruitful and increase in number; fill the earth and subdue it. Rule over the fish of the sea and the birds of the air and over every living creature that moves on the ground." Then God said, "I give you every seed-bearing plant on the face of the whole earth and every tree that has fruit with seed in it. They will be yours for food. And to all the beasts of the earth and all the birds of the air and all the creatures that move on the ground—everything that has the breath of life in it—I give every green plant for food." And, it was so. (Gn 1:27-30)

God made covenants with Noah (Gn 9:8-16), Abraham (Gn 12:1-3), and David (2 Sm 7:8-16). All these covenants point to His blessings on the nation Israel, and all other nations.

God's covenant with Moses clearly placed the choice between life and death in the hands of humans. Humans knew the will of God through the Old Covenant.

> See, I set before you today life and prosperity, death and destruction. For I command you today to love the Lord your God, to walk in obedience to him, and to keep his commands, decrees and laws; then you will live and increase, and the Lord your God will bless you in the land you are entering to possess. But if your heart turns away and you are not obedient, and if you are drawn away to bow down to other gods and worship them, I declare to you this day that you will certainly be destroyed. You will not live long in the land you are crossing the Jordan to enter and possess. (Dt 30:15-18)

God gave the nation of Israel a comprehensive law to guide all aspects of their life and existence—spiritual, economic, political, social and material (Ex 20-23). God's conditions could not be clearer. If they obeyed the laws of God, they would have life. If they failed to obey the laws of God, they would have chosen death.

The people of Israel were commissioned, not only to obey the law, but also to teach God's laws to their children in every generation. They were to talk about these laws at home and in public places. God said to them,

> Hear, O Israel: The Lord our God, the Lord is one. Love the Lord your God with all your heart and with all your soul and with all your strength. These commandments that I give you today are to be on your hearts. Impress them on your children. Talk about them when you sit at home and when you walk along the road, when you lie down and when you get up. Tie them as symbols on your hands and bind them on your foreheads. Write them on the doorframes of your houses and on your gates. (Dt 6:4-9)

They were to choose to do the will of God if they wanted to live. Effectively, the Old Testament revealed the inability of humans to do what they knew was right. The people of Israel failed to obey the laws of God consistently. It was actually impossible for them to obey because of the sin nature they shared with all humans. However, this failure was to point to the necessity for a New Covenant. The Old Covenant served the purpose of leading humanity to the New Covenant.

The Old Covenant was not defective in itself. What made it ineffective in leading people to enter into the blessings promised by God was the sinful nature of humanity. The law is holy and spiritual, yet is limited in its blessing effects by the lack of holiness and spirituality in humans. The Apostle Paul said:

> So then, the law is holy, and the commandment is holy, righteous and good. Did that which is good then, become death to me? By no means! Nevertheless, in order that sin might be recognized as sin, it used what is good to bring about my death, so that through the commandment sin might become utterly sinful. We know that the law is spiritual; but I am unspiritual, sold as a slave to sin. (Rom 7:12-14)

This encounter between the holy law and the sinful tendencies in humans produces a struggle, which leads people to a place where they appreciate salvation from God. People realize the issue is not lack of knowledge about what is right; it is possible to have knowledge about what is right. It is also not about the will to do right; it is possible for people to have the will to do what is right. Therefore, knowledge and will are not enough to make people holy and spiritual. This encounter between the holy law and sinful humans leads to frustration with the human inadequacy to meet the standards of God. It is difficult for us as humans to meet standards we set for ourselves based on what we know is right; it is even more difficult to meet the perfect standards of God. It is simply impossible for humans to meet the standards of God. This is the Apostle Paul's frustration, which led him to cry out, "Wretched man that I am!" The following is Paul's testimony:

> For I know that good itself does not dwell in me, that is, in my sinful nature. For I have the desire to do what is good, but I cannot carry it out. For I do not do the good I want to do, but the evil I do not want to do—this I keep on doing. Now if I do what I do not want to do, it is no longer I who do it, but it is sin living in me that does it. (Rom 7:18-20)
>
> What a wretched man I am! Who will rescue me from this body that is subject to death? Thanks be to God, who delivers me through Jesus Christ our Lord! (Rom 7:24-25)

The Apostle Paul concluded that Jesus Christ provided the way of escape from this condition of frustration when he said,

> For what the law was powerless to do because it was weakened by the flesh, God did by sending his own Son in the likeness of

sinful flesh to be a sin offering. And so he condemned sin in the flesh, in order that the righteous requirement of the law might be fully met in us, who do not live according to the flesh but according to the Spirit. (Rom 8:3-4)

The helplessness of humans led to hopelessness for salvation through human efforts. God intervened by sending His Son Jesus Christ to fulfill the demands of the law through His holy living, because He does not share in the fallen sinful nature of humans. He is holy and perfect. Therefore, He was able to live a perfect life. The law was not made ineffective by His sinful nature. He was able to obey the demands of the law perfectly. The uniqueness of Jesus Christ's life is not only His perfection, but also His eternal and omnipresent nature. This means He could live His perfect life for all of human history and for all people. Because of this, there is now no condemnation for those who are in Christ Jesus (Rom 8:1).

Paul attributed this victory to a new law operating within Him— the law of the Spirit of life. This is contrary to the law of the sinful nature. How does the law of the Spirit of life work? We need to go back to the promises of God that pointed to the New Covenant. In the New Covenant, God Himself will put His laws in the minds of people and write it on their hearts. This will be through the ministry of the Holy Spirit.

> "The days are coming," declares the Lord, "when I will make a new covenant with the people of Israel and with the people of Judah. It will not be like the covenant I made with their ancestors when I took them by the hand to lead them out of Egypt, because they broke my covenant, though I was a husband to them," declares the Lord. "This is the *covenant* I will make with the people of Israel after that time," declares the Lord. "I will put my law in their minds and write it on their hearts. I will be their God and they will be my people. No longer will they teach their neighbor, or say to one another, 'Know the Lord,' because they will all know me, from the least of them to the greatest," declares the Lord. "For I will forgive their wickedness and will remember their sins no more" [italics added]. (Jer 31:31-34)

The Holy Spirit will be in the lives of the people of Israel, helping them know the will of the Lord, and granting them the power to obey His statutes (Ez 36:26-28).

> I will give you a new heart and put a new spirit in you; I will re-
> move from you your heart of stone and give you a heart of flesh.
> And I will put my Spirit in you and move you to follow my de-
> crees and be careful to keep my laws. Then you will live in the
> land I gave your ancestors; you will be my people, and I will be
> your God.

This experience of regeneration and ongoing empowerment is what
enables Christians to obey God and live victoriously. Empowered
Christians are able to say "no" to the demands of the sinful nature
and choose to walk in accordance with the desires of the Spirit.

This New Covenant will also extend beyond the people of Israel.
God promises to pour out His Spirit on all flesh in the last days.
Peoples of all nations will receive the blessing of the Holy Spirit, learn
the things of God through the Holy Spirit, and be empowered by the
Spirit to do the will of God. The prophecy of Joel speaks clearly to the
extension of the works of the Spirit beyond the nation of Israel to
cover all peoples across the world, "And afterward, I will pour out my
Spirit on all people. Your sons and daughters will prophesy, your old
men will dream dreams, your young men will see visions" (Jl 2:28).

To make this universal twist possible, it was necessary for the
demands of the law to be fully met in order to free humans from the
penalty of the law and be fully reconcilable to God. This requirement
is what called for the coming of God's Son to live a perfect life and to
satisfy the demands of the law on behalf of all humanity. He faced
the penalty for transgressing the law in the past, present and future
sense, in order to excuse humans from the wrath of God for their sins.

After the death and resurrection of Jesus Christ, the fulfillment
of the Father's promise occurred on the day of Pentecost; the Church
universal was born. Now, it is possible for people to experience the
new life in the Spirit.

In the first Creation, God breathed into Adam and Eve and they
became living souls. In the second Creation, the Holy Spirit comes
into human beings and they once again become living souls. This
is a *rebirth* experience, reversing the death, which came through the
Fall of humankind. It is for this reason that, except a human being is
born again through the inner regeneration of the Holy Spirit, he or
she cannot be in the kingdom of God.

The Concept of the Kingdom of God and the Gospel
Throughout the scriptures, the phrase "kingdom of God" is used; its significance is underscored by its frequent usage to explain God's plan for the nations and people by Jesus Christ. An earlier reference to the concept of the kingdom of God was when God made a promise to David to establish a kingdom through his lineage that will last forever.

> ...The Lord declares to you that the Lord himself will establish a house for you: When your days are over and you rest with your ancestors, I will raise up your offspring to succeed you, your own flesh and blood, and I will establish his kingdom. He is the one who will build a house for my Name, and I will establish the throne of his kingdom forever. (2 Sm 7:11[b]-13)

The immediate application was Solomon, who succeeded his father David as king. During his reign, Israel enjoyed rest from her enemies. It was a period characterized by peace. The reign of Solomon, as a king of peace, was also a pointer to the Messiah, the Son of David, King of Salem, who will reign forever as the King of Israel. Isaiah prophesied about the Messiah,

> For to us a child is born, to us a son is given, and the government will be on his shoulders. And he will be called Wonderful Counselor, Mighty God, Everlasting Father, Prince of Peace. Of the greatness of his government and peace there will be no end. He will reign on David's throne and over his kingdom, establishing and upholding it with justice and righteousness from that time on and forever. The zeal of the Lord Almighty will accomplish this. (Is 9:6-7)

The Messiah is to reign over David's kingdom and to lead in justice and righteousness. The reign is supposed to be eternal.

The vision of Nebuchadnezzar graphically illustrates the eternal nature of the throne of the kingdom of the Son of David. Nebuchadnezzar saw a statue representing the kingdoms of the earth. The head of the statue was made of pure gold, its chest and arms of silver, its belly and thighs of bronze, its legs of iron, and its feet partly of iron and partly of baked clay. While Nebuchadnezzar was watching, a rock was cut out of a mountain, but not by human hands. It struck the statue on its feet of iron and clay and smashed them. The rest of the statue was broken to pieces and became like chaff. The wind swept the chaff away without leaving any trace. However, the rock that struck the statue became a huge mountain and filled the whole earth.

Daniel explained that the four parts of the statue, made of different minerals, represented four kingdoms that would have world influence. We understand the head of gold represented the Babylonian kingdom; the chest and arms of silver represented the Persian kingdom; the belly and thighs of bronze represented the Grecian kingdom; and the legs of iron and feet, partly made of iron and partly made of burnt clay, represented the Roman kingdom. Daniel explained to King Nebuchadnezzar that the God of heaven bestows upon men the opportunity, power and authority to rule in the kingdoms of men. God's harsh judgment, followed by the removal of Nebuchadnezzar from office, was due to the failure of Nebuchadnezzar to acknowledge that heaven rules over the affairs of men through human governments (Dn 4:26).

The rock cut off by no human hands represents the kingdom of God, which will be set up to crush and bring an end to the kingdoms of men; this also includes religious kingdoms. The kingdom of God will grow over a period of time and eventually fill the whole earth, so that God's kingship will be on earth as it is in heaven. The existing mountain, from which the hand of God cut the rock, represents the kingdom of heaven.

The significance of the rock being cut from the existing mountain is that the kingdom of God, which will utterly cover the whole earth, is supposed to be exactly like the kingdom of God as it is in heaven. This is consistent with the Lord's Prayer, in which we are taught to pray for the kingdom of God to come and the will of God to be done on earth as it already is in heaven. The kingdom of God as it is in heaven should be the model for anything we are doing on earth in relation to the building of God's kingdom on earth.

Jesus as the King of the kingdom had to be likened to a stone cut with no human hand. His virgin birth was, therefore, necessary. He was born of Mary, but conceived of the Holy Spirit. He had to be, at the same time, the Son of David and the Son of God. The genealogy of Matthew was careful to establish Jesus as coming from David's line. He was born not only as Savior, but also as Lord. Therefore, He was called Christ the Lord. The lordship of Jesus Christ is directly linked to His being the King of the kingdom of God. He is Lord over all because He is the eternal King of the kingdom of God. He is the most qualified to be Savior of all because He is Lord over all. In essence, Christ the Savior, Lord and King, is Himself the good news. His various titles and functions only present His person and His functions from different perspectives.

When Jesus Christ's ministry started, He preached the *gospel of the kingdom*; His message to the people of His time was that the kingdom of God had come upon them. The King of the kingdom was in their midst. The hope for the kingdom yet to come was also a reality because Christ is the King for both the kingdom now, and the kingdom yet to come. All the blessings intended by God for humanity are experienced in the kingdom of God. The kingdom of God is the *community of the blessed*. Appropriately, the gospel of Jesus Christ is called the gospel of the kingdom (Mt 4:23; 9:35; 24:14; Mk 1:14-15).

The gospel of the kingdom points to the kingdom yet to come. Yet, the launching of the kingdom in the now by Jesus Christ is in itself a necessary tasting and demonstration of the promise of the gospel.

The Concept of Good News or Glad Tidings and the Gospel
The prophets in the Old Testament used the phrases "good news" or "glad tidings" to announce a good turn of events. While defeated and ruled by Assyrians and then Babylonians, the Jews used the phrases in the context of their deliverance from the oppression of their enemies. They looked forward to a Savior who would restore the times of *shalom* they had enjoyed under the leadership of Solomon. The Messiah was to be the King of Salem whose reign will never end.

The prophet Isaiah foresaw the announcing of liberty to the people of Israel. In spite of the difficulties and sufferings under the rulers of other nations, the good news Isaiah proclaimed was for the people of Israel to be aware that their God was still the King over all the nations of the earth. He still reigned and He had not lost control. Isaiah, therefore, prophesied:

> How beautiful on the mountains are the feet of those who bring *good news*, who proclaim peace, who bring *good tidings*, who proclaim salvation, who say to Zion, "Your God reigns!" [italics added]. (Is 52:7)

The good news about God's reign was also an announcement of deliverance for His people. Because God reigned, He was going to bring salvation to His people; a link existed between salvation and the kingship of God. Those who came down from the mountains proclaimed the good news of a new day, a day of salvation for the people of God. It was also an encouraging reminder that the God of the people of Israel had not forgotten His people. He had not become powerless in the face of the kingdoms of men. He indeed was on the throne as the King over all nations, and the Deliverer of the people of Israel. His mighty arm would bring salvation to His people. The prophet Nahum also presented the same message:

> Look, there on the mountains, the feet of one who brings *good news*, who proclaims peace! Celebrate your festivals, Judah, and fulfill your vows. No more will the wicked invade you; they will be completely destroyed [italics added]. (Na 1:15)

God will bring deliverance and usher in a time of peace for His people. The people of God will not forever remain prey for the wicked. The prophet Isaiah explained God's plan to bring deliverance by personally visiting His people. The eternal God was going to visit His people, dwell amongst them, and bring them salvation. The good news was linked to the experiencing of salvation and peace on the part of God's people.

> You, who bring *good news* to Zion, go up on a high mountain. You who bring *good news* to Jerusalem, lift up your voice with a shout, lift it up, do not be afraid; say to the towns of Judah, "Here is your God!" [italics added]. (Is 40:9)

In Isaiah 40, the good news was about God's visit to His people. This was a prophecy about God visiting His people in the person of Jesus Christ. The angels, John the Baptist, and later on, the disciples shared the good news of great joy—the coming of Jesus. The angel of the Lord appeared to a group of shepherds, who were keeping watch over their flocks at night, to announce to them,

> Do not be afraid. I bring you *good news* that will cause great joy for all the people. Today in the town of David, a Savior has been born to you; He is the Messiah, the Lord [italics added]. (Lk 2:10-11)

The disciples of Jesus Christ in our time also have reason to announce the good news of God coming to dwell among His Creation in the person of Jesus. We can proclaim to the people of our generation the good news that, through Jesus Christ, our God has revealed Himself to us in human flesh!

Jesus secured the salvation of the Jews and the rest of humanity by laying down His own life as a ransom; He died to ensure that the unrighteous who place their trust in Him would be saved. He conquered death through His resurrection. His name was, therefore, exalted above all other names, so that at the mention of the name of Jesus, every knee will bow and every tongue confess that He is Lord.

We can conclude with the position that the scriptures present the gospel through different concepts. These include the concepts of blessings, the New Covenant, the kingdom of God, and glad tidings or good news. The gospel is, therefore, presented as the original blessings intentions of God, or the New Covenant, or the kingdom of God, or glad tidings. Looking at the gospel from all these perspectives provides a richer and more comprehensive understanding. There is what we may call the *gospel time line*. There is a past, present and future perspective on the gospel. Concerning the past, God, through His Son Jesus Christ, paid the price for our salvation. He gave His Son so that none will perish. This is good news.

In the present, God reigns as King over all nations, powers and authorities. Christ, the King of God's kingdom, is at work in the present to empower those who believe so that they can experience, even in part, the full benefits of salvation promised for the future. Christians do not have to live as victims of sin or Satan. Christ the King, who reigns in power, continues to work powerfully in and through the lives of believers to give them victory. This is good news.

Regarding the future, God will completely transform all He created so there will no longer be sin or its effects. We will dwell together with God forever in His kingdom. There will be no more death or suffering, or tears. The people of God will break out in singing, with shouts of joy that salvation belongs to Jesus Christ. This is good news! From the past, present and future perspectives, we understand the gospel as God's blessings being showered on humankind.

Modifiers of the Gospel
Other modifiers of "the gospel" in the New Testament can shed further light on its meanings and implications. These modifiers allow us to look at the gospel from different perspectives (Keathley, 2000): the gospel of Jesus Christ (Mk 1:1; 1 Cor 9:14); the gospel of His Son (Rom 1:9); the gospel of the grace of God (Acts 20:24); the gospel of the kingdom (Mt 4:23; 9:35; 24:14); the gospel of peace (Eph 6:15); and the

eternal or everlasting gospel (Rv 14:6). From these we know that the gospel is about the Son of God and His kingdom.

The gospel is an act of God's grace and should be received as such. It is not a result of human effort. It is the gift of God, so no one can boast about making the gospel possible in any human experience. The gospel is about the peace of God; the peace or *shalom* of God is a state of wholeness and total wellbeing resulting from a right relationship with God and it is the blessing promised by God. The benefits of the gospel are not only for now, but also for all of eternity.

God's Strategy for Blessing the Nations

God promised to bless Abraham as the father of the nation of Israel and that he would be a blessing to all other nations. Israel was chosen by God as both the object of blessing and the channel of blessings to all nations.

The Nation of Israel as Witness

God's strategy was to build the nation of Israel on His nature and laws. The nation of Israel would then be an example to other nations. God made His plan clear in the following statement:

> See, I have taught you decrees and laws as the Lord my God commanded me, so that you may follow them in the land you are entering to take possession of it. Observe them carefully, for this will show your wisdom and understanding to the nations, who will hear about all these decrees and say, 'Surely this great nation is a wise and understanding people.' What other nation is so great as to have their gods near them the way the Lord our God is near us whenever we pray to him? And what other nation is so great as to have such righteous decrees and laws as this body of laws I am setting before you today? (Dt 4:5-8)

God's purpose in choosing Israel was to establish it on godly principles as an example for other nations. The nations will observe:

- The righteous decrees and laws of Israel.
- The wisdom and understanding of the people of Israel.
- The closeness of God to the people of Israel, demonstrated through answered prayers.

In this way, the nation of Israel was meant to be a light to other nations. Being a light means a nation is governed by righteous decrees, the citizens are filled with knowledge, wisdom and understanding, and God is supernaturally showering His blessings on the nation.

The level of knowledge, wisdom and understanding of the citizens of nations is a true reflection of their level of development. When a people develop a culture of pursuing and applying knowledge and wisdom, and do so with godly motives, their development is not only good, but also exemplary. God's favor is directed towards nations governed by righteousness, justice, and godly wisdom.

The call to be witnesses for God is not limited in its focus to individuals. God also expects communities and nations to be His witnesses. The role of Christians in society is to call their nations to such leadership, governance and development that make them witnesses of God. The call to make disciples of nations, therefore, includes discipling leaders and citizens in godly leadership, governance and development principles. When done successfully, this is when the nations become witnesses to the wisdom and power of God. The nations effectively become examples of, and as such, pointers to the kingdom of God yet to come. The affairs of such nations are governed with the constant focus and prayer that God's will be done in these nations as it is in heaven.

Making disciples of all nations is not only about making individual disciples within the nations; it is also about governing the nations based on the nature and principles of the kingdom of heaven.

The Church as the New Nation
According to the Apostle Peter, the Church, as a community, is the new nation of God. It is a community of people called from the nations of men to constitute a new universal nation of people, who submit to Jesus Christ as their Head. The Head of State for the new nation of God's people is Jesus Christ. This new nation is called to declare, even more powerfully, the wisdom, power and plan of God. The Apostle Peter wrote:

> But you are a chosen people, a royal priesthood, a *holy nation*, God's special possession, that you may declare the praises of him who called you out of darkness into his wonderful light. Once you were not a people, but now you are the people of God; once you had not received mercy, but now you have received mercy. Dear friends, I urge you, as foreigners and exiles, to abstain from sinful desires, which wage war against your soul. Live

such good lives among the pagans that, though they accuse you of doing wrong, they may see your good deeds and glorify God on the day he visits us [italics added]. (1 Pt 2:9-12)

The Church, as the new nation of God, is called to declare the praises of God, pursue holiness, and practice good deeds in such a way that those outside this community of faith cannot but glorify God. This compares well with the admonishing of Jesus Christ when He said, "In the same way, let your light shine before others, that they may see your good deeds and glorify your Father in heaven" (Mt 5:16).

It is important to note that the prophecies about Israel are not annulled by the creation of the universal Church as a new nation. The Church universal is a broadening of the blessings of God to all humanity beyond the nation Israel; it is not a replacement of the nation Israel. It also emphasizes an Abraham-like faith as the condition for belonging to God's community of the blessed, not biological genetic connection.

Communities can choose governance by the principles and laws of the kingdom of heaven. Such communities, if properly governed, can be witnesses to other nations of the wisdom, power and plan of God. However, the new nation of God—the Church, is called to be light. The Church has no option but to ensure that she is governed in a way that is exemplary to other peoples. It should be the best government on earth, showing forth the wisdom of God and the power of Jesus Christ as the Head of this universal nation.

The Nations as an Inheritance of Jesus Christ
A biblical study of God's strategy for blessing the nations is helpful for understanding how the message and blessing intentions of the gospel should influence Christian missions today. Psalm 2 has a recording of the conversation between God, as Father, and His Son, as Messiah, regarding the blessing of the nations. The Father said to the Son:

You are my Son; today I have become your Father. Ask of me, and I will make the nations your inheritance, the ends of the earth your possession. You will rule them with an iron scepter; you will dash them to pieces like pottery. (Ps 2:7[b]-9)

In this passage, there is a direct link between making the nations an inheritance of the Son and the rulership of the Son over the nations. The Father desires to give the nations to His Son as an inheritance. This plan of God is best understood in the context of the Creation story of the Bible. According to the New Testament, God created the world through His Son and there is nothing created, which did not involve the Son. Nevertheless, more importantly, God created all things *for* His Son. Therefore, everything belongs to the Son by God's original intention.

Those who lay claim to aspects of God's Creation need to understand who is the rightful owner. If properly understood, all owners of elements of God's Creation are only trustees, appointed or allowed by God, to exercise stewardship on behalf of His Son. If we apply this understanding of ownership, trusteeship and stewardship to nations, we quickly appreciate that all leaders of nations are not outright owners of the people they lead. To act as such is to take an opposing stand to God's intended purpose for His Son to be the rightful owner of all nations. All leaders of nations are but trustees, appointed or allowed by God, to exercise good stewardship on behalf of His Son—who has been revealed to us in the person of Jesus the Christ. Leaders who recognize this will also do well to seek ways of "stewardship-leadership" consistent with God's agenda and as such please Him.

These approaches to "stewardship-leadership" rightfully acknowledge God as the source of power and authority, and demonstrate accountability towards God. They acknowledge God as the source of all blessings. We seek blessings for nations through "stewardship-leadership": recognizing God as the source of all authority and power, and exercising leadership in ways consistent with the character and plans of God.

If properly followed, God's plans for the leadership of nations will lead to an understanding and acceptance of His Son as the First Trustee who is sharing responsibility for the stewardship of His Father's Creation with earthly representatives. This is the reason Psalm 2 continues with a warning and admonition to the kings of nations:

> Therefore, *you kings*, be wise; be warned, and you rulers of the earth. Serve the Lord with fear and celebrate his rule with trembling. *Kiss his son*, or he will be angry and your way will lead to your destruction, for his wrath can flare up in a moment. Blessed are all who take refuge in *him* [italics added]. (Ps 2:10-12)

This conversation between God, as Father, and Jesus, His Son, presents a unique perspective on the Great Commission mandate. The leaders of nations, who are privileged to be making policies and determining values that shape the cultures and lives of their people, need to acknowledge the higher authority of God and His Son. They are admonished to make peace with the Son of God, to love and embrace His purposes, and to serve God with fear, joy and trembling. Leaders of nations will have to answer as to how they lead, and how they relate to God and His Son. All leadership authority comes from God. All leaders need to be aware of their accountability to God.

When the thoughts of leaders are taken captive by the good news, to the obedience of God and His Son, then the nations they lead are directed by the purposes of God and shaped by the values of God. Effectively, Jesus Christ becomes the recognized ruler of such nations. Such nations become, in actuality (though imperfectly), the inheritance of Jesus Christ, waiting for the ushering in of the eternal kingdom when they become the perfect eternal inheritance of Jesus Christ.

The call to recognize the Son of God as the ruler over all the nations is universal. This universal nature is justified because the nations of the world are seeking the Son of God. When one studies the aspirations and cries of the nations, it becomes obvious that they are seeking One like the Son of Man, even Jesus Christ. The prophet Haggai makes a good note of this:

> This is what the Lord Almighty says, 'In a little while I will once more shake the heavens and the earth, the sea and the dry land. I will shake all nations, and what is desired by all nations will come, and I will fill this house with glory,' says the Lord Almighty. (Hg 2:6-7)

This passage is generally agreed to be a messianic passage speaking of Jesus the Christ as the desired One of all nations. A universal quest for Jesus Christ is the implication here. This means that Jesus, if properly presented and understood, is not only recognizable by all nations and cultures, but is also desired or wanted by all peoples. This reality should be a motivation for presenting Christ to all nations as the One they have been desiring and seeking. This is one of the reasons the message of the Christ is good news to all nations.

A careful look at Psalm 2 shows that leaders of nations are admonished *now* to align with God's plan to give the nations as an inheritance to Jesus Christ. They are told to kiss the Son of God; this means accepting and loving Him. This message, particularly directed to the kings of the nations, is similar to the admonishing in scriptures to pray for those in authority (1Tim 2:1-2). Praying for those in authority is with the purpose of living peaceful lives in all godliness and holiness. This is also God's desire for nations in the present age. God does have a desire for nations to be led with godly and righteous values in the present, so that they are actually under the kingship and rulership of Jesus Christ, the Son of God, albeit imperfectly.

The image of dashing the nations to pieces in Psalm 2 is consistent with the vision in Daniel 2, where the kingdoms of men are dashed to pieces by the rock cut with no human hands. They are gradually replaced by the kingdom of God, which fills the whole earth. Two things are obvious from this part of Psalm 2. First, it confirms again that the rulership of the Son of God in question is that of the kingdom now. Second, when nations come under the rulership of the Son of God in the present, it serves as a witness to God and His kingdom. Kings and other citizens see the difference made in a nation when leadership submits to the rulership and principles of Jesus Christ. They are then encouraged to rise above the kingdom now and sign up for the eternal kingdom yet to come.

Is the Church, as the new nation, the only inheritance of Jesus Christ, or is Christ also the Head of all nations and as such inviting them to acknowledge His rulership? The answer to this question will greatly affect our approach to missions. The Church is under Christ's mandate to be the light for all nations. However, all nations are still invited to follow the example of the Church and acknowledge the supremacy of the wisdom, nature, and plans of God. The nations are invited to accept the Lordship of Jesus Christ and be governed by His Christ-like values and principles.

The Church develops leaders as oaks of righteousness (Is 61:3) who see themselves as ambassadors of Jesus Christ wherever they find themselves in society. They see themselves as ambassadors in the marketplace. They are kingdom ambassadors; they represent the kingdom of God wherever they are and show how things work on earth based on how things work in the kingdom of heaven. They live their lives, and do their work (as lawyers, engineers, financial managers, doctors, etc.) based on kingdom principles. They see the way they do their work as part of their witness for Jesus Christ.

God's strategy begins with the Church, within the nation, living by the principles and values and laws of Jesus Christ. As an example or light, the Church engages the rest of the nation in a discipleship relationship, which is expected to lead to the nation being gradually transformed into Christ-likeness. Such transformation is never perfect or complete, but it is different enough to be a shining example to society, and a pointer to the perfect and coming kingdom of God. Leadership and governance in the Church and of the Church in society through service are an essential part of Christian witness.

The Gospel and Christian Missions

Christian mission is essentially about bringing the good news to people in every nation. The understanding of Christian mission comes from what we refer to as the Great Commission.

The Great Commission

The Great Commission is a call to make disciples of all nations. We are called, first, to be disciples of Jesus Christ and then, to help make disciples among all other peoples. The phrase "all nations" needs to be understood in the context of its biblical usage throughout the Old Testament. The Great Commission is the means to effecting God's purpose of blessing all nations that embrace Abraham as father. Through Jesus Christ, One greater than Abraham, all nations become a part of God's eternal family; the eternal "blessed community." The blessings are for this age and the ages to come.

The Great Commission is a call to make disciples of all nations, not just make disciples in all nations. The difference in meaning and implications is significant. Making disciples within a nation could simply focus on individuals as disciples. Making disciples of nations means not only the discipling of individuals, but also of communities to ensure they build themselves on godly principles, honoring Christ. However, the process for discipling nations begins with the building of communities of disciples (churches) as the new nation within the nation. The communities of disciples are able to engage nations in discipleship processes, opening the nation to receive the blessings of God, which should not be looked at in the popular sense as essentially consisting of material blessings. God's blessings are holistic and primarily seek to bring the people of a nation relationally closer to God.

What is the exact nature of these blessings? Through the teaching of nations to obey the teachings of Jesus Christ, they are able to experience life as God intends it. The Holy Spirit, working through the Church, brings blessings touching all spheres of human society.

The areas addressed in Deuteronomy 8 are still relevant in the New Covenant, and for that matter, the Great Commission. God's call is for His people to obey all His commands. Jesus Christ repeated this call when He asked that His disciples learn and teach others to observe all of His commandments. In Deuteronomy 8, we see God's priorities in relation to His blessing intentions. When He took the Israelites through the wilderness for 40 years, it was to humble and teach them that humans should not be preoccupied mainly with their daily bread or basic material needs, but rather should prioritize living by all of God's revealed Word (Dt 8:3). Jesus repeated this lesson to His disciples when He commanded them to not worry about their basic needs. Instead, they should be eager to seek first the things pertaining to the kingdom and righteousness of God (Mt 6:33). God, therefore, commands His people to prioritize living by His Word—seeking first His kingdom and His righteousness; these priorities make spiritual blessings foundational to all other blessings.

However, it is important to note God's intentions to expand His blessings to cover other dimensions of life. He cautioned the Israelites about the temptation to take credit for the blessings of God. Jesus also carefully used the phrase "…and all other things shall be added to you." Added blessings strongly indicate that the blessings come from God, not from human might or intelligence. When God blesses individuals and a people, He expects them to be thankful to Him for the blessings—not to be arrogant and proud in thinking they have accomplished great things for themselves. God also expects people who are experiencing His blessings to continue living by His Word. God's priority is to help us learn more about Him and His ways. Sometimes this could mean losing material blessings in order to relearn how "man does not live by bread alone but by every Word that comes from God" (Dt 8:3).

Prioritizing the spiritual is not a call to exclusivity of focus on the spiritual; it is also not a call to shy away from seeking wealth in the other spheres of life. We are to always seek abundant blessings in all dimensions of life whilst prioritizing the spiritual aspect. What is constant is the wholehearted commitment to all of the Word of God with focus on relational intimacy with Him. This relational intimacy is the blessing of God's presence in the lives of those who are dedicated to Him. In John 14:21, Jesus promises this abiding presence to those who obey God's command. He promised that the Son and the Father would reveal more and more of themselves to those who obey God's commands.

The second important commitment after prioritizing the spiritual is learning to continue to rejoice in the blessed presence of God, both when there is abundance of material blessings or scarcity of material blessings (Phil 4:11-13). We should constantly pursue abundant blessings in all spheres of life, but be flexible, as God in His sovereignty allows different levels of blessings in the material or physical sphere of life for the higher purpose of transforming us into the image of His dear Son, Jesus Christ.

Some Essential Characteristics of the Great Commission
The following are some essential characteristics of the Great Commission:

The Great Commission is based on the New Covenant.

The Great Commission is based *on faith.*

> i. It moves away from dependence on what humans are able to do to obey the laws of God, to faith in what Jesus Christ has done to fulfill the demands of the law on behalf of all people.

> ii. There is also a shift from dependence on human faculties to obey God's laws, to dependence on the enabling power of the Holy Spirit.

The Great Commission is about *all nations* and not only the nation of Israel.

The Great Commission *expands* the blessing intentions of God from the temporary to the eternal.

The Great Commission is not a shift from focusing on blessings in the now to eternal spiritual blessings reserved for the age to come; it prioritizes the spiritual and eternal, but is supposed to encompass all other spheres of life in the present as well as in the future.

The manifesto of Jesus Christ in Isaiah 61 illustrates this point well. Jesus said to His disciples: "As the Father has sent me, I am sending you" (Jn 20:21b). In our approach to helping fulfill the Great Commission, we are truly called to follow the example of Jesus Christ.

The nature of the mission of Jesus Christ is well explained in the prophecy of Isaiah read by Jesus in the temple:

> The Spirit of the Sovereign Lord is on me, because the Lord has anointed me to proclaim *good news* to the poor. He has sent me to bind up the brokenhearted, to proclaim freedom for the captives and release from darkness for the prisoners, to proclaim the year of the Lord's favor and the day of vengeance of our God, to comfort all who mourn, and provide for those who grieve in Zion—to bestow on them a crown of beauty instead of ashes, the oil of gladness instead of mourning, and a garment of praise instead of a spirit of despair. They will be called oaks of righteousness, a planting of the Lord for the display of His *splendor.* (Is 61:1-3)

When Jesus identified Himself with this prophecy, it shook the religious leaders of His time because it was the conclusive identification with the Messiah they were expecting.

The Benefits of the Great Commission
From Isaiah 61:1-6 and related passages, the benefits for those who become plantings of the Lord to display His splendor can be grouped into the following categories:

- **Economic**
  Rebuilding ancient ruins
  Aliens shepherding your flocks
  Foreigners working your fields
  Food for the hungry and water for the thirsty (Ps 107:8-9)

- **Spiritual**
  Release from darkness
  Becoming priests of the Most High
  Becoming oaks of righteousness

- **Emotional**
  Everlasting joy will be theirs
  Gladness instead of mourning
  Spirit of praise instead of spirit of despair

- **Political**
  Justice to the nations (Is 42:1 and 3b)
  Freedom for the captive (Ps 107:10-16)

In order to avoid the common temptation to engage in a pseudo-spiritualizing of Isaiah 61, we need to turn to Isaiah 58 for some explanation of the intended meaning of the words and phrases used by Jesus Christ:

> Is not this the kind of fasting I have chosen: to loose the chains of injustice and untie the cords of the yoke, to set the oppressed free and break every yoke? Is it not to share your food with the hungry and to provide the poor wanderer with shelter—when you see the naked, to clothe them, and not to turn away from your own flesh and blood? Then your light will break forth like the dawn, and your healing will quickly appear; then your righteousness will go before you, and the glory of the Lord will be your rear guard. Then you will call, and the Lord will answer; you will cry for help, and he will say: Here am I. If you do away with the yoke of oppression, with the pointing finger and malicious talk, and if you spend yourselves in behalf of the hungry and satisfy the needs of the oppressed, then your light will rise in the darkness, and your night will become like the noonday. The Lord will guide you always; he will satisfy your needs in a sun-scorched land and will strengthen your frame. You will be like a well-watered garden, like a spring whose waters never fail. Your people will rebuild the ancient ruins and will raise up the age-old foundations; you will be called Repairer of Broken Walls, Restorer of Streets with Dwellings. (Is 58:6-12)

Fasting is one of the most difficult spiritual disciplines; we fast in order to commune effectively with God. However, God views spirituality differently. Although He commends fasting, God also entrusts us to practice other deep spiritual disciplines, which invite His blessings. These include: fighting for justice for the weak, feeding the hungry and providing shelter for the wanderer.

One of the challenges of present day Evangelical Theology is that what God considers spiritual actions, we prefer to reference with a sense of spiritual pride as social action. Yet, social action, when done with godly motivation and purpose, becomes a spiritual act of worship. Psalm 107 also throws much light on the relevance of this passage to the other areas of human life and existence mentioned above.

In Ezekiel chapter 36, we see another example of God addressing the economic aspects of His blessing intentions to the nation Israel. In characteristic figurative language, God speaks to the mountains of Israel; His message was to condemn the unrighteousness of the people of Israel for their pollution, or corruption, of the mountains and the rest of the land. Therefore, here we find a direct link between the spiritual lives of a people and the blessing potential of the land of the people. The idolatry and immorality of the people of Israel caused God to limit the economic benefits of their land.

Later in the chapter, God promises healing to the land and blessings for the people. A simple conclusion from the figurative speech is that God cares about the mountains and the land He has gifted to nations. It is His desire for the land to remain fruitful. When this is the case, the land will fulfill the God-intended purpose of providing food, shelter and the pleasure of beauty to the inhabitants. We should not make any more claims from the Ezekiel 36 passage other than to observe how the passage presents a link between the spiritual condition of the people and the fruitfulness of their land. This is understandable when we revisit our proposition that blessings in all spheres of life come from God.

We, however, have to keep in focus the main objective of the Great Commission. The object of the Great Commission is to help reconcile people of every nation to God. God is in the process of reconciling humanity to Himself. The gospel is, therefore, a message of reconciliation. There are two dimensions to reconciliation. The vertical dimension is reconciliation to God. People of every nation are spiritually separated from God without Jesus Christ. They are all aliens to the kingdom of God. When people, through the hearing and understanding of the gospel, turn from their sins and enter into saving relationships with God through Jesus Christ, they are reconciled to God. This in turn leads to the horizontal dimension, which is the reconciling of humans to one another. A powerful effect of the gospel is the breaking down of all walls of hostility between humans so that in the place of divisions there is oneness (Eph 2:14-16).

God is also in the process of reconciling the rest of His material Creation to Himself. All of Creation is groaning and waiting in eagerness for redemption and transformation, so the corruption there now, because of the Fall, is replaced with perfection (Rom 8:19-22). God is, through Christ, reconciling all things to Himself, whether in heaven or on earth, making peace by the blood of His cross (Col 1:20). The cross of Jesus Christ, therefore, becomes a symbol of the reconciling of all

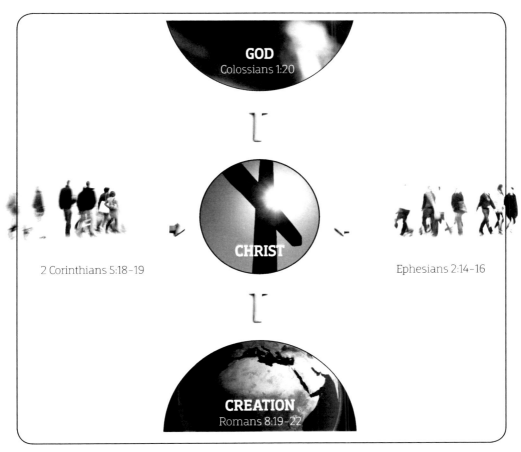

FIGURE 1 – God through Jesus Christ reconciling all things to Himself

things to God.

The Great Commission is about the reconciling of all things to God through Jesus Christ. This then is what provides the framework for Christian mission. Though individuals and institutions will play their different parts in this process of reconciliation, God is working through all the Great Commission efforts to accomplish the overall objective of reconciling all things to Himself.

God is redeeming, reconciling and transforming all that He has made; He is returning all things to their original state of blessing. God will look again at all He has redeemed, reconciled and restored, and will say, "It is good." God will also restore humans to their stewardship-leadership responsibility over His Creation as co-heirs with Jesus Christ, the Chief Steward.

This vision of the future hope of the gospel provides a framework for Christian missions in the present. Christian missions should not only focus on spiritual redemption, though this is the unquestionable priority. Missions should also demonstrate, albeit imperfectly, the heart of God for all of His Creation. Those who are reconciled to God should share in the heart of God for the reconciliation of humans to one another, and the rest of Creation to God, through Jesus Christ.

Christian missions throughout history have been faced with the tension of either focusing almost exclusively on the spiritual, or on all aspects of human life and Creation.

Historical Shifts in the Understanding and Approaches to Christian Missions

The 1st century of Christianity was concentrated in the Middle East, North Africa and Europe. The early disciples, who were directly influenced by the Lord Jesus Christ, laid the foundation. Legend has it that Mark went down to Egypt to spread the good news. Thomas is believed to have taken the new faith to India. Paul was largely responsible for the spread of the faith in the Near East and parts of Europe (Greece, Rome, Cyprus, etc.). Philip, in obedience to the Holy Spirit, introduced the good news to the rest of Africa by helping convert the Cushite (Ethiopian eunuch) from the north of Khartoum, in present-day Sudan.

Christian states were established in the 4th century. In 301 A.D., King Tiridates III established Christianity as the sole religion of Armenia, making it the first Christian nation in history (Babayan). The second was in the Roman world and occurred when Constantine's first edict concerning Christians was given in Rome in 312. This edict was lost, however, Constantine's edict of 313, in Milan, recognized Christians and granted them free religious worship ("Constantine" in EarlyChurch.org.uk). Two young men, Frumentius and Aedisius converted King Ezana of Axum to Christianity. Around 340, Ezana was baptized and Christianity became the official religion of the Axum Empire in present day Ethiopia (Nosotro, 2009).

Constantine was disturbed by the doctrinal conflicts amongst Christians. The members of the primal religions at the time lived together peacefully. This was, however, not the case for the Christians. In response, Constantine organized the first meeting of government and Christian leaders in Nicene, in present day Turkey, in 325. This was in direct response to the Arian heresy, which denied the deity of Jesus Christ (Slick, 2009). The result from this Council was the Nicene Creed, which was revised at the second Ecumenical Council held in 381 in Constantinople. The meeting in Constantinople was in response to the Macedonian or Pneumatomachian heresy, which denied the divinity of the Holy Spirit (Slick, 2009). The third Ecumenical Council was held in Ephesus in 431.

> The fourth ecumenical Council at Chalcedon in Asia Minor (what is now Turkey) met in 451 to address the idea that Jesus lacked a human nature (along with other ecclesiastical issues). Chalcedon attempted to define a middle way that balanced Jesus' divine and human aspects by emphasizing that Jesus had two natures unified in one person, so that he was genuinely human and yet truly divine. Chalcedon was also careful to avoid saying that Jesus was two persons, a position called Nestorianism that had already been rejected at the third ecumenical Council at Ephesus in 431. (Bratcher, 2009)

The Athanasian Creed was named after Athanasius, but is believed to have been developed in the 6th or the early 7th century.

These Councils were held to ensure that the many factions and variations of Christianity did not obscure the teachings of Jesus Christ and the early apostles. What we know today as Orthodox Christianity was the result of these Councils. One must be quick to point out that the Councils did not eliminate disagreements. The remaining doctrinal agreements, among other things, led to different orthodox traditions—Syrian, Greek, Roman, Egyptian, etc. In the following centuries, there were many efforts to preserve orthodox Christianity, some commendable and others regrettable. It was not until the 16th century when a radically new Christian tradition emerged in reaction to some of the fundamental assumptions of Orthodox Christianity, particularly that of Rome.

In 1454, Johannes Gutenberg invented printing in Europe. At the time, there were only 30,000 books in all of Europe. By 1500, there were nine million books ("Gutenberg" in English Translation of the

Bible, 2009). The Roman Catholic Church established the Canon of scripture at the Council of Trent in 1546 (Marlowe, 1848). On October 31, 1517, All Hallows' Eve, Martin Luther nailed his 95 Theses to the door of the Castle Church at Wittenberg (Kreis, 2002). Luther's attention was captivated by the realization from scripture that, "the just shall live by faith." Salvation is only possible through faith. This was followed by John Calvin's lecture on All Saints Day in 1533, in which he defended justification by faith alone (Kreis, 2002). After the Reformation, the Western Church became divided between those who accepted the authority of the Pope in Rome and those who did not. The Church of England did not.

> The Church of England was among the churches that broke with Rome. The catalyst for this decision was the refusal of the Pope to annul the marriage of Henry VIII and Catherine of Aragon, but underlying this was a Tudor nationalist belief that authority over the English Church properly belonged to the English monarchy. In the reign of Henry's son Edward VI, the Church of England underwent further reformation, driven by the conviction that the theology being developed by the theologians of the Protestant Reformation was more faithful to the teaching of the Bible and the Early Church than the teaching of those who continued to support the Pope. In the reign of Mary Tudor, the Church of England once again submitted to Papal authority. However, this policy was reversed when Elizabeth I came to the throne in 1558. ("A Reformed Church," 2004).

There was a movement of people who thought England's break from the Catholic Church in 1535 did not go far enough. In their view, substituting the King of England for the Pope was simply recapitulating a corrupt and even idolatrous order ("Pilgrims and Puritans: Background"). The Puritans believed religious authority should be grounded solely in scripture and not in the Pope, king or the Holy Catholic Church. The increasing dissemination of scripture, and the emphasis on it for spiritual meaning, led to growing individualism. This individualism led to the dispersion of authority, moving away from the centralization of authority in the king or the Pope. The authorities in England feared this growing movement of individualism and resorted to persecution.

The Puritans were separatists who believed in coming out from among those who did not accept the sole authority of scripture, or did not interpret scripture properly. They first went to Holland in 1608. They wanted freedom in new lands to build communities of faith based on Puritan beliefs. After 12 years, the Puritans returned to England complaining about the hard way of life in Holland. They wanted an easier place to raise their children and ensure the continuation of strong families. It would seem they feared the "ungodly" influences on their children in Holland. They also saw a possible migration to the New World as an opportunity to advance the kingdom of Christ in distant lands. Migrations from Europe to the New World began in 1620 (Palfrey, 2007). The Puritan migrants hoped to build a model society. John Winthrop expressed his vision for this model city as: "... We shall be as a city upon a hill. The eyes of all people are upon us."

The children of the migrants did not always remain faithful to the Christian beliefs and values of their parents. This led to the culture of evangelical revivals in America. The first sermons of Solomon Stoddard in Northampton, Massachusetts, resulted in revival breaking out as early as 1679. Jonathan Edwards, George Whitefield, and others preached new messages to re-establish the place of God in society. Their messages focused on sin, repentance and the personal experience of conversion. Revivals broke out across America and led to the shaping of American Evangelical Christianity (Wake Forest University Web site, 2009).

This new evangelicalism thrived on the culture of individualism. Every individual was to continually seek spiritual renewal and revival as a necessary foundation for the new communities that were to be light for the rest of society. The culture of individualism amongst the Puritans, which emphasized scripture as the sole authority for life and faith, was to be coupled with the acceptance of John Calvin's rule that those who are to perform any public function in the Church should be chosen by common voice ("Pilgrims and Puritans: Background"). This led to what Americans later called democracy. The culture of democracy in North America, even though an asset from the Reformation, posed its own problems to Western Christianity. Popular views were now in contention with traditional Christian beliefs. Democracy became the new religion challenging Evangelical Christianity.

A second challenge to Evangelical Christianity was the European Enlightenment, which encouraged a departure from the tradition of uncritically accepting Christian beliefs. Rationality, as a new value, elevated "reason" to new heights in Western society. Reason was applied to scriptural claims to investigate their sensibility and acceptability.

This ushered in the age of Modernity, which sought to establish truth through scientific reasoning. The pietistic movement resulted as a reaction to this modern version of Christianity. Pietism sought to preserve commitment to the literal meaning of scripture with openness to the spiritual or supernatural. Modern theology, which was a by-product of "Enlightenment Christianity," challenged the illogical supernatural claims of scripture.

The scientific age following the Enlightenment also challenged the traditional uncritical acceptance of a Christian worldview as proposed by leaders in the Church. Isaac Newton's *Principia Mathematica*, in the 17th century, put traditional religious beliefs under pressure. Newton's works, and those of other scientists, seemed to minimize the gap between God and humans. The Church had to now contend with a growing perception in society that man had the ability to discover the secrets of the universe and thereby control his own destiny. Hitherto, man's destiny was believed to be solely in God's hands. The situation became more serious with the introduction of Darwin's Evolution Theory. This theory challenged the basic Christian assumption that God created the world. It questioned, albeit indirectly, the very existence of God. These new developments challenged the otherwise taken for granted privilege of Christianity to be the religion that was shaping society in the present and future sense.

A characteristic of the scientific age was the optimism that science had the potential of ushering in an era of utopia. What has become so characteristic of the Church is that what goes on in the world determines not only the agenda of the Church, but also the theology of the Church. In the 18th and the 19th centuries, the Church developed scientific methods for Bible interpretation believed to have the potential of leading students of the Bible to the same truth if applied correctly. The pioneers of the hermeneutical methods, therefore, laid claim to the "truth" regarding biblical passages and claims. The religious commitment given to defending these "truths" contributed significantly to the founding of many new denominations and movements in Christianity.

This new era of optimism due to the Enlightenment and the scientific age continued until the First and Second World Wars in the early parts of the 20th century. The hope in the new utopia that was going to be ushered in by science was shattered. This resulted in a new skepticism, which ushered in the era of relativism. The Church has not escaped this era of relativism. Truth is relative. Post-modernity has taken the place of Modernity. Experience is given more prominence than the discovery of truth through scientific biblical interpretation. Evangelical Christianity has fully met its giants.

One of the greatest challenge to Christianity has been the shift on the part of Evangelical Christianity from seeking to create communities of faith that would be a light for society, to focusing on "spiritual individual salvation." With the hopelessness that faced the world after the World Wars, Evangelical Christianity defined Christian missions narrowly, as mainly the rescuing of souls from God's damnation. There was no point in building model societies since all things were soon to be destroyed for the establishment of a new heaven and a new earth. This sense of urgency for the salvation of souls before the world would come to an end resulted in a narrow theology of salvation that focused primarily on the spiritual and the eternal.

The shattering of the hope in science to usher in a new world, due to the two World Wars, was crisis enough in the 20th century. But, the greater crisis of the 20th century has been the moral failure of the Church worldwide. Since the time of slavery to the time of colonialism, the Church has failed on a significant number of occasions to distinguish herself as a moral agent who would serve as the conscience of society; the light for a dark world. It is ironic that the Bible Belt in the southern part of the United States was the last region to accept that slavery was a crime against God and humanity. There was also surprise and dismay that the Bible was used to help people develop, justify, and promote apartheid in South Africa. Along with the partnership of some missionaries and the perpetrators of colonialism, each of these situations contributed to a loss of confidence in the Church to be the voice of God crying and calling for righteousness and justice in a dark world of sin. The Church was also not loud enough during the genocide against the Jews that saws the destruction of the lives of six million Jews. Finally, and unfortunately, the Church was not found innocent during the 1994 genocide in Rwanda, and the 2008 massacres in Kenya.

These moral failures have affected the credibility of the Church as an agent of change in our world. What is even more significant is that the Church has lost confidence, as well as her sense of mission, in being God's sole agent for holistic change in society founded on righteousness and justice. The Church has therefore, opted for a "safe approach" to issues of societal change. Instead of engaging the world in order to bring the logos of God to bear on all issues of life, the Church is content with specializing in spiritual matters, avoiding controversies, and being a harmless friend to society from a safe distance. The question of Jesus Christ to Church leaders today could well be this: "How can you please God if you seek the praises of men?"

The 21st century presents us with a world that has lost faith in "truth." People are now exploring for a religion-less spirituality and morality. For many, truth does not really exist. It is an age of relativism. The contribution of the Church to society has been confined to the arena of optional private spirituality. No longer do people view the Church as having much to contribute to the big ideas, which address the challenges facing our world today. The implication is that our Christian theologies today have not influenced our work ethic and, as such, are not fundamental to social and economic development, as was the case after the Reformation in Europe and the migrations to America. This irrelevance is further pronounced by the increasingly plural nature of modern society.

Even though Christian population is on the increase in the new Christian regions like Asia, Africa and Latin America, there does not seem to be a corresponding improvement in morality, integrity, effective leadership, social peace, and development. The reason is that these new Christian regions of the world have borrowed their theologies primarily from Europe and North America. The question of the growing irrelevance of the Christian faith, and its seeming ineffectiveness in addressing issues of injustice, poverty, and discrimination, are raising new questions about the role of the Church in society. Discussions have renewed, especially in the non-Western world, about the kind of relationship that should exist between Church and State. Can the Church and the State renew the discussion about the nature of the partnership that should exist between them, as they both look at improving the quality of life of citizens? What should be the mission of the Church as she seeks to impact society as the light and salt of the world?

The Gospel and Christian Missions—The Way Forward
To recover the mission of the Church in relation to society, it is important to revisit the biblical story of salvation. The goal is to appreciate essential principles from the story of salvation that should shape our

understanding and practice of mission.

The Three Tracks of Missions

The gospel is a story of the redemptive act of God, which brings reconciliation towards restoration. The gospel brings reconciliation of all created things to God through Jesus Christ. All things are reconciled to God through Jesus Christ, in order to restore all things to their original God-intended state of blessing.

There were three results from the Fall, which call for three mission-shaping responses from God. The first result from the Fall was a *relational disconnection from God*. On the day of the Fall, humankind suffered death; that is spiritual separation from God. This relational distance was in the place of the original design of God to have relational intimacy with humankind. The second result from the Fall was a *misalignment with the purposes of God*. A characteristic of God's Creation was order; everything was created for a purpose. After the Fall, the tendency was for everything God created to fall out of line and be misaligned with the purposes of God.

The third result from the Fall is the *distortion of God's image in Creation*. God created humans in His own image. The Fall has, however, caused distortion in this image of God in humans, and the rest of Creation. Everything God created reflects aspects of His image. However, humans were created to reflect more fully the image of God. The distortion in the image of God affects all aspects of human life—spiritual, emotional, intellectual, social, and physical.

These three negative results from the Fall of humankind call for three responses. The relational disconnection from God calls for relational reconnection to God. The misalignment with the purposes of God calls for realignment with the purposes of God. Finally, the distortion of God's image in Creation calls for the restoration of God's image in humans and the rest of Creation. Each of these responses speaks to an aspect of Christian mission. The relational reconnection speaks to the relational aspect of mission, the realignment with God's purposes speaks to the leadership aspect of missions, and the restoration of God's image speaks to the transformational aspect of missions.

Christian missions should, therefore, involve three areas—*relational, leadership and transformational*. In the relational aspect we present the gospel of reconciliation, inviting people into a saving relationship with Jesus Christ. This relationship is nurtured with the goal of encouraging an intimate walk with God. The leadership aspect of mission involves inviting humans to first realign their lives with the purposes of God. Secondly, the leadership aspect involves engaging people in exercising stewardship-leadership over the rest of God's Creation seeking to align everything to God's original intended purposes. God Himself is in this process of realignment. The main missional responsibility here is to partner with God in His ongoing work of realignment. The transformational area of mission involves first the invitation of humans to allow God's Spirit to continually transform their lives from one degree of glory to another in the process of regaining God's perfect image in their lives (2 Cor 3:18). The second aspect involves humans partnering with the Spirit of God in encouraging the transformation of other humans and other elements in God's Creation. God's work of alignment and transformation is ongoing in the present. It will continue until the coming of Christ, when the perfect takes the place of the imperfect. Until then, God invites us as agencies through which He will do His work of realignment and transformation. These works in the present are necessary acts of mercy to meet the needs of God's Creation. They are also demonstrations of what is to come. The imperfect works of realignment and transformation are pointers to the perfect realignment and transformation that is coming.

God does not invite Christians to a passive, observation role of His works of realignment and transformation. He actually invites us into an active, responsible stewardship engagement with Him in what He is doing. Granted that we are only instruments, God has chosen to work through His people, who will seek to know what He is doing today and align themselves to His works.

The ultimate purpose of the relational, leadership and transformational elements of mission is to participate with God in His work of restoring all things to their original intended states of blessing before the Fall. God calls us in the present to participate in His restoration mission and in the future to be co-heirs of His Creation with His Son Jesus Christ. God's reason for inviting us to participate with Him in His works of restoration is to deepen our understanding and appreciation of the beauty and purpose of His Creation. It is also an invitation to share in His blessings in the present. We are blessed with discovering ourselves, and our place in God's plans, as we engage with God in His restoration ministry in the present.

In sum, we can affirm that God is reconciling all things to Himself through Jesus Christ. He has invited redeemed humanity, as both messengers of the message of reconciliation and instruments of His work of reconciliation in the rest of Creation. Therefore, through Christ all things are being restored to their original God-intended states of blessing. Christian missions is about being instruments of God in the restoration of all of Creation to their original God-intended condition of blessing. This work begins and ends with Christ. When Christ inaugurates His eternal kingdom on earth, the imperfect will give way to the perfect. The processes of reconnection, realignment, and transformation will end as all of Creation transforms in the twinkling of an eye to a perfect, eternal blessed state. We are eagerly praying, hoping, and waiting for this future. We await this future, not as passive observers, but as active and caring partners with God in His necessary work in the present to continually reconnect, realign, and restore from one degree of glory to another, until the imperfect gives way to the perfect. All things left to themselves will move towards higher disconnection from God, greater misalignment with the purposes of God, and more chaotic states of distortion of the image of God. This tendency is a result of the sin nature, which has deeply characterized all of God's Creation. This tendency, in part, calls for God's intervention in the present. God's intervention in the present to restore all things through reconnecting, realigning, and transforming all of Creation is what shapes our understanding and actions in missions.

The Kingdom of God in the Now
This intervention in the present is a demonstration of the kingdom of God in the present. The King of the kingdom, Jesus Christ, announced the new chapter of His kingdom in the present when He told the religious leaders of His time and His disciples that the kingdom of God was amongst them (Mt 12:28). The King of the kingdom was in their midst; the presence of the King was the essence of the inauguration of the kingdom. It was in fulfillment of the prophecy of Zachariah: "Rejoice greatly, Daughter Zion! Shout, Daughter Jerusalem! See, your king comes to you, righteous and victorious, lowly and riding a donkey, on a colt, the foal of a donkey" (Zec 9:9). When Jesus rode on a donkey to Jerusalem, it was a fulfillment of the prophecy of the coming of the King of Zion. God made the King of Zion, who comes with salvation and righteousness in His hands, the King of all nations.

Another chapter of the kingdom of God in the now was opened when the risen Christ was enthroned at the right hand of God. From there He rules and reigns over all nations. An interesting question is this: "What is Jesus Christ doing now during His reign?" Here are some of the things that Christ is doing in the present as King of the kingdom of God:

a. He is working with the Father in pouring out the Holy Spirit on all flesh (Jl 2:28-32; Acts 2:14-21).

b. He is praying for His followers (Heb 7:25).
   i. He is serving as High Priest.
   ii. He is praying for the unity of the Church (Jn 17).
   iii. He is praying that His followers are sanctified by the truth (Jn 1:17).

c. He is supporting the works of those spreading the good news with miracles (Mk 16). This is to also accredit His true followers, as well as the gospel message (Acts 2:22).

d. He is saving people (Heb 7:25).

e. He is revealing Himself to people, to call them to Himself and/ or to call them to ministry in various aspects of the Great Commission. Paul of Tarsus is one example.

f. He is supporting those involved in making disciples of all nations with His authority and power (Mt 28:18-20).

"All authority in heaven and on earth has been given to me... And surely I am with you always, to the very end of the age."

g. He is pruning His followers for greater fruitfulness; that is, developing them into effective leaders (Jn 15).

h. He is preparing a place in the kingdom of heaven for His followers (Jn 14).

i. He is serving the poor, the needy (Mt 25).

j. He is serving as an Advocate/Defense for His followers before God (1 Jn 2:1-2). Satan is the accuser of believers; Jesus is their advocate.

k. He is destroying all dominion, authority and power until He has put all His enemies under His feet (1 Cor 15:24-25); the last enemy is death.

The above actions speak to Christ's present works in the kingdom of God. The reason Christ and His followers are involved in aligning the world to God's agenda and promoting transformational restoration in the present is that any other leadership results in oppression. When people are led by following theories and concepts based on falsehoods, whether intentionally or unintentionally, the result is oppression and false comfort (Zec 10:1-2). God cares for His Creation in the present and holds leaders and shepherds responsible for the present plight of His Creation. When Jesus saw the crowd harassed as sheep without a shepherd, He had compassion on them. God raised up Jesus as the cornerstone to lead with others, so as to provide God's blessings to His people in the present, and for eternity (Zec 10:4-5).

Redefining the Role of the Church in Missions
The tendency of Creation to increasingly be relationally disconnected from God, misaligned with the purposes of God, and corrupted in the reflecting of the image of God is largely due to the stubborn determination of Satan to derail God's plans for humankind and the rest of Creation. It is because of these wicked schemes of Satan that God's intervention in the present through His kingdom is necessary. This involvement demonstrates the heart of God for His Creation and the wisdom and goodness of His plans for Creation. It is not possible for God or His Christ to be passive regarding the present in order to simply act in the future to usher in a kingdom of justice, righteousness and peace. God is working now in order to reach people with His mercy and justice.

The Church is called to be both a messenger of the gospel of Jesus Christ, and an instrument for bringing the promises of the gospel into human experience. The priority of the Church in missions has to be the relational reconnection of people to God through Jesus Christ. The greatest blessing human beings can look forward to is being in the eternal presence of God. Dwelling in God's presence and enjoying intimate relationships with Him is the most satisfying human experience in the present, and the most excellent aspiration for the future.

The priority of the relational and eternal should not lead to an exclusive focus on the relational-eternal aspect of God's works of redemption, reconciliation, and restoration. Because God is at work in the present, reconciling the world to Himself, missions should also involve promoting relational reconciliation amongst people

characterized by love, righteousness, justice, and peace. The difference
between the Church's approach and that of other human institutions
is the eternal perspective of the Church. The Church is positioned for
temporal reconciliation within the context of God's plan for an eternal
reconciliation. So, the Church engages in the mission of reconciliation
in the present, with an invitation to the eternal reconciliation with God
and fellow humans. This invitation should be present in the Church's
efforts at reconciliation. If the Church engages only in the temporal
and not the eternal, then she misses the big picture of God's heart for
reconciliation. The temporal is a necessary act of mercy on the part
of God in the present. But, it is also meant to be a demonstration and
pointer to eternal reconciliation that will be fully experienced in the
coming kingdom of God.

The third focus of missions is to promote the reconciling of the
rest of God's material Creation to God in the present, within the
context of eternal reconciliation. In the present, mission should involve stewardship-leadership over all of God's Creation, based on the
understanding of God's intended purposes for His Creation. It is the
responsibility of Christians to investigate what God's purposes are for
His Creation, and how to ensure that our human relationships with
Creation are aligned to the purposes of God in the present. The efforts
at aligning material Creation to the purposes of God will yield limited
results, because the perfect is not possible in the present. But, once
again, it is necessary for life to work reasonably in the present, and it
is also a necessary demonstration and pointer to God's perfect plan for
reconciliation that will be fully realized in the kingdom yet to come. It
is the calling of the Church to participate and lead in the aligning of
stewardship-leadership of material Creation to the purposes of God
in the present, whilst at the same time inviting human agencies that
are partners or beneficiaries to participate in God's plan for eternal
and perfect alignment to His purposes. When we properly engage in
the stewardship-leadership of God's Creation within the context of
God's eternal vision, the results of transformation in the social and
material aspects of life do not only serve the needs of humanity and
Creation in the present, but also provide hope for the perfect and
eternal restoration that is yet to come.

Leadership and government in the Church are essential aspects
of the Christian witness. The Church, as the new nation, should be
governed in such a way that it is actually viewed as a good example

of what leadership and government should be in broader society. The Church should consider it as part of her Christian witness to engage and equip kingdom leaders in every sphere of society, and entire nations to lead with the same biblical and godly principles. Why would this work in a religiously plural society? The reason is that the biblical and godly principles of leadership and government are essentially universal principles. Though they are universally true and applicable, they are not universally accessible. It is the Church that has the whole truth through nature, the revealed Word of God, and Jesus Christ as the embodiment of all truth. The Church therefore, has the duty to share this knowledge of truth with leadership and government in other spheres of society.

The Church should also challenge society to acknowledge that God, the Father of Jesus Christ, is the source of all blessings. It is understandable that this would not be easy in plural societies. However, it is part of the mission of the Church to keep this challenge before leaders of different segments of society and nations. Part of the gospel message is that God, the Father of Jesus Christ, reigns today over all nations. It is therefore an appropriate witness to leaders to challenge them to acknowledge Jesus Christ as the higher authority over them, and all other institutions and nations. One way in which this has been done successfully in many nations is to set aside a day each year for national prayer. Christians usually organize these national prayer events, but all leaders are invited to participate. At these events, explanation and encouragement are offered to the leaders to attribute all blessings to God.

Every society has "power centers" where decisions are made that affect the lives of the majority of people. The assumptions and beliefs that shape the values, perspectives, and paradigms for leadership and government of power centers determine what happens in society. A society is blessed when those values, principles, and paradigms are based on truth. When a people are guided by lies—oppression, injustice, and unrighteousness characterize society. When a people are guided by truth, freedom, righteousness, and justice characterize society. The Spirit of truth and power is committed to engaging the false spirits behind ungodly power centers in order to bring freedom, justice, righteousness, and peace into human experience. One of the implications of the kingship of Jesus Christ in the present is that through the working of the Spirit of God, He brings deliverance, righteousness, justice, and peace into human experience in the present. The kingship of Jesus Christ in the present is a reality demonstrated through the supernatural intervention of the Holy Spirit in human experience, to bring the temporary experiencing of the blessings of the gospel as a promise of the perfect and eternal blessings to which God is restoring His people (Mt 12:18-21).

It is not possible to speak of nations becoming the inheritance of Jesus Christ, when their power centers remain unchallenged by the claims of the gospel. Christian mission should seek to take every thought captive to the obedience of Jesus Christ. The power centers of societies need to be challenged with the gospel of the Son of God, the truths of God, and the reality of the kingdom of God in the present. The result of this is ongoing transformation that reconstructs, to greater degrees, the distorted image of God in humans, and realigns people and Creation, to greater degrees, to the purposes of God.

Christ-honoring transformation of society must begin with the Church. A transforming Church is an effective agency in the hands of God for transforming society.

Conclusion

In order to fulfill her role as God's agency for Christ-like change in society, the Church should:

- Commit to a broader understanding of the blessing intentions of God, not only spiritual, but also economic, political, social, scientific, and technological.
- Engage in national transformation and not only individual evangelism and discipleship.
- Commit to both the kingdom now and the kingdom yet to come.
- Posit "spiritual salvation theology" in the broader context of "kingdom theology."

The gospel message must not only be limited to the salvific act of God in history through Jesus Christ, but the declared purpose of the gospel. The message is not only about what happened, it also addresses the "So what?" question. Christ died for our sins; He rose again from the dead…"So what?" So that people from all nations can enter into the experience of God's blessings now and forever more.

The blessings for people from all nations will include relational reconnection with God. Experiencing intimacy with God, through His dwelling presence, is the foundation for all other blessings promised through the gospel. The blessings will also include realignment to the purposes of God and the transformation of saved humanity and all of God's Creation. When our imperfect world gives way to the perfect kingdom of God's Son, Jesus Christ, we will experience these blessings in their fullness for all eternity.

Yet, we can begin experiencing these blessings now. Though imperfect, the blessings of the gospel are a foretaste of the perfect blessings awaiting all of God's Creation. The gospel cannot be proclaimed only as a promise for the future. The gospel does not come to us only in word. It also comes through the demonstration of the power of God in our human situations in the present (1 Thes 2:13). For the kingdom of God is not a matter of talk, but of power (1 Cor 4:20).

Christian mission is about presenting the gospel message of Jesus Christ and through it, inviting all people to enter into God's intended blessings in the fullest sense, beginning from the present to eternity. In the present, the experiencing of God's blessings is partial, and imperfect. However, the perfect and eternal experiencing of God's blessings will replace the imperfect and temporal experiencing. For this reason all efforts by Christian missions to bring people into God's blessings should never lose focus of the promised, eternal, and full experiencing of God's blessings. The partial and imperfect experiencing of the blessings in the present should always be a pointer to the full and eternal experiencing of God's blessings in the future; it is the responsibility of Christian missions to ensure this is always the case.

Christian missions are also about being the hands and feet of Jesus Christ in extending the blessings of God to people and nations in the present. These acts of blessings are only a tiny fraction of the blessings God has in store for His people. As it is written, "No eye has seen, no ear has heard, no mind has conceived what God has prepared for those who love him" (1 Cor 2:9). All efforts of helping people experience God's blessings in the present, through the demonstration of the power of the gospel, must necessarily point to the full and eternal blessings promised by God to all who choose to live in His eternal kingdom.

Dr. Célestin Musekura serves as President and International Director of African Leadership and Reconciliation Ministries, Inc. (ALARM) based in Nairobi, Kenya. He is an ordained Minister who was born and raised in Rwanda. He received a Bachelor of Theology at Kenya Highlands Bible College, a Master of Divinity at Nairobi Evangelical Graduate School of Theology (NEGST) in Kenya, a Master of Sacred Theology and a Ph.D. in Theological Studies at Dallas Theological Seminary (USA).

A major focus of his studies has been on Conflict Resolution, Mediation, and Reconciliation and he spent six years serving as a Pastor in Rwanda. Musekura is married to Bernadette and they have four children.

Conflict Resolution, Transformation and Development in Africa

Célestin Musekura, Ph.D.

Introduction

The theme of this year's forum is *The African Church in Mission and Transformation*. The focus of this paper is *Conflict Resolution, Transformation and Development in Africa*. The goal is to sensitize and inspire leaders of religious groups, governmental and non-governmental institutions, as well as civil and local communities, to work in partnership for peace, transformation, and the development of Africa. This paper will attempt to remind the reader about the causes and costs of conflicts in Africa. We will look at approaches to resolve these conflicts and to build peace on the continent, without which development cannot occur.

I will begin with a brief reminder of the blessings we have as Africans by looking at our God-given resources, as well as the meaning of transformation and development in the context of Africa. In view of the need for African leaders to engage in societal transformation and economic progress, I will discuss the task of preventing and resolving conflict for the successful transformation and development of a nation. Since this mission requires a different kind of leadership, I will propose five kinds of leadership needed for Africa to rise up to the current challenges and become a player in world affairs.

Bad governance and destructive leaders in Africa have played major roles in fomenting, encouraging, fueling, funding and supporting local, national and regional violence. For this reason, emerging leaders need to learn skills and acquire tools to build their capacity to respond to conflicts productively. To this effect, I humbly suggest a list of courses and topics for incorporation in the formal and informal systems, where the minds of our leaders are opened and character is formed.

African Continent, Transformation and Development

The understanding of divine privilege, and the concepts of transformation and development, will help us to visualize possibilities in using African resources to develop capacities that will, in turn, move Africa from a war zone to a life-giving continent.

African Continent

Most of us here are Africans or friends of Africa. No matter the complexion of your skin, your height, the shape of your nose, your socio-economic status, or even your religious affiliation or doctrinal convictions, we share Africanism, a God-given identity. The Apostle Paul reminds us of the divine design through which God has fixed times and periods for every nation, and has set geographical boundaries with a plan in mind (Acts 17:26). Africa and Africans were in the mind of God when He designed this continent. We are not an accident. We are here by divine design.

God intended Africa to be one home, a large family, with diversity of tribes, tongues and cultures. Unfortunately, the greed of the West, and their desire for control and dominance, messed up divine boundaries by creating artificial boundaries, which have contributed to conflicts in many parts of Africa. From the early days of conquest, plunder and exploitation, instead of being a home, Africa became a war zone. In the hands of Europeans, Africa experienced its own tower of Babel. Only this time it was not God who confused the languages, but nations that wanted African resources to build their small towers.

Transformation

You are the salt of the earth…You are the light of the world. (Mt 5:13-14)

The kingdom of heaven is like yeast that a woman took and mixed into about sixty pounds of flour until it worked all through the dough." (Mt 13:33)

The word transformation means that a new identity has taken over an old one. The concept is different from interposing one identity on the top of another. When talking about the transformation of Africans, we are implying a total change of the total person and the environment. The whole person changes; he/she transforms into a new self. This implies that no area of life remains untransformed.

For transformation to take place, a multi-disciplinary approach, with multiple tools and a diversity of instruments, needs to be used. For Africans, such transformation will require a holistic approach to the diverse needs of the continent. It is not economy alone, nor preaching alone, nor evangelism alone, nor good governance alone, nor defeating HIV/AIDS alone, nor eradicating poverty alone, that will help bring about transformation. Only by bringing all instruments of transformation together, and by developing partnerships and cooperation among all players, will the transformation of Africa take place.

For years, leaders of the Church, civil society, and communities have operated independently of each other, as if they are dealing with different clients. In many instances, they worked against each other. The Church in Africa has not effectively worked with governments and non-governmental institutions for holistic transformation of her communities. For the most part, the Church has been "too spiritual" to be relevant in dealing with social justice, political, and security concerns. This kind of approach makes it difficult for the Church to be the "salt and light of the world." It is too heavenly-bound to be earthly-involved.

On the other hand, African politicians, economists, scientists, health professionals, lawmakers, jurists, lawyers, military leaders, and leaders of civil society, have failed to recognize the power of the Christian faith to transform individuals and communities. Politicians have not realized that, "the African is a radically religious person, religious to the core of his or her being. Africa's communal activities, and their social institutions, are inextricably bound up with religion and the spirit world. Africans seem unable to explain life and its mysteries without some reference to the supernatural" (Pobee and Ositehu, 1998:9). Change will take place when Church leaders, pastors, members of parliament, economists, city planners, strategists, etc. work in partnership and share responsibility and accountability for the transformation of the beloved continent.

Development
> "However, there should be no poor among you, for in the land
> the Lord your God is giving you to possess as your inheritance,
> he will richly bless you." (Dt 15:4)

When talking about the development of Africa among Africans, one hears two major views about the future of Africa: the pessimistic and the optimistic perceptions.

The Pessimistic Perspective
For pessimists, Africans seem cursed; only calamity and trouble are their lots. These pessimists point out too many ills and woes for the continent, from her colonization to the recent genocides of the 20th and 21st centuries in Rwanda and Darfur, Sudan. They talk about the massacres of innocent people in Burundi, eastern Congo, and southern Sudan, as well as the brutality in Sierra Leone and Liberia, and the post-election violence and brutality of army and police forces in Kenya. They ask questions such as: *Can Africa recover from these evils? Will Africa ever know peace, justice, righteousness, social justice, and democracy? Does God care about Africans?* African pessimists throw their hands in the air and opt to live only for today, because life is too short to do anything else.

The danger of the African pessimists, or those pessimistic about Africa, is slipping into fatalism—a belief that we are powerless to do anything, because no matter what we do, things are not going to change. This group of people believes in a "system in which human choices and decisions really do not make any difference. Therefore, it is futile to attempt to influence the outcome of events or the outcome of our lives by putting forth any effort or making any significant choices, because these will not make any difference anyway" (Grudem, 1994:674).

This pagan view of the purpose of life has led many African leaders to grab, kill, rob, swindle, exploit, and embezzle public and Church funds for their pleasure. They take what they can, and spoil the national resources for themselves, because they are only here today, since tomorrow they will die. The prophet Micah speaks against these acts of injustice in these words:

> "Woe to those who plan iniquity, to those who plot evil on their
> beds! At morning's light they carry it out because it is in their
> power to do it. They covet fields and seize them, and houses,

and take them. They defraud people of their homes, they rob them of their inheritance. Therefore, the Lord says: 'I am planning disaster against this people, from which you cannot save yourselves. You will no longer walk proudly, for it will be a time of calamity.'" (Mic 2:1-3)

While we can clearly see the social evils, injustice, and structural evil resulting from this pessimistic and fatalistic view of many of our leaders, it is very important to realize there is a foundational issue—namely, the lack of trust in the God who created Africa. This is the same God who provided abundant resources and who continues to call Africa to play her divinely given role in the destiny of the world. Our brethren have followed a traditional saying of the Egyptians in which they exhibited a skeleton during banquets to remind their guests of the brevity of human life, and saying, "Eat, drink and be merry, for tomorrow we die" (Brewer's, 2005:434).

The Optimistic Perspective
While pessimists and fatalists focus on problems and barriers, optimists look at the reality of the blessings and the potentials of Africa. They trust in God, who is in the business of restoring and reconciling communities and nations. While optimists share the pain, heartache, and discouragements with pessimists, they dream of a new Africa, and they intentionally act and move towards new horizons.

While preparing this paper, I came across a portrait with the figures of Martin Luther King, Jr. and that of President Barack Obama side by side. Above the picture of King were the words "I have a dream" and above President Obama were the words "I am the dream." This picture is a reminder of how optimism, coupled with courage, determination and sacrifice by leaders, can motivate and empower people for change even when the odds are against them. How do we convert our pessimistic brethren and friends from despair, hopelessness and a defeatist attitude to the, "Yes, We Can" attitude?

For pessimists to recover from this state of despair and hopelessness, the African Church must recapture and regain the belief and trust in the Sovereign God who always meets Africans at their crossroads. God, who created and who cares about Africa, has promised restoration if we turn to Him in repentance of our greed, corruption, murder, tribalism, idolatry, infidelity, etc. If our national leaders lead us into national repentance, we may hear God's Words to the children of Africa: "I will repay you for the years the locusts have eaten—the great locust and the young locust, the other locusts and the locust swarm—my great army that I sent among you. You will have plenty to eat, until you are full, and you will praise the name of the Lord your God, who has worked wonders for you; never again will my people be shamed" (Jl 2:25-26).

The optimism of a few leaders in Africa reflects undisputable factors signaling hope for the continent: (1) Africa's human resources, (2) natural resources, (3) agricultural land, and (4) recent trends in direct foreign investment in Africa.

Africa's Human Resources

Africans comprise one-eighth of the world's population and we continue to grow by birthrate, while many Western populations are dwindling by aging and low birthrates. Africans are a people of great resilience and hard work. If the energy and excitement of all Africans were properly channeled towards constructive behavior and attitude, Africa would rise up to her destiny quicker than economists have predicted. What Africa needs for its prosperity is building and strengthening human capabilities and human development, namely, "to lead long and healthy lives, to be knowledgeable, to have access to the resources needed for a decent standard of living, and to be able to participate in the life of the community" (UNDP Website, Human Development Concept, 2009).

Natural Resources

Africa is blessed with natural resources. In one country such as Congo, you can find diamonds, gold, uranium, rubies, coltan, platinum, oil, timbers, forests, rivers, etc. There is plenty of copper, petroleum, natural gas, and oil everywhere in Africa. In the article, "Racing for New Riches: Russian and Chinese investors are battling for African resources to fuel their growing empires," Owen Matthews (2007) says that:

> Today emerging market giants are fighting for oil, gas and metal ore in Africa as energetically as 19th century European colonists grabbed land. The Chinese have been more aggressive, with more than 700 companies active in 50 countries…But Russia; the second most active emerging market power is gaining. Pushed by the profit motive and by a Kremlin eager to build economic empires and restore its international position, Russian businessmen are heading south.

Considering these riches of Africa, it is shameful today to read about poverty, hunger and starvation in many African countries. It is even more tragic when such poverty is seen in countries with the most natural resources on the earth such as Congo, Sudan, and Nigeria. Unfortunately, we have turned God's blessings into curses and we even have produced, "blood diamonds and conflict diamonds" in the Democratic Republic of Congo, Liberia, Sierra Leone, Angola, etc.[1]

Agricultural Land

Africa's enormous agricultural potential is still untapped. Africa's arable land can feed the rest of Africa if only conflicts, which displace people and interrupt their agricultural and farming activities, could be stopped. If all the farming land in the south of Sahara was managed well, it has been said, there should be no famine on the African continent. The application of modern farming, farm management disciplines, and the introduction of farmland techniques would increase crops and yield vast returns for farmers and nations. Africa could be a food-basket of the world if her land was put under good stewardship and responsible management.

Foreign Direct Investment

Today, foreign direct investment is rising in Africa. In the past, Africa was characterized by political instability and viewed as an unhealthy environment for business. International corporations and foreign investors adopted an exploitive approach to dealing with Africa as foreign companies, "sought to extract as many resources from the ground as they could in the shortest period of time possible. As a result, they never bothered to invest in African's long-term development and instead left gaping craters in the countryside or waste dumps as lingering reminders of their operations" (Kapstein, 2009:125-126). Foreign investors are engaged in long-term investment because of different reasons:

- African banks are healthier than many banks in the West after the financial crisis in the West.
- There is economic growth in certain countries of Africa despite some level of ethnic violence.
- African businessmen and women, trained in the West, are building business-advertising networks with Western investors.

- Many countries are rising up from years of violence and are building strong economies, as well as providing opportunities that are attracting regional and international investors.
- Some leaders in Africa are actively inviting Western technocrats and business experts as advisors and investors in the national economies.

These are a few of the signs of hope for Africa's development.

Root Causes and Costs of African Conflicts

"What causes fights and quarrels among you? Don't they come from your desires that battle within you? You want something but don't get it. You kill and covet, but you cannot have what you want. You quarrel and fight. You do not have, because you do not ask God. When you ask, you do not receive because you ask with wrong motives, that you may spend what you get on your pleasures. " (Jas 4:1-3)

In the last century and early this century, Africa has known the bloodiest conflicts on earth. Two genocides in Rwanda and Sudan, and atrocities and murder in eastern Congo, marked Africa as a troubled and bloody continent in recent history. The general causes of conflicts in postcolonial Africa range from social inequalities, political exclusion, economic exploitation, tribalism and ethnicity, bad governance, corruption, abuse of power, group victimization, the demonization of one group by another, exclusion, persecution, and humiliation of some groups by others, power struggles, etc.

For the sake of this presentation, the primary causes of conflict are summed up in three categories: (1) internal (2) external, and (3) the cost of these conflicts, which in reality fuels more internal and external causes.

Internal Causes of Conflicts
It is difficult to clearly define and distinguish between the internal and external causes of African conflicts. These are not simple categories because they intertwine, and are not always in white and black, since they feed on each other. However, there are two major internal causes of conflicts in many African countries: (1) tribal fragmentation, and (2) destructive leadership. Tribalism and ethnicity remain the decisive factors and sources of major conflicts in Africa. Political and

religious leaders with self-interest have manipulated our God-given diversity of tribes. Our natural identity and resources are used, not for prosperity, but for the destruction of human lives in the name of tribe, ethnic group, color or race.

The second internal cause of African conflicts is bad and destructive leadership. Most of the main conflicts in Africa are the result of the deliberate choices of elite political and military leaders who foster hatred, fear, suspicions, and tribalism in order to keep themselves in power. Western countries have also been known to support these destructive leaders without accountability and transparency, as long as they support their foreign agenda.

External Causes of African Conflict
Though Africans should take the blame and accept responsibility for the many conflicts after independence, one should not forget that most African countries still suffer the consequences of colonialism. Africans were not left alone, even after independence. There is no doubt that external actors and interest groups were, and still are, playing a major role in instigating, facilitating, aggravating, or prolonging conflicts in Africa for the sake of their gains and at the expense of African lives.

The greed of nations and the effects of their greed are not limited to international foreign countries. Recent wars in Congo have clearly shown that due to the immense natural resources in this vast nation, which does not have strong leadership, various foreign regional nations have been part of looting the resources, and in the process have encouraged and supported tribal and ethnic wars in eastern Congo. In October 2002, the UN panel of experts on the illegal exploitation of natural resources of the Democratic Republic of the Congo accused 85 companies of conducting shady business activities in Congo. The panel identified 12 nations in the region through which goods originating from the DRC may be passing. They include Burundi, Rwanda, Uganda, and Zimbabwe, as well as other regional states such as Angola, the Central African Republic, Kenya, Mozambique, the Republic of Congo, Tanzania, and Zambia.

Cost of African Conflicts
Consider human tragedy resulting from conflicts in East and Central Africa: one million Tutsis and moderate Hutus perished in the 1994 Rwanda Genocide and 2.5 million people died in Congo, in what has

been described as Africa's First World War, the deadliest conflict since World War II. The internally displaced in eastern Congo, as well as refugees in Rwanda, Uganda, Burundi, and Kenya number over 1.5 million. The Khartoum government and Arab Muslims have killed more than 2.5 million black Christians and animists from southern Sudan in the war with the Sudan People's Liberation Army/Movement (SPLA/M), while another four million, from 1956-2004, were displaced or exiled. More than 200,000 Darfurians were killed in what has been called the first genocide of the 21st century. Because of this same war, two million people live in refugee camps in Chad or in Internally Displaced People (IDP) camps inside Sudan. The human tragedy of African conflicts is beyond imagination. Human life seems to have no value anymore.

Peace: A Prerequisite for Development
No Peace…No Development
Peace is a prerequisite for sustainable development. Peace is the heart and soul of development. Any dream of democracy or social and economic development can only be realized in a stable and peaceful society. No nation on earth can prosper when her citizens are at war with each other and running in different directions for safety. In 2000, the UN and Western countries established what they called Millennium Development Goals (2000) known as MDGs, to enable Africa to reduce poverty by half, provide free universal primary education, reduce infant mortality, achieve gender equality, increase access to clean water, etc. Unfortunately, conflicts and unstable governments in Africa have frustrated those efforts. The 2008 G8 Summit, addressing the problems of civil wars in Africa, declared that, "peace and security are fundamental to stability to meet the needs of their people. Fragile and post-conflict states remain farthest from reaching the MDGs."

The exiled refugees hardly participate in the development of their country of origin. They also interrupt the development of the country of refuge. Most of the people in this forum are aware that many of the current wars and atrocities in eastern Congo are the result of the presence of Hutu refugees, who fled the advance of the Rwanda Patriotic Front army in 1994, following the genocide against Tutsi and moderate Hutus. The attack of the defeated members of the Rwandan Army on Rwanda from the refugee camps in eastern Congo prompted the Rwandan government to raid those camps in 1996, and start the rebellion to overthrow Mobutu. This began a war, in which the death toll estimates are at 5.4 million people, most of them civilians.

The existence of Internally Displaced People (IDP) within the border of many of our African countries, and the large number of refugees who have crossed into neighboring countries, are indicators that Africa is far from being stable enough to engage in socioeconomic development. "In 2004, some 3.5 million African refugees were outside their countries, and some ten million were displaced within their own countries. Most were not fleeing natural disasters, but internal political violence and power struggles that feed on religious, tribal and ethnic differences" (Musekura, 2006:321). Even with progress made in the last five years, we still have a long way to go to secure peace in the region. According to Human Rights First (July 2009), "Currently, Africa hosts approximately three million refugees fleeing war, persecution and massive human rights violations."

To accelerate personal and national development in Africa, all national, regional and international actors must labor for peace and the stability of Africa. All dreams for social and economic development must begin with ending all kinds of social disruption. A people on the run are a people without dreams, and without dreams, there is no hope for development. There can be no sustainable development without the active participation of the population and civil society. When citizens are safe in their homes, communities and within their borders, they can then freely and creatively engage in development activities that foster their wellbeing.

Approaches to Managing and Resolving Conflicts

"Blessed are the peacemakers for they will be called sons and daughters of God." (Mt 5:9)

"Bear with each other and forgive whatever grievances you may have against one another. Forgive as the Lord forgave you." (Col 3:13)

People in conflict can generally resolve their disputes by varying means, depending on the formality of the process, the privacy of the approach, the people involved, the authority of the third party (if there is one), the resulting type of decision, and the amount of coercion exercised by or on the disputing parties.

It is vital that African leaders learn to manage, resolve and transform conflicts before they turn into violence. Conflicts are a normal part of life, and are inevitable in real-life situations where two people or groups interact with each other. What is abnormal is when individuals or groups allow conflicts to turn into violence, instead of using conflicts to improve their situation, and strengthen their relationships. While a conflict is defined as "a relationship between two or more parties (individuals or groups) who have, or think they have, incompatible goals; violence consists of actions, words, attitudes, structures, or systems that cause physical, psychological, social, or environmental damage, and/or prevent people from reaching their full human potential" (Fisher, *et al.*, 2000:4).

For Africa to be peaceful and stable, leaders must learn how to respond to conflicts. Because of the limitation of space, we will mention in passing the key approaches to managing, resolving, and transforming conflicts into healthy relationships.

Informal Problem-Solving Discussion
An informal problem-solving discussion is probably where the majority of disagreements end in daily life. When avoidance is no longer possible, or tensions become so strong that the parties cannot let the disagreement continue, they usually resort to this approach.

Negotiation
Negotiation is a bargain relationship between parties who have a perceived or actual conflict of interest. Unlike the informal discussion, this is a structured process of dialogue between conflicting parties; each one maintaining different opinions that could potentially damage their relationship.

Mediation
Mediation is an extension or elaboration of the negotiation process. This involves the intervention of an acceptable third party who has limited or no authoritative decision-making power. Mediation is usually initiated when the parties no longer believe they can handle the conflict on their own and they need a third party to help them clarify and talk about the problem. The third party facilitates the dialogue and allows the parties to arrive at a mutually agreed upon solution.

Arbitration
Arbitration is a voluntary process in which people in conflict request the assistance of an impartial and neutral third party who listens to the arguments and renders a binding decision on the contested issues. The

task of arbitrators is to listen to all the sides of the arguments and then decide what the solution should be. Most of the time, arbitrators are respected peers, leaders, community/traditional elders, religious leaders, spiritual directors, mentors, teachers, etc., who in the past have been known to be men and women of integrity, fairness, and discernment.

Forgiveness

Forgiveness is a letting go of resentment and the need for revenge. To forgive someone means we release him or her from the debt of suffering punishment or penalty, despite the harm or injury caused to us or to others. In forgiveness, the victim gives up the negative judgment against the offender and develops compassion and goodwill towards him/her. There are five basic actions in the forgiveness process:

We ask God to change our hearts and He fills us with grace.

We surrender our right to revenge or punishment.

We discover a shared humanity with our offender.

We develop compassion for, and benevolence to, the offender.

We wish our offender well. Forgiveness leads to restoration and reconciliation.

Reconciliation

Reconciliation is the desired result of forgiveness and any approach to conflict. Reconciliation is the restoration of friendship after an offense-created enmity and caused separation and division between former friends. It is a commitment to restore relationships and start to live in harmony because of valued relationships.

Vision for a Stable and Developing Africa

"Where there is no vision, the people perish." (Prv 29:18, 21st Century King James Version)

"Men of Issachar who understood the times and knew what Israel should do." (1 Chr 12:32, NIV 1984)

"My people are destroyed from lack of knowledge. Because you have rejected knowledge, I also reject you as my priests; because you have ignored the law of your God, I also will ignore your children." (Hos 4:6, NIV 1984)

The hope for Africa is in the African people and their leaders. Ordinary African women and men must dream of a better future for their lives and their nations in an environment enabling them to envision possibilities to grow, develop and strive. Instead of being refugees, Africans must receive protection and defense against all forces keeping them in darkness and despair.

I propose five kinds of leadership needed to provide a vision of a stable and developing Africa: a visionary leadership, a peaceful leadership, a protecting leadership, a responsible leadership, and a skillful leadership.

A Visionary Leadership

> "The men of Issachar, understood the times and knew what Israel should do." (1 Chr 12:32, NIV 1984)

The progress of any community depends greatly on the quality of its leaders and the health of its people. A stable and developing Africa is possible through visionary and transformative leaders. The Bible clearly teaches that where there is no vision and understanding, nations perish. (Prv 29:18) Talking about the need for visionary and transformational leaders for a progressive Africa, Nelson Mandela (1999) observed that:

> Africa is beyond bemoaning the past for its problems. The task of undoing that past is on the shoulders of African leaders themselves, with support of those willing to join the continental renewal. We have a new generation of leaders who know that Africa must take responsibility for its own destiny, that Africa will uplift itself only by its own efforts in partnership with those who wish her well.

A visionary leadership is committed and dedicated to national public service. It is genuinely committed to the national interest. Visionary leaders face present, hard realities and tough challenges with an optimistic view of what the nation could become. They focus not on the obstacles, but rather on what is beyond the mountains, and they lead people to that end.

This hope for visionary leadership is not a fantasy. In recent years, we witnessed a visionary leader in former President Mandela of South Africa who turned the nation, from many years of pain and the ills of apartheid, into a democratic country. Another visionary leader is

His Excellency President Paul Kagame of Rwanda, who has turned a country that was compared to a valley of dry bones 15 years ago, into an oasis of hope and development by fighting corruption, promoting reconciliation, embracing information technology, insisting on national pride instead of tribal pride, etc. We can also mention the former President of Botswana, Sir Ketumile Masire; Presidents Thomas Boni Yayi of Benin, and Mrs. Ellen Johnson-Sirleaf of Liberia. They are examples of visionary leaders emerging on the African continent. These are signs of a new era for Africa.

A Peacemaking Leadership
In this 21st century, African leaders should not be praised for stopping wars and resolving conflicts they started in the first place. Rebel leaders who start the so-called "wars of liberation," instead of using negotiation to address their grievances, should be prosecuted, even after they declare themselves victors or "saviors." No amount of progress and achievement can replace the blood of innocent civilians and children shed in the name of liberation, especially when it is a brother or a sister killing another brother or sister. Those who ascend to leadership at the expense of the blood of their brothers, sisters or neighbors should be put on "the list of shame" for all Africans to see. Political excommunication and social isolation should be the lot of these African leaders.

A peacemaking leader is aware that security and stability are keys to progress. Consequently, he or she strives to unite, reconcile, and model personal and communal reconciliation. It is the role of the leader to build bridges between tribes and communities by advocating for inclusive policies enabling communities to embrace each other in just and genuine ways. Peacemaking leaders work against the natural instincts of all tribes and races for self-preservation at the exclusion of others. As Peter Paris (1988:118) puts it:

> Since most of our associational life is rooted in the natural instinct of self-preservation and self-enhancement, and since our social groups are characteristically impious to the admission of alien elements into their respective domains, the basic problem of our time is how we can break out of our parochialism and expand our moral communities for the sake of justice.

Peacemaking leaders boldly and genuinely make efforts to establish equity and fairness, foster peacebuilding and conflict prevention, thereby helping create a culture of peace in the community and nation. Burundi is a success story of how a committed leader, His Excellency President Pierre Nkurunziza, boldly and sacrificially pursued dialogue, and embraced the major political parties and different rebel groups. Today, Burundi is emerging as a promising democracy in this region. No nation is peaceful and safe when some of her children are forced to live in the bush as refugees, rebels, militia, mercenaries, or stateless people. Peacemaking leaders create room for negotiation, mediation, political forgiveness, apologies, pardons, and reconciliation with personal and political opponents. He or she strives to bring all children home, including prodigal sons and daughters. All leaders in Africa must remove obstacles that turn citizens into enemies of the State.

A Protecting Leadership

"When the wicked rise to power, people go into hiding."
(Prv 28:28, NIV 1984)

Like a good parent, protecting leaders provide a sense of safety and security to all citizens, national institutions, values and principles. The significant role of protecting leadership is "to provide security for an institution and its particular way of life, its cultures, values, beliefs and interests. It seeks to strengthen institutional functions, processes, and values at the same time it guards against excessive opportunism" (Terry, 2002:60). Africa needs leaders who see their roles as protectors of human and natural resources. All citizens, guests, foreigners, and aliens must feel protected by the leadership in order to engage in productive social and economic life.

Protecting and caring leadership is aware of the importance of good neighbors, as well as the bad bedfellows. Because no nation or people live in isolation, leaders have the duty to protect their citizens from internal and external threats. However, the best protection of our own nation begins by protecting neighboring nations. When one nation allows its soil to be a staging place for political and physical attacks, and the destabilization of her neighboring country, experience has shown us that the wind will blow the flames back to its origin. The Rwanda-Congo scenario is a classic example of how dangerous border-crossing conflicts can be. The trend of cross-border insecurities and the tendency for conflicts from one country to flow into a neighboring country are also seen between Uganda and Congo, between Sudan and Uganda, Sudan and Chad, Eritrea and Ethiopia, and between Somalia and Sudan. A protecting and peacemaking leadership will do everything possible to avoid such overflow of conflicts into a neighboring country.

Responsible Leadership

> "Learn to do right! Seek justice, encourage the oppressed, defend the cause of the fatherless, plead the case of the widow." (Is 1:17)

Irresponsibility and bad governance in Africa pose a threat to all development efforts. Irresponsible leaders in Africa have long rewarded corrupt leaders by allowing politicians and military leaders to plunder national resources with the help of foreign and regional accomplices. What we have today is a leadership enabling "military officials and dictators [to] monopolize economic activities, providing few, if any incentives for legitimate entrepreneurs to do business. It comes as no surprise that under these circumstances Africa suffers from low growth rates and high levels of poverty" (Kapstein, 2009:120).

One of the sources of Africa's woes is a lack of responsible and competent leaders capable of identifying and responding to the critical challenges of their nations. Robert Rotberg (2004:14) was right in his assessment that:

> Africa has long been saddled with poor, even malevolent leadership: predatory kleptocrats, military-installed autocrats, economic illiterates, and puffed-up posturers. Such leaders use power as an end in itself, rather than for the public good; they are indifferent to the progress of their citizens; they are unswayed by reason and employ poisonous social or racial ideologies; and they are hypocrites, always shifting blame for their countries' distress.
>
> While the international community may assist Africa in stimulating economies and reducing poverty, only Africans can and must take responsibility in fostering responsible and transformational leadership capable of developing policies requiring accountability and transparency in the management of resources.

Capacity-building programs should focus on the development of talented emerging leaders into future transformational leaders. These young leaders must pursue skills in areas such as international relations, international economy and development, good governance, policy development, business administration, conflict management, international diplomacy, natural resource management, modern farming techniques, information technology, etc.

A Skillful Leadership
New challenges require new skills and tools. Effective leadership forms a foundation for good governance. There is a shortage of skilled leaders with the competence and capacity to lead Africa into the global economy. The current challenges facing Africa require the skills to move the continent away from the traditional and colonial legacies that have perpetuated ineffective leadership.

To encourage effective leadership in Africa, the John F. Kennedy School of Government at Harvard University brought together a group of prominent African leaders who met in 2003 and 2004. These leaders established the African Leadership Council with an objective to strengthen, nurture, and encourage high quality elected leadership in Africa. The council "promulgated a code of African leadership with 23 commandments, issued a Mombasa Declaration, promoting better leadership, and proposed a series of courses to train their political successors in the art of good government" (Rotberg, 2004:16). The proposed curriculum has 25 topics that are relevant to current African realities (World Peace Foundation, 2004). However, one wonders if the list may be too ambitious, given the lack of funded institutions on the continent regularly offering these courses to emerging and promising leaders.

AFRICAN LEADERSHIP COUNCIL
Capacity Building for Elected African Leaders
Mombasa, 20 March 2004

Proposed Curriculum Topics:
- Nature and Theory of Leadership
- Leadership Best Practices
- Models of African Leadership for Good (Botswana, etc.)
- Governance and Good Governance
- Public Management for Public Officials
- Essentials of Democracy: Theory and Practice
- Constitutionalism and Elections and Electoral Laws
- Coalition Building: Various Methods
- Rule of Law Fundamentals

- Ethics and the Ethical Leader
- Accountability and Its Uses
- Dealing with the Media: Strengthening Leadership
- Fundamentals of Macro and Microeconomics
- Fundamentals of Good Fiscal Management
- Nature and Potentials of Internet Technology
- Science and Technological Knowledge: The New Frontier
- Nurturing Civil Society: Building Social Capital
- Conflict Prevention and Conflict Resolution
- Peacekeeping, Peace Enforcement, and Peacebuilding
- Security Issues: Armies and Police Forces
- The International Legal and Political System
- Medical Frontiers and Practices
- Educational Frontiers and Practices
- Environmental Frontiers and Practices
- Managing Diversity

The curriculum of the African Leadership Council is an important starting point and, if implemented, has the potential to develop a leadership that creates vision, empowers followers, and encourages them to explore new possibilities through networking and collaboration. Indeed, Africa needs transformational leadership—"a type of leader that is attentive to the needs and motives of followers, and helps followers reach their fullest potential" because it is inseparable from followers' needs (Northouse, 2007:176).

Topics for Capacity-Building in Conflict Resolution

The current conflicts and wars in Africa require skills and strategies in conflict prevention, conflict resolution, peacemaking and tribal reconciliation. Those who are truly interested in a stable Africa must give attention to these skills and make the allocation of enough funding for conflict resolution, and peacebuilding initiatives a priority. True friends will help us prevent deadly conflicts and will journey with us in the resolution of those we cannot prevent.

In order to build capacity for peacebuilding and conflict resolution, I propose a list of topics which, when covered, will equip leaders with the tools and skills necessary to respond confidently and productively to national, regional and international conflicts:

- Understanding Peace and Justice
- Understanding Conflict and Conflict Analysis

- Conflict Transformation and Conflict Resolution
- Human Rights and Human Responsibilities
- Democracy and Peacebuilding
- Building Strategies to Prevent Conflict
- Leadership in a Divided Nation
- Gender in Conflict and Conflict Resolution
- Good Governance and Leadership
- Conflict and Challenges to National and Regional Security
- Peacebuilding and the Peacekeeping Process
- Post-War Rehabilitation and Restoration
- Religions, Violence and Peacebuilding
- Mediation, Negotiation and Arbitration
- Regional and International Intervention
- Understanding International Terrorism
- Forgiveness, Justice and Reconciliation

This list is not exhaustive and the order is not important. Each country and community should decide which courses are critical for that nation's particular context. The list, however, provides key areas of study that would not only avoid violent conflict, but would also equip leaders to respond to conflict in a more productive way. Preventing and limiting conflicts in Africa must be a vocation and a calling for all who love and care for Africa.

Conclusion

Leaders of governmental and non-governmental institutions, religious groups and civil societies in Africa must undergo training in contemporary challenges in order to lead the continent on a path of peace, justice and development. All institutions that train and develop leaders in Africa will make a great contribution to the healing and hope of Africa when topics on conflict resolution are integrated in the educational system for the skill development and character formation of our leaders.

National and regional institutes for conflict management for leaders need to be established. Short courses must be offered for grassroots and community leaders through existing universities, seminaries and colleges, so that the art of conflict prevention, peacebuilding, and reconciliation does not become a prerogative of the elites, who are in most cases untouched by the effects of these conflicts. Monitoring and encouraging emerging leaders must be a practice of every good and successful leader. Leaders leave a long-lasting legacy if they invest their lives in other leaders who will follow their footprints. Discipleship is not only a Christian concept, but also a leadership principle. By investing His life into a group of a few disciples, Jesus' teachings changed, and continue to change, the world. A successful leader prepares his successors to succeed.

Africa needs transformational leadership in all sectors of life. Conflict prevention and resolution, peacebuilding, forgiveness and reconciliation must be both a personal and national vision. Africans must be intentional in developing skills that will heal Africa from the wounds of trauma and the years of lost dreams. Our suffering will be in vain if we fail to lead the world in peacebuilding after rising above our painful experiences of genocides in Rwanda and in the Darfur region of Sudan, mass murder in the northern and western regions of Rwanda, eastern Congo, and Burundi, and the senseless killings and atrocities in northern Uganda, Liberia, Angola, and Sierra Leone. It is the conviction of the organizers of AFREG 2, and this presenter, that conflicts in Africa do not have to be destructive. They should be transformed into opportunities for national growth and development.

May all the sons and daughters of Africa become peacemakers for the sake of the development of African communities and the divided world in need of grace, mercy, and forgiveness!

> "He has showed you, O man, what is good. And what does the Lord require of you? To act justly and to love mercy and to walk humbly with your God." (Mi 6:8, NIV 1984)

Dr. Setri Nyomi is married to Akpene Esther and they have three children. He received a Ph.D. in Pastoral Theology from Princeton Theological Seminary, USA.

As a theologian from Ghana, he currently lives in Geneva where he serves as General Secretary of the World Communion of Reformed Churches (WCRC).

He has served as Parish Pastor in both Ghana and the USA. Nyomi has served in a number of international roles, often breaking new ground. He constantly addresses injustice in any form, and the call for Christians to place value on the sacredness of life, human wholeness and dignity.

The Environment and Our Christian Calling

Setri Nyomi, Ph.D.

God Created the World

In the record of how God created the world and everything in it, there is a clear indication of our first human parents being given a task of stewardship of the environment. In Genesis 1:28, we read:

> "God blessed them, and God said to them, 'Be fruitful and multiply, and fill the earth and subdue it; and have dominion over the fish of the sea and over the birds of the air and over every living thing that moves upon the earth.'"

The Hebrew wording of "subdue" and "have dominion over" can be understood more accurately as "take care of and be responsible for." These are words of stewardship rather than a notion giving human beings permission to plunder and display power over the rest of Creation. Therefore, the question becomes, "Are we, as human beings in Africa, especially as believers in Christ, taking good care of the environmental resources God has placed at our disposal?"

Luke 12:22–34 is an account filled with many insights. Traditionally, the Church has only grasped part of the message there. This is such a familiar account in the Bible that it is very easy to miss some of the insights it provides. The Church has often interpreted it as a moral lesson in getting rid of our anxieties. Such a simplistic view of the passage leads us to often respond to serious challenges that friends and family members are facing with a rather lame quick response "Don't worry!" Assuming that once we have said it, the worry is supposed to jump out of the window. While the passage is certainly addressing the futility of worrying, it goes much deeper than the simplistic meanings we have often given it. A close look at this passage demonstrates some helpful insights. We can identify the key verse in this passage as "Seek first God's kingdom, and all other things shall be added on to you." In Luke's Gospel, our Lord Jesus contrasts seeking first the kingdom of God with what we worry about—not whether or not we worry.

In other words, the main message of this passage is—rather than worry about those things that satisfy us as human beings, we should seek first the kingdom of God. This is a challenge to two things:

1. A self-centered life that does not care about what God cares about.

2. A merely anthropocentric view of life that focuses on our satisfaction to the point that we neglect all other elements of Creation.

The passage rejects any selfish and self-serving interests. It points out how anxiety about meeting our needs, rather than seeking God's kingdom, is unhealthy, demonstrates a lack of faith on our part and is shortsighted. This is what gives us a passion for mission and for bringing the good news of the salvation in our Lord Jesus Christ to people without knowledge of Him. Self-centered people cannot be committed to proclaiming this good news. They will be too busy worrying about what will satisfy their egos. Therefore, if African Christians are going to make a difference, we should begin by stepping forth in faith and choosing carefully, what we focus our worries on.

It also rejects anthropocentric views. Even Christians can think only of the centrality of human beings, and not care about all other forms of Creation. It is interesting that even as African Christians celebrate success, they often take on the same patterns as non-Christians. So for example, many Christians see God's blessings in the bigger, more prestigious cars. They do not even stop to ask how the energy consumption patterns of these cars are depleting the earth's resources.

Our Lord Jesus describes the exclusive focus on what will satisfy us as futile exercise. In this passage, the Lord opens up our horizons—to show that a simple focusing on worrying about what will satisfy us as human beings is what non-believers focus on. This is what the nations of the world strive after. These are worldly values. Christian values go far beyond and include all of Creation, for "life is more than food, and the body more than clothing" (Luke 12:23). Then, for the Christian, He uses very vivid pictures of other elements of Creation or ecology to illustrate how human beings tend to narrowly focus on and worry about their own needs. This shortsightedness, on the part of human beings, contrasts with God's desire for us to focus on all of Creation. The beauty of the birds of the air, flowers and lilies of the field—part of what God cares about—far surpasses the splendor of the well-known King Solomon. This is a humbling lesson for our monarchs and political leaders who may revel in the splendor of the positions they hold. God sees and cares about all human beings—women and men—and the entire Creation. In any case, God knows our needs and is ready to take care of us. We as human beings limit God when we so focus on ourselves that we do not take care of anything else about which God cares.

Christians who truly seek first the kingdom of God will be able to focus on caring about all that God cares for. Micah 6:8 raises the question:

"What does the Lord require of you?"

Then it proceeds to answer:
"Justice, kindness and to walk humbly with your God."

The human tendency to want and get only for ourselves is not sustainable. It makes us use ecology rather than live in harmony with ecology in sustainable ways. We destroy trees and other vegetation to put up what we have seen as symbols of development and wonder why rain patterns have changed. We buy into the false notion of measuring success in life by how many material things we have accumulated for ourselves. The bigger the car, the better: even if it contributes immensely to destroying the ecology. We often do not take time to think of how the food we eat gets to our tables, even if the food is a result of injustice. So long as it meets our needs, we seem okay.

Those who walk with our Lord Jesus should remember that, rather than focus on our needs; we should focus on the kingdom of God. We should strive for the values of the kingdom of God. We get a glimpse of some of those values in the vision Isaiah portrays in the prophecy around the expected Messiah that is to come (Is 11:1–9). Isaiah says that the coming of our Lord will usher in the reign of God in a way, which reverses the disharmony in nature and the ecology caused by sin as portrayed in Genesis 3. This is where sin affected the harmony between humanity and other created beings. Isaiah saw a different picture in which there will be ecological balance. Where normally ferocious animals would live at peace, and lie together with their prey, and where even infant human beings will live at peace with snakes without fear. The picture of the reign of God has that harmony.

As believers, we are expected to strive for the reign of God and that includes a better care for the environment. Unfortunately, some of the foreign theological directions coming to this dear continent of ours seem to encourage us to disobey God in this direction. Those theologies tell us to focus on our needs and ourselves. We even seek for places of worship in terms of whether or not the Church meets our needs. Does the worship style satisfy *me*? Those theologies teach us that the more faith we have, the more we can acquire material wealth to meet our needs as human beings. Very little is taught about offering our lives as living sacrifices to the Lord (Rom 12:1-2), to be agents of God's transformation, ushering in a new reality characterized by the values of God's kingdom. This is part of the slippery road of focusing only on ourselves, rather than on God's reign.

Care for ecology and the environment is not simply a fad that arose in the 21st century. It is at the heart of living with values of the reign of God. This year, 2009, my family of churches—the Reformed and Presbyterian family—is celebrating 500 years after the birth of John Calvin on 10th July 1509. Therefore, it is appropriate to quote from one of John Calvin's sermons.

On 20 December 1555, John Calvin preached a sermon on Deuteronomy 20:16–20. He focused on the 19th verse (NIV UK), which reads,

> When you lay siege to a city for a long time, fighting against it to capture it, do not destroy its trees by putting an axe to them, because you can eat their fruit. Do not cut them down. Are the trees of the field people, that you should besiege them?

A few sentences from this 16th century sermon illustrate how concern for ecology has been in John Calvin's understanding of living faithful Christian lives.

Calvin proclaimed:

> When we find ourselves driven by wickedness or some evil thoughts to the point of destroying trees, houses and other

such things, we have to control ourselves and reflect: Who are we waging war against? Not against creatures, but against the one whose goodness is mirrored here. Not against one man only, but against each and everyone, ourselves included.

John Calvin (1555) continued elsewhere in the same sermon:

Today, such cruelty is even greater among those who call themselves Christians…For today they go about scorching and burning the land, which is worse than cutting throats…Human beings have distanced themselves from God and become brutish as a result.

This is John Calvin, in December, 454 years ago, not a 21st century ecological activist. In his conclusion, Calvin shows us a justice that must permeate our whole lives:

Let us therefore take care not to uproot any fruit trees, but since the Word of God is the seed of life, let us endeavor to scatter it widely, so that it can put down strong roots and produce a tree that is not unfruitful, but one that produces much fruit.

In its document called the *Accra Confession*, the World Communion of Reformed Churches, (WCRC) the organization in which I serve, followed this tradition of Calvin. It calls on us Christians to stand firm in rejecting lifestyles and actions that result in irresponsibility regarding the environment. Let me quote a couple of verses of the *Accra Confession* (2007):

We believe that God calls us to stand with those who are victims of injustice. We know what the Lord requires of us: to do justice, love kindness, and to walk in God's way. (Mi 6:8) We are called to stand against any form of injustice in the economy and the destruction of the environment, "so that justice may roll down like waters, and righteousness like an ever-flowing stream." (Am 5:24)

Therefore, we reject any theology that claims that God is only with the rich and that poverty is the fault of the poor. We reject any form of injustice, which destroys right relations—gender, race, class, disability, or caste. We reject any theology, which affirms that human interests dominate nature.

We believe that God calls us to hear the cries of the poor and the groaning of creation and to follow the public mission of Jesus Christ, who came so that all may have life and have it in fullness. (Jn 10:10) Jesus brings justice to the oppressed and gives bread to the hungry; He frees the prisoner and restores sight to the blind (Lk 4:18); He supports and protects the downtrodden, the stranger, the orphans and the widows. Therefore, we reject any church practice or teaching which excludes the poor and care for creation, in its mission; giving comfort to those who come to "steal, kill and destroy" (Jn 10:10) rather than following the "Good Shepherd" who has come for life for all. (Jn 10:11)

The references in the *Accra Confession* (2007) to "any theology which affirms that human interests dominate nature," "the groaning of Creation," and the "care for Creation," are meant to draw attention to the environment. In this confession, WCRC took very seriously the need to act against economic injustice and environmental degradation.

When we do not take care of the environment God has given us, when we think ecological issues are to be taken for granted, we do this against God, against the values of God's reign, and against ourselves.

God's promise still holds true: if our thoughts are focused on striving for God's kingdom and not narrowly on what will satisfy us, we become God's agents of transformation as we take better care of the totality of Creation, including its ecology. The good news is God knows both the needs of the entire Creation, and our needs as well, and God will not abandon us.

Question: Are we striving for the kingdom of God and the values of God's reign or are we simply seeking what will satisfy us? Among other values of the kingdom, let us step forth in faith as Africans and take better care of the land, the environment and the resources that God has given us—and all other things shall be added to us.

The Environment and Our Christian Calling

Rev. Charlotte Opoku-Addo received God's call to full-time ministry in 1976. She worked as a traveling secretary for Scripture Union in Ghana; then she took short courses at the Haggai Institute, Singapore and the London Institute for Contemporary Christianity. She studied Urban Evangelism and Pastoral Studies at the Centre for International Christian Ministries in the U. K. and became a licensed Minister of the Pentecostal Churches of Great Britain.

Rev. Opoku-Addo was ordained in 1992 and lectured at the CICM; she also served as Pastor/Evangelist for Finsbury Park Christian Fellowship in London. She returned to Ghana and became National Evangelism Director of the Ghana Congress on Women's Ministry (GHACOE); she currently serves as National Director of GHACOE.

The Role of the Church in Societal Transformation: The Church in Mission and Transformation

Rev. Charlotte Opoku-Addo

Introduction

Understanding Key Concepts

To effectively discuss the topic, there is the need to clearly understand the key concepts in my presentation. The key concepts in this paper are "Church" and "Societal/Social Transformation."

For many people the word "church" means a building where Christians meet. To Christians it usually means the place where they meet with other believers to worship God. According to the Bible, the word "Church" also refers to all Christian believers. The word church/Church thus means both a place and a group of believers.

Jesus first used the word that is translated "church" in Matthew's Gospel, (Mt 16:18). He used it to describe the gathering of people who believed in Him—His followers. The first disciples believed Jesus was the long-promised Christ and the Son of God. After the crucifixion and resurrection of Jesus, these disciples—inspired by the Holy Spirit—played a key part in establishing the early Church with the community of Jesus' followers.

For this presentation, the word "Church" broadly describes churches and all church/faith-based organizations involved in mission/development work.

Transformation is defined simply as positive change that is radical and lasting. A resource manual for leadership in Lay Training (ACLCA, 2000) defines social transformation as a process by which a group of people decide to change their way of living in a positive manner. It involves the liberation and realization of oneself. It is a change in societal structures, norms and ethics.

According to Max Assimeng (1989), religion has played an important role in the evolution of civilizations, particularly in the areas of ethical development and social organization. He further argues that the social functions of religion for a particular society include:

- Maintenance and support of the social order
- Control of activities of men in their encounter with the social and natural environment
- Regularization of the network of social relationships

Jesus was very clear, from His example and His words that serving the kingdom of God meant more than just preaching. Through His example and His teaching, He challenged us not just to talk about our faith, but also to put it into action by caring for the poor, the sick, and those suffering from injustice. It is, therefore, not enough for the Church to preach the good news of the gospel, but also the Church must go out to transform their communities.

The Church is the basic unit of Christian society. As portrayed in the New Testament, churches were made up of people who had experienced transformation through receiving Jesus Christ as their Savior, acknowledging Him as Lord, and incarnating His servant ministry by demonstrating the values of the kingdom both personally and in community (Mk 10:35-45; 1 Pt 2:5; 4:10). Today, similar examples of transformed lives abound in churches worldwide.

We recognize that over the centuries the Church has been the vehicle for the transmission of the gospel of Jesus Christ. Its primary role, which is a threefold ministry, has been: a) the worship and praise of God; b) the proclamation, in word and deed, of the gospel of the grace of God; and c) the nurture, instruction and discipleship of those who have received Jesus Christ into their lives. In this way, transformation takes place in the lives of the people as individuals, families, and communities/society; through their words and deeds, they demonstrate both the need and reality of ethical, moral and social transformation.

However, kindly note that without the performance of the Church's secondary role of bringing development to the society, its primary role would not be effectively achieved, thus, there would not be a complete transformation of the society.

To achieve this development role, the Church must first see itself as the conscience of the society/nation. In this regard, the Church is expected to be able to point out abuses and work to protect and defend the rights of all, especially the marginalized and vulnerable, within society (i.e. women, children, the poor, people affected by and infected with HIV/AIDS). This is just what Christ saw as His role, as stated in Luke 4:18–19:

> "The Spirit of the Lord is upon me, because he has anointed me to proclaim good news to the poor...to proclaim freedom for the prisoners and recovery of sight for the blind, to set the oppressed free..."

The Church has therefore, been commissioned by Christ to transform society and bring about social change by performing these roles:

a. Provide prophetic witnessing

b. Oppose human rights abuses in society

c. Build awareness on morality and human rights issues

d. Provide moral education and seek moral transformation through direction and advocacy

e. Speak against bad leadership in the society, especially in Africa, and promote good governance, transparency and accountability

f. Support the poor and vulnerable by complementing the efforts of the State in bringing development to the people in terms of education, training, healthcare, and entrepreneurial development

Africa's Situation and the Church

A look at Africa today reflects scenes of failed economies leading to deprivation and extreme poverty, wars and religious conflict, famine, brain-drain, corruption, greed, poor leadership, unemployment, diseases (HIV/AIDS and malaria), child labor and trafficking.

Studies have shown that Christianity is growing faster in Africa than any other continent, but the sad and contradictory aspect is that the people of Africa are rapidly becoming poorer, and the moral and social fabric of the society is disintegrating. Currently most countries in Africa are experiencing the feminization of poverty, meaning that more and more women are falling below the poverty line.

One can conclude that the Church is not making the needed impact on African nations. The big question we need to reflect on is, "Why are we in this situation?"

- Is it that the Church has failed to apply the gospel to the whole life and limited it to spiritual life only?

- Are we reading the scriptures selectively and not placing emphasis on the verses that matter to humanity—that is justice, material wellbeing and the dignity of people?

It is about time we realize that the Church can no longer pretend not to know the pains and sufferings of the people. The Church must rise up to its duty as the conscience of the society by guiding our continent and serving as agents of social transformation. According to the former President of Tanzania, Julius Nyerere, the relevance of the Church depends on its involvement in effecting changes in the social structures that condemn humanity to poverty.

In discussing the role of the Church in societal transformation, this paper focuses on the Church's roles in relation to issues affecting women and children. Although the Church recognizes God's Creation of men and women in His own image, as equals in human dignity but having different roles, in many parts of Africa women are insecure, overworked, exploited and made to feel insecure. There are deep-seated prejudices against women, which need consideration in order to ensure the total liberation of women in society.

The Situation of Women and Children in Ghana
During His ministry on earth, Jesus Christ paid a lot of attention to women and children. For instance, we note that Christ revealed some of the critical tenets of our faith to women. To Martha, He said, "I am the Resurrection and the Life" (Jn 11:25); to the Samaritan woman, He indicated the need to worship God in Spirit and truth, and that He is the Messiah (Jn 4:14-26) and the source of life. To Mary, the risen Christ revealed Himself and gave her a charge for evangelism (Jn 20). He also reached out to vulnerable women like Mary Magdalene the prostitute, the woman with the issue of blood, the bent over woman, and several

others. Jesus Christ asked His disciples to allow the children to come to Him because theirs is the kingdom; He also noted that unless we receive the kingdom like a child, we shall not enter (Mt 19:14; Mk 10:15).

Unfortunately, due to the situation of women and children, they have not been able to fully access the liberating and fulfilling message of Christ. God encouraged Esther, an alien, refugee and orphan girl to become queen, administrator and strategist. In the same way, let us reach out more to women and children, rather than leave them to fall prey to teenage pregnancy, drug abuse, HIV/AIDS, maternal deaths, poverty, prostitution, non-fulfilling economic roles and other more frightening fates.

Since the United Nations Decade for Women (1976-1985), there has been an increasing awareness of the need to enhance the status and participation of women in national development. The United Nations Convention on the Rights of the Child states that every child has a right to an adequate standard of living and the highest attainable standard of health and education based on equality of opportunity. The 1990 Summit for Children urged countries to prioritize the needs of children to ensure their survival, protection, development and participation.

In September 2000, 189 Heads of States made a commitment to achieve the eight Millennium Development Goals (MDGs), each of which has women as critical to their achievement by the set date of 2015. These goals are:

1. Eradicate extreme poverty and hunger

2. Achieve universal primary education

3. Promote gender equality and empower women

4. Reduce child mortality

5. Improve maternal health

6. Combat HIV/AIDS, malaria and other diseases

7. Ensure environmental sustainability

8. Develop global partnerships

Women in Ghana constitute about 51 percent of the population and contribute immensely to national development through the performance of productive income-generating activities, as well as their traditional and domestic roles. Women are constrained by a number

of factors in their production ability and in the scale of their operations. Due to multiple roles, they are hampered by their lack of time;
they lack education (with literacy rates at 23 percent for females as
compared to 42 percent for males); they have limited access to critical
resources such as credit, land, information, labor and markets.

An assessment of women's involvement in economic activities
shows that:

- In manufacturing, their efforts have been in undertakings
  such as bead making, oil processing, food processing, making
  indigenous soaps and creams, which are considered informal
  and unimportant.

- In commerce/service, women are generally involved in petty
  trading and hawking.

- In agriculture, women are more involved in food crop farming
  than in export crop farming and their activities are limited
  by access to land, credit and service delivery.

The National Human Development Report (2007, chap. 2) classi-
fies one-third of all Ghanaians as poor, with women and young people
seen as the most vulnerable. Evidence shows that increasingly, female-
headed households (a growing phenomenon) have increased from 29
percent in 1984, to over 35 percent in 2007. Ghana seems to be experiencing the "feminization of poverty," with women in the northern
parts of the country being the most vulnerable.

According to Oxfam GB (2000), governments and development
organizations should be concerned about gender inequality because
the majority of the world's poor are women. Around 70 percent of the
1.3 billion people who live in extreme poverty (on less than one dollar
a day) are women and girls. Two-thirds of the children denied primary
education are girls, and 75 percent of the world's 876 million illiterate
adults are women. Every extra year a girl spends at school could reduce child mortality by ten percent (UN, World's Women 2005). More
than half a million women die in pregnancy and childbirth every year.
Of these deaths, 99 percent are in developing countries. In parts of
Africa, maternal mortality rates are one in 16 (UN, World's Women,
2005), and domestic violence is the biggest cause of injury and death
to women worldwide. Gender-based violence causes more deaths and
disability among women aged 15 to 44 than cancer, malaria, traffic ac-

cidents and war (World Bank Discussion Paper #255, see Heise, 1994).

Gender discrimination or the denial of women's basic human rights is also a major cause of poverty. Men and women experience many aspects of poverty differently and ignoring these differences risks further entrenchment of poverty and the subordination of women.

HIV/AIDS, since its outbreak, along with STDs, is a serious threat to the development and survival of humanity, especially women and children. The disease has orphaned more than 14 million children and this number is expected to more than triple by 2010. In the developing world, AIDS is reversing development by cutting down men and women in their productive years, eroding both societal and family structures. Estimates show that 50 percent of all new HIV infections occur among young people and 30 percent of the 40 million people living with HIV/AIDS are in the 15 to 24 years age group (WHO, 2004). Generally, women appear to be more vulnerable to sexually transmitted diseases, including HIV/AIDS, than men. Gender disparities are also more pronounced in the age bracket of 15 to 29 years, where women account for 76 percent of all reported cases of HIV/AIDS.

Women and children are subjected to violence in the home, work place, school and the community. The issue of violence against women and children, which is injustice, can be traced to the imbalance of power relations and harmful cultural practices, which impinge on their fundamental human rights. Categories of violence against women and children include: domestic violence, which occurs within the home; cultural violence, which involves acts of humiliation; and physical violence perpetuated on women and children in the name of culture. For instance, puberty rites, issues of inheritance, forced marriages; female circumcision, and widowhood rites are all forms of cultural violence. The scripture enjoins us to take good care of widows and orphans (and the weak in general), yet the Church looks on helplessly as women, even those in the Church, are forced to go through such dehumanizing rituals. Other acts include forced labor, prostitution, child trafficking and sexual harassment.

Other problems generally facing children in Ghana include "streetism" (issues surrounding and affecting homeless individuals), drug abuse, HIV/AIDS, poverty, and limited avenues for education and training. All these issues negatively affect the spiritual, economic, physical and emotional wellbeing of women and children. Christ tells us He has come so that we may have life abundantly. The question then is "Are women and children (generally the vulnerable in society) experiencing the abundant life promised to all by Christ?"

Unfortunately, when we come to the Bible, there appears to be male dominance in most of the stories, many of which have been over-exploited to the disadvantage of women and children. For instance, in the Bible male persons are much more prominently presented than women. Most of these men have a name, but we meet many nameless women in the Bible. They are the mother, the wife, or the sister, or the daughter of…and then a man's name follows. For example, Saul's mother, Noah's wife, Lot's daughters, etc.

When there is a discussion on women's positions within the Church, we often hear about the subordination of women. Two very famous Bible verses are 1 Corinthians 14:34-35, which states "As in all congregations of God's people, women should keep silent at the meeting. They have no permission to talk, but should keep their place as the laws direct." Why do we not often quote the text from Galatians 3:28 (NIV), "There is neither Jew nor Gentile, neither slave nor free, nor is there male and female, for you are all one in Christ Jesus"? The text is clear—in Christ, we are one. In Christ, it does not make any difference if you are a man or a woman—everybody is valuable.

Clearly, not only the selection, but also the interpretation of Bible verses place women more or less in a secondary position. Most sermons on the history of Creation make that clear. In the Church, we often hear preaching on Genesis 2 "first man was created by God and after that the woman was created from the man's rib." For that reason a woman should be subordinate to a man. Yet, in Genesis 1:27, we read how God created human beings in His own image: male and female. We do not note any distinction between man and woman. Why has the Church not given more value to this text instead of the text from Genesis 2?

The recognition and full participation of women and children in the Church are firmly rooted in the Bible. There are many texts and stories in the Bible, which demonstrate this involvement, but we need to re-read them and realize that in Jesus' life, death and resurrection, we have the true authority. We have to take Jesus Christ as our model. His life shows us that for Him, men and women are equal; in Christ, there is no male or female! He broke down all the barriers that discriminated one person from another, in order to proclaim the message of liberation.

The Role of the Church

In Ghana, the Church has played the lead role in the education and training of women since the time of the missionaries in the Gold Coast in the 19th century. Indeed, missionaries introduced formal education to this area. The wives of missionaries mobilized young Ghanaian women, giving them training in domestic science, knitting, sewing, personal hygiene and home management. They also taught them to read the Bible and sing church hymns in some Ghanaian languages.

The main aim was to make these women and girls, good mothers/wives and homemakers. This strong foundation laid by the missionaries formed the basis for the growth of the Church and especially the women's ministry/fellowship.

Today in Ghana, the Church has been involved in a holistic ministry by actively engaging in the development of communities by bringing them the Word of God and by meeting their physical needs. Notably, the Church is a key partner with government in the reaching communities through the provision of education, health, agricultural extension, and rural development, to communities. Some specific projects have also targeted women and children; the focus of these projects has normally been in the areas of health, including nutrition, maternal and child health, STDs, and HIV/AIDS education. Others have included literacy programs and vocational/technical training.

The Church's physical and spiritual interventions are not always as effective as they ought to be. Many believe that since the Church is generally gender blind, we are effectively influencing the lives of people in communities with the Word of God and development initiatives. However, we have not fully realized the effect of these initiatives on women and children. Perhaps this is because many of these efforts are not planned and implemented while considering the practical and strategic needs of women and children; additionally, thought must be given to the issues of equality and power relations, access to and control over the allocation of resources, as well as benefits and decision making, both within the Church and the society.

This means that many grey areas still exist for exploration into missions for women and children, especially those, which will enhance their total transformation. As Christians, we are to see our mission to women and children as a command from Christ to us, to reach out to the whole, noting that women and children represent the majority of the human race.

The Importance of Reaching Out to Women and Children

The issues raised so far clearly show an urgent need for the Church to reach out to women and children, especially those in vulnerable situations, in order to give them a fulfilled life in Christ. The underlying problem we must confront is poverty. We must address the economic, social, emotional, environmental and spiritual needs of the poor, especially women and children. Nevertheless, the greatest need of the vulnerable, as with all people, is the need to be reconciled with God to escape His wrath.

As described earlier, two-thirds of the world's poor are women and therefore, any mission/ministry to the peri-urban poor and rural communities should target women. The fundamental theme throughout the Old Testament is the upholding of God as the protector of the poor and needy. The motive of God's defense of the needy is made unmistakably clear: God rescued His people when they were strangers and slaves in Egypt; hence His redeemed people should act in like manner towards the helpless in their midst (Ex 22:21; 23:6).

God created the world in a state of glorious perfection, but the Fall of humankind brought an end to the *shalom* of Eden. The mission of the God of Creation is to restore peace to His Creation, calling a special people to be in communion with Him as recipients of His blessings and agents of *shalom*. Jesus Christ modeled the "*shalom* ministry" and summed up His mission as preaching the good news to the poor, proclaiming freedom for the prisoners, restoring sight to the blind, releasing the oppressed and proclaiming the year of the Lord's favor (Lk 4:18-19). Scripture gives hope, life, dynamism and immense possibilities beyond human imagination; reflection upon scripture is critical to human transformation and is something that differentiates Christian development from secular development.

The need to reach out to women and children, especially those in peri-urban and rural areas, is critical in the sense that they lack the material essentials to sustain a life of dignity and responsibility in their communities. Their situation is not only the result of economic factors, but also social, structural and spiritual causes. There is generally no motivation to seek education, thus they are normally semi-literate or ignorant. They experience conditions of severe deprivation of basic human needs including food, safe drinking water, sanitation facilities, health, shelter and education. They are in a vicious cycle of poverty and thus are vulnerable. The girls are prone to early sex and produce children early; they become even poorer by their circumstances.

The conditions in which we find the poor are like those of Ezekiel's audience—helpless (Ez 37:7-14). Therefore, reaching out to such people should be applied as the mediation of the creative power of our Lord, the ultimate basis of our life and mission.

Transformational development is the expression of the mission of *shalom*; it is the act of responding positively to God's call to a partnership with Him in re-building His kingdom. Transformational development seeks to respond to the needs of the poor in a holistic manner; it seeks to follow Christ in the way He went about doing His ministry—encompassing the physical, spiritual, social and cultural dimensions of personal and societal life. This kind of transforming development hopes and works for change in people towards the ideals of the kingdom of God, self, others and the environment. The strategies and approaches of transformational development affirm the dignity and work of people as created in the image of God.

We must be committed to care for people with a concern for their spiritual, physical, mental, social and emotional wellbeing. The poor should learn skills allowing them to be self-employed, which can lead to financial empowerment. Non-formal education should be given to illiterate women to narrow the gap between the literate and the illiterate. The Church must respond to the strategic and practical needs of women, teaching them about marriage, home management, childcare, etc.

Ministry to the poor is a challenge and it must take the collective efforts of government, churches, NGOs, other organizations and individuals. These efforts must be coordinated and well planned.

The Case of GHACOE Women's Ministry

GHACOE Women's Ministry was born at the first Ghana Congress on Evangelization held at the Kwame Nkrumah University of Science and Technology (KNUST), Kumasi in July 1977. Seventy women among the 600 participants responded to the evident challenge for a more consistent walk with Christ and, in total obedience to Him, to help Ghanaian women understand and live life more fully through Christ.

Over the years, GHACOE has worked to promote the spiritual, moral and material development of women in Ghana and in other parts of Africa. Towards its mission of promoting the holistic develop-ment of women and, through them, strong families and communities, GHACOE Women's Ministry has provided opportunities for women from all over the country to fellowship, pray and grow together. Their participation in the ministry has also provided them with access to counseling and prayer support. In recognition of the impact of their material status on their spiritual wellbeing, the organization has also initiated training and credit interventions to strengthen wom-en's income-generation activities. Up-to-date, GHACOE has over 120 branches in all ten regions of Ghana, with a staff strength of 19 and more than 500 active volunteers working at the local level.

Strategies Adopted by GHACOE in Its Holistic Mission to Women and Children
Recognizing the vulnerable situation most women and children find themselves, GHACOE has worked through a holistic development ap-proach, seeking to empower the poor and marginalized people in society. GHACOE's strategies include:

- **Evangelism**—Leading married, single women and teenage girls to Christ and discipling them through Bible study, music, etc.

- **Study**—Molding the lives of women as they study GHACOE's manual, *The Challenge of Being a Woman.*

- **Leadership Development**—Developing leadership qualities and the talents of Christian and non-Christian women in Ghana and Africa through teaching and training.

- **Domestic Skills Training**—Giving home management and productivity skills, with the aim of enabling them to become productive and self-reliant, by setting up income-generating ventures to effect change in their home, church and commu-nity and, thereafter, by imparting their acquired skills to others. Skills imparted are batik making, screen-printing, soap making, cosmetics production, flour confectionery establishment, business management, and biblical teaching.

- **Cross-Cultural Training**—Using the power of the Word of God to break down cultural barriers, educate the rural and peri-urban poor people and bring them together to form multi-purpose productive units.

- **Gender Sensitization**—Adopting a gender–based approach, focusing on rural women's immediate needs in specific communities.

- **Church and Community Partnerships**—Working with local churches and community leaders to gain acceptance and encourage community ownership of programs for women, and use this support to address the underlying cultural and social structures, which make women and children more vulnerable.

- **HIV/AIDS Awareness Education**—Giving HIV/AIDS awareness and education to rural communities for behavioral change.

- **Care for AIDS Patients**—Giving care to AIDS patients in the Upper West and Northern regions of Ghana.

Achievements of GHACOE Women's Ministry

- **Evangelization, Counseling and Small Business Development**—Since its establishment, GHACOE has worked with commercial sex workers in Kumasi, with the aim of liberating them from this trade. Programs with these women include evangelization, counseling and the provision of seed capital to start a business. With the advent of HIV/AIDS, GHACOE has witnessed some of these women dying of the disease, yet they died knowing Christ. Some have also successfully engaged in other economic activities.

- **Development Partnerships**—GHACOE has collaborated with development partners such as UNDP, German Development Service and Tearfund, UK to bring skills training to unemployed women and a number of men. Beneficiaries of these training programs include the unemployed, under-employed, physically impaired, wives of ministers and army officers, commercial sex workers, street children, etc.

- **Leadership Training**—Helping to give women the training and skills needed to be useful in their churches and communities.

- **Marriage Counseling**—The bedrock of the family and the nation is under constant attack from the enemy. The ministry focuses on teaching couples how to save and improve their marriages.

- **Ministry to Prisons**—Reaching out to and evangelizing women in prisons, providing for their material wellbeing and giving them skills for their return to the community. We also hold open-air evangelistic crusades for Kumasi Central Prisons in Ghana. The Lord has used the crusades to save many condemned criminals.

- **Visitation**—The Greater Accra Region has adopted a ward at the Accra Psychiatric Hospital and meets with patients for a meal once a month and to share the Word of God.

- **Bible Studies**—Sessions based on GHACOE's Manual, *The Challenge of Being a Woman*, monthly educational retreats, evangelism/leadership training programs, prayer, council and regional meetings, and annual conferences.

- **Teen Group Meetings**—Monthly and annual meetings organized by GHACOE. The aim is to catch them young.

- **Gender Sensitization**—Men in the north are realizing that their women are not "useless" (as they previously thought). They are able to feed the household through the skills imparted to them by GHACOE. Drugs, food and the gospel have been given to the people living with HIV/AIDS (PLWHA), giving them hope and the strength to go on living.

Conclusion

I wish to conclude this paper with a reminder in the words of the former President of Tanzania, which sums up the role of the Church in societal transformation (Lawford, 1989:37).

Unless we participate actively in the rebellion against those so-cial structures and economic organizations, which condemn men to poverty, humiliation and degradation, then the Church will become irrelevant to man and the Christian religion will degenerate into a set of superstitions accepted by the fearful. Unless the Church, its members and its organizations, express God's love for man by involvement in the present conditions of man, then it will become identified with injustice and persecution. If this happens, it will die—and, humanly speaking, deserves to die—because it will then serve no purpose comprehensible to modern man.

President Julius Nyerere

ENDNOTES FOR
Societal Transformation

1 The UN General Assembly on 1 December 2000 recognized the role of conflict diamonds in fuelling war in Angola and Sierra Leone. The UN defines conflict diamonds as "diamonds that originate from areas controlled by forces or factions opposed to legitimate and international recognized government, and are used to fund military action in opposition Council (www.un.org/peace/africa/diamond.html, accessed July 21, 2009.

Blood diamonds refers to diamonds mined in a war zone and sold to finance an insurgency, invading army or a warlord's activity usually in Africa. "Blood Diamond," http://in.wikipedia.org/wiki/Blood_Diamonds; Internet accessed: 21 July 2009.

Reference List

"A reformed church" in *The archbishops' council of the church of England*. (2004). Retrieved (n. d.) from http://www.churchofeng-land.org/about-us/history/detailed-history.aspx

Abah, A. (Ed.). (2003). *Understanding African missions*. Jos, Nigeria: Grace Foundation Media Services.

Adadevoh, D. (Ed.). (2007). *Building leaders of integrity to transform Africa*. Orlando, FL: ILF Publishers.

Adadevoh, D. (2008). *Leading transformation in Africa*. Orlando, FL: ILF Publishers.

Adadevoh, D. (n. d.). Quotation from International Leadership Foundation (ILF) files. Orlando, FL: ILF Publishers.

Adeyemo, T. (July 2009). *Africa's enigma and leadership solutions*. Nairobi, Kenya: WordAlive Publishers.

African Progress. (2004). *The African leadership capacity development project*. [On-line]: Available: http://www.africanprogress.net/

African Studies Center at Michigan State University. (n. d.). *Exploring Africa: Introduction to religion in Africa*. In module 14 of the Exploring Africa curriculum. [On-line]: Available: http://exploringafrica.matrix.msu.edu/

Ali, A. Y. (2001). *The Qur'an translation*. (7th ed.). Elmhurst, NY: Tahrike Tarsile Quran, Inc.

Ali, M. (1999). *Islam reviewed*. Ft. Myers, FL: Fish House Publishing.

Al-Masih, A. (1996). *The main challenges for committed Christians in serving Muslims*. Villach, Austria: Light of Life.

Amadi, S. (2004a). *Freedom of religion and plural democracy: The sharia as a critique of liberal legality*. Unpublished doctoral dissertation. Cambridge, MA: Harvard Law School.

Amadi, S. (October 18, 2004b). *Theological ambivalence and democratic accountability.* Paper presented at the Pentecostal-Civil Society Dialogue, Lagos, Nigeria.

Annan, K. (March 22, 2005). *Opening address.* United Nations 50th Session of the Commission on the Status of Women. United Nations, New York, NY.

Appleby, S. (2000). *The ambivalence of the sacred: Religion, violence and reconciliation.* Lanham, MD: Rowman and Littlefield.

Aquinas, St. T. (c. 1270/1920). *The summa theologica of St. Thomas Aquinas.* Fathers of the English Dominican Province (Trans.). (Second and revised ed.). Kevin Knight (2008). (Ed.) for New Advent. [Online]: Available: http://www.newadvent.org/summa/

Assimeng, M. (1989). *Religion and social change in West Africa.* Accra, Ghana: Universities Press.

Association of Christian Lay Centres in Africa. (ACLCA). (2000). *Equipping the laity for social transformation: A resource manual for courses on leadership in lay training.* Accra, Ghana: Asempa Publishers.

Augsburger, D. W. (1992). *Conflict mediation across cultures: Pathways and patterns.* Louisville, KY: Westminster/John Knox.

Babayan, Y. *ArmenianHistory.info.* Retrieved 11 August 2009 from http://www.armenianhistory.info

Barclay, W. (1960). *The mind of Jesus.* Great Britain: SCM Press, Ltd.

Battle, M. J. (1997). *Reconciliation: The ubuntu theology of Desmond Tutu.* Cleveland, OH: The Pilgrim Press.

Blood diamond, *n.* Retrieved July 21, 2009 from http://en.wikipedia.org/wiki/Blood_diamond

Bourdillon, M. (1990). *Religion and society: A text for Africa.* Gweru, Zimbabwe: Mambo Press.

Bratcher, D. (Ed.). Retrieved August 11, 2009 from http://www. crivoice.org/creedsearly.html

Brewer's Dictionary of Phrase and Fable. (2005). *Eat, drink and be merry, for tomorrow we die.* New York: Cassell Publishers, Ltd.

Brink, P. (2003). "Debating international human rights: The middle ground for religious participants" in *Review of faith and international affairs 1* (2): 13-20. [Online]: Available: http://www.rfiaonline.org

British Broadcasting Corporation (BBC). (October 26, 1997 , 6:39 GMT). Radio announcement in Zambia of *coup* attempt by Captain Stephen Lungu.

Brown J. L. (n. d.). *HIV/AIDS alienation: Between prejudice and acceptance.* Dissertation presented for the Degree of Doctor of Theology, University of Stellenbosch, South Africa.

Budziszewski, J. (1992). *True tolerance: Liberalism and the necessity of judgment.* New Brunswick: Transaction Publishers.

Burrowes, P. C. (2001). "Black Christian republicanism: A southern ideology in early Liberia, 1822 to 1847" in *The journal of negro history, 86* (1), 30-44. (Winter, 2001).

Calvin, J. (December 1555). *Sermon on Deuteronomy 20.*

Carter, I. (2004). *Mobilising the church: A PILLARS guide.* Resources Development Unit–Tearfund, U. K.

Carter, S. (1993). *The culture of disbelief: How American law and politics trivialize religious devotion.* New York: Basic Books.

Catholic Bishops of Zambia. (July 23, 1990). *Economics, politics and justice: A pastoral statement of the Catholic bishops of Zambia.* Lusaka, Zambia: Catholic Secretariat. [On-line]: Available: http://www.afcast.org.zw

Catholic News Service (October 11, 2004). *Bishops say Zambia should not be called Christian in constitution.* [On-line]: Available: http://www.catholicnews.com/

Carmody, B. (March 4, 2002). "The Catholic Church and Zambia's elections" in *America magazine: The national catholic weekly, 186* (7). [On-line]: Available: http://www.americamagazine.org

Chapman, A. and Spong, B. (2004). *Religion and reconciliation in South Africa: Voices of religious leaders.* Philadelphia and London: Templeton Foundation Press.

Chiluba, F. (December 29, 1991). *Inaugural address of President Chiluba, Zambia.* Presented at the State House in Lusaka, Zambia. Retrieved June 18, 2009 from http://www.servingthenations.org/old/nations/inaugural_address_chiluba.htm

Chiluba, F. (October 26, 1997). "Prayer of confession." Presented during *An address to the nation* from Zambia National Broadcasting Corporation, Radio 2.

"Christian Words You Should Know." *Bible Study Planet.* Retrieved May 2011, from http://biblestudyplanet.com/christian-words-you-should-know-gospel/

"'Christian' Zambia: Heaven on earth?" *in Americans united for separation of church and state.* (April 2000). [On-line]: Available: http://findarticles.com/

Church, F. (Ed.). (2004). *The separation of church and state: Writings on a fundamental freedom by America's founders.* Boston, MA: Beacon Press.

Combès, G. (1927). *La doctrine politique de Saint Augustin.* Paris: Librairie Plon.

Constantine, *pron. EarlyChurch.org.uk.* (2009). Retrieved August 11, 2009 from http://www.earlychurch.org.uk/constantine.php

Constitution of Zambia - Part III. (1996). *Protection of fundamental rights and freedom of the individual.* Retrieved June 24, 2009 from http://www.thezambian.com/Constitution/1996partiii.aspx#19

Constitution of Zambia—Preamble. As amended by Act No. 18 of 1996. Gateway to Zambia—the Zambia. [Online]: Available: http://www.thezambian.com/Constitution/1996preamble.aspx; Internet accessed: 24 June 2009.

Constitution of Zambia. (1996). [On-line]: Available: http://www.elections.org.zm/constitution/

Covey, S. R., A. R. Merrill, and R. R. Merrill. (1994). *First things first.* UK: Simon and Schuster, Ltd.

Coward, H. and Smith, G. (2003). *Religion and peace building.* Albany, NY: SUNY Press.

Crwys-Williams, J. (Ed.). (1999). *In the words of Nelson Mandela.* South Africa: The Penguin Group.

Davidmann, M. (2005). *Church and state, government and religion: Social policies (doctrine) of the Roman Catholic Church: An evaluation.* [On-line]: Available: http://www.solhaam.org/

Durham, Jr., W. C. (2007). "Recognizing religious communities in law" in *Review of faith and international affairs, 5* (3).

Emerson, R. W. (n. d.). From "Power" in *The conduct of life.* Retrieved from http://www.notable-quotes.com/e/emerson_ralph_waldo.html

Falk, P. (1979). *The growth of the church in Africa.* Grand Rapids, MI: Zondervan.

Fernandez, J. (1982). *Ethnography of the religious imagination in Africa.* NJ: Princeton University Press.

Fisher, S., *et al.* (2000). *Working with conflict: Skills and strategies for action.* London: Zed Books, Ltd.

Fonjong, L. (September 2001). "Fostering women's participation in development through non-governmental efforts in Cameroon" in *The geographical journal, 167* (3).

Fortunate, E. (March 8, 2008). "The harm women: Critical role in peace building," in *The standard,* 17, Col. 1-5.

G8 Summit (July 8, 2008). *Declaration on development and Africa.*

Gandhi, M. (n, d.). 1-Famous-Quotes.com. Retrieved July 4, 2011, from http://www.1-famous-quotes.com/quote/84533

Gathirimu, P. (2009). Interview with Gathirimu, consultant physician and registrar at the Department of Internal Medicine, University of Nairobi.

George, S. (1994). *A fate worse than debt: A radical analysis of the third world debt crisis.* New York: Penguin Book Group.

Gingerich, M. (1968). *The Christian and revolution.* PA: Herald Press.

Gospel, *n.* Retrieved May 2011 from http://biblestudyplanet.com/ christian-words-you-should-know-gospel/

Grace Foundation Media Services. (2003). *Understanding African missions.* A. Abah (Ed.). Jos, Nigeria.

Grudem, W. (1994). *Systematic theology: An introduction to biblical doctrine.* Grand Rapids, MI: Zondervan Publishing House.

Guroian, V. (1999). "Evangelism and mission in the orthodox tradition," in J. Witte, Jr. and R. C. Martin (Eds.), *Sharing the book: Religious perspectives on the rights and wrongs of proselytis.* New York: Maryknoll/Orbis Books, 231-244.

Gutenberg, *pron.* "English Translation of the Bible" in *DidYouKnow. org.* Retrieved August 12, 2009 from http://www.didyouknow.org

Hamurger, P. (2002). *Separation of church and state.* Cambridge, MA: Harvard University Press.

Hasting, A. (1981). "The Christian churches and the liberation movements in southern Africa" in *Oxford journal of African affairs, 80* (320), 345-354.

Haynes, J. (1997). "Religion, secularization and politics: A postmodern conspectus," in *Third world quarterly, 18* (4), 709-728.

Heilman, B. and Keisser, P. (2002). "Religion, identity and politics in Tanzania," in *Third world quarterly, 23* (4), 691-709.

Heise, L., J. Pitanguy, and A. Germain. (1994). "Violence against women: The hidden health burden." *World bank discussion paper #255.* World Bank: Washington, DC.

Henriot, P. (February 12, 1998). *Being a Christian in a Christian nation: Lack of clarity.* Jesuit Centre for Theological Reflection. [On-line]: Available: http://www.jctr.org.zm/

Henriot, P. (March 16-18, 2005). *Church in the modern world of Africa: the Zambian experience.* Paper presented at Vatican City conference: The call to Justice: The legacy of gaudium et spes 40 years later.

Hobbes, T. (1651/2007). *Leviathan.* USA: Wilder Publications.

Human Rights First. *Refugees in Africa.* [On-line]. Available: www.humanrightsfirst.org/intl_refugees/africa/africa.htm

Iwe, J. I. (2005). "Enhancing women's productivity in the library and information sector in Nigeria," in *The electronic library, 23* (3).

Isizoh, C. D. (2009). *Christianity in dialogue with African traditional religion: The changing attitude of the Catholic Church.* [On-line]: Available: http://www.afrikaworld.net/

James, W. (1982). *The varieties of religious experience: A study in human nature.* Hammondsworth, England: Penguin Books.

Jesuit Centre for Theological Reflection. (October 2005). *Observation and comments on interim report and draft constitution of constitution review commission.* [On-line]: Available: http://www.jctr.org.zm/downloads/jctrsubcrc-251005.pdf.

Kapstein E. B. (July/August 2009). "Africa's capitalist revolution: Preserving growth in a time of crisis," in *Foreign affairs, 88* (4).

Karongo, C. (October 2007). "Banking on women," in *Business in Africa.*

Keathley, J. H. (2000). "What is the Gospel?" from *Bible.org.* Retrieved June 2011 from http://bible.org/article/what-gospel

Kline, M. G. (1972). *The structure of biblical authority.* Grand Rapids, MI: William B. Eerdmans.

Kolakowski, L. (1997). *Modernity on endless trial.* Chicago: University of Chicago Press.

Kreis, S. (2002). "Lecture 3: The Protestant Reformation" in Lectures on Early Modern European History from *HistoryGuide.org.* Retrieved August 12, 2009 from http://www.historyguide.org/earlymod/lecture3c.html

Kuhlman, K. (1973). Unpublished sermon entitled, *"The secret power of the holy spirit"* given in Pittsburgh, PA.

Ladd, G. E. (1974). *The presence of the future: The eschatology of biblical realism.* New York: Harper and Row.

Lawford, I. (August 1989). *Salt in the stew—Theological basis for Christian participation in social transformation.* From the All Africa Conference of Churches (AACC). Nairobi, Kenya: Research and Development Consultancy Service.

Lihinag, T. (2007). *Les vraies valeurs de la jeunesse.* Yaoundé, Cameroon: Familytimes, (Ed.).

Lincoln, A. (n. d.). 1-Famous-Quotes.com. Retrieved July 4, 2011, from http://www.1-famous-quotes.com/quote/21354

LINKS. (July 1998). "Lessons from the gender mapping project" in *Newsletter on gender for OXFAM GB.*

Little, P. and S. Lauver (April 2005). "Engaging adolescents in out-of-school time programs: learning what works," in *The prevention researcher,* 7-10.

Locke, J. (1689/2004). *Two treatises on government.* Whitefish, MT: Kessinger Publishing.

MacIntyre, A. (1984). *After virtue: A study in moral theory.* (2nd ed.). Notre Dame, IN: University of Notre Dame Press.

Maduekwe, O. (2005). *Raising the bar.* Ibadan, Nigeria/Channel Islands, U.K.: Spectrum Books in association with Safari Books.

Malanda, R. (January 2009). "What African women really want," in *New African woman.*

Mandela, N. (January 1997). *Renewal and renaissance—towards a new world order.* Lecture given at the Oxford Centre for Islamic Studies, Oxford, England.

Mandela, N. (January 29, 1999). *Address to the world economic forum.* Davos, Switzerland.

Manent, P. (1995). *An intellectual history of liberalism.* NJ: Princeton University Press.

Manuh, T. (April 1998). "Women in Africa's development: Overcoming obstacles, pushing for progress," in *Africa recovery briefing, 11.*

Maritain, J. (1998). *Man and the state.* Washington, DC: Catholic University of America Press.

Marlowe, M. D. "Canons and Decrees of the Council of Trent" English translation by James Waterworth (London, 1848) in *Bibleresearcher.com*. Retrieved August 11, 2009 from http://www.bible-researcher.com/trent1.html

Marshall, K. (2001). "Development and religion: A different lens of development debate," in *Peabody journal of education*, 76 (3 and 4), 339-375.

Mathenge, R. (July 8, 2007). "Dying young" in the *Daily nation newspaper*. Nairobi, Kenya.

Mathur-Helm, B. (2004). "Women in management in South Africa," in Davidson, M. and Burke R. (Eds.). *Women in management worldwide: Facts, figures and analysis*. Aldershot: Ashgate Publishing Company.

Mathur-Helm, B. (2005). "Equal opportunity and affirmative action for South African women: A benefit or barrier?" in *Women in management review, 20* (1) 56-71.

Matthews, O. (November 19, 2007). "Racing for new riches: Russian and Chinese investors are battling for African resources to fuel their growing empires" in *Newsweek* [On-line]: Available: www.newsweek.com/id/68910

Mbiti, J. S. (1999). *African religions and philosophy*. Portsmouth, NH: Heinemann: A Division of Reed Publishing (USA), Inc.

McGrath, A. E. (2001). *Christian theology: An introduction*. Victoria, Australia: Blackwell Publishing.

McLoughlin, M. (1997-2005). "Serving God's purposes in business." [On-line]: Available: http://www.scruples.org/web/seminars/pssb/chapter0/serving.htm

Moltmann, J. (1984). *Human dignity: Political theology and ethics*. (Trans. M. Douglas Meek). London: SCM Press.

Morgan, D. (July 13-17, 2008). *Women in Africa's development: Pushing for progress through entrepreneurship education complemented by ongoing coaching sessions.* Paper presented at the fifth commonwealth forum on open learning. UK: University of London.

Morsink, J. (1999). *The universal declaration of human rights: Origins, drafting, and intent.* PA: University of Pennsylvania Press.

Mouw, R. J. (2005). "A Christian declaration on human rights." Miller, Allen O. (Ed.). In *Theology today, July 1978, 35*(2). [Online]: Available: http://theologytoday.ptsem.edu/search/index-search.htm

Mumba, N. (1997). *The national christian coalition launching.* Press conference speech, September 4, 1997. Lusaka, Zambia: Pamodzi Hotel.

Mumba, N. (2006). *Vision and plan for a new Zambia: Mumba for president of Zambia.* Retrieved July 4, 2009 from http://www.neversforpresident.com/plan.cfm

Murray, J. C. (1960). *We hold these truths: Catholic reflections on the American proposition.* NY: Sheed and Ward.

Murray, J. C. (1966). "The declaration on religious freedom: A moment in its legislative history," in J. C. Murray (Ed.), *Religious liberty: An end and a beginning.* New York: Macmillan and Company.

Murray, J. C. (1993). *Religious liberty: Catholic struggles with pluralism,* Hooper, J. L. (Ed.). Louisville, KY: John Knox Press.

Muraya, E. (November/December 2008). "A visionary business leader" in *Biashara Leo.* Nairobi, Kenya: Asante Media, Limited.

Musekura, C. (2006). "Refugees," in T. Adeyemo (Ed.), *Africa bible commentary: A one-volume commentary written by 70 African scholars.* Nairobi, Kenya: WorldAlive Publishers.

Mwilu, L. and G. Chellah. (September 7, 2006). "Clergymen differ over candidate to back for president," in *The Post,* Retrieved June 4, 2009 from http://allafrica.com/stories/200609070523.html

Mwanakatwe, J. (2003). *Teacher, politician, lawyer: My autobiography.* Lusaka, Zambia: Book World Publishers.

Nation, *n.* (2009). *Wikipedia.org.* [Online]: Available: http://en.wikipedia.org/wiki/Nation

Nehls, G. and W. Eric. (2003). *The church in Africa encounters the challenge of Islam: Workshop papers for Christian leaders.* Nairobi, Kenya: Life Challenge Africa.

New Partnership for Africa's Development, NEPAD. (2003). *Comprehensive African agricultural development programme.* [Online]: Available: http://www.nepad.org/foodsecurity/agriculture/about

Newbigin, L. (1989). *The gospel in a pluralist society.* Grand Rapids, MI: Wm. B. Eerdmans Publishing Company.

Niebuhr, R. (1934). *Moral man and immoral society: A study in ethics and politics.* New York: Charles Scribner's Sons.

North Africa Mission, *Reaching the Muslim today: A short handbook.* Loughborough, Leicestershire: North Africa Mission.

Northouse, P. G. (2007). *Leadership: Theory and practice.* Thousand Oaks, CA: Sage Publication, Inc.

Nosotro, R. (2009). "The History of Christianity in Ethiopia" in *HyperHistory.net.* Retrieved August 11, 2009 from http://www.hyperhistory.net/apwh/essays/cot/t1w12ethiopia.htm

Obenga, T. (2007). *Appel à la jeunesse africaine: Contrat social africaine pour le 21ème siecle.* Paris: Editions Ccinia Communication.

Ogutu, E. (August 9, 2008). "A woman's best friend" in *The standard,* 6, Col. 1-5.

Olsen, T. "One African nation under god," in *Christianity today magazine*, February 4, 2002. Retrieved June 13, 2009 from http://www.christianitytoday.com/ct/2002/002/3.36.html

Olukoju, A. (2006). *Culture and customs of Liberia.* Westport, CT and London: Greenwood Press.

Omar, O. (2004). "A qualitative evaluation of women as managers in the Nigerian civil service," in *The international journal of public sector management, 17* (4).

Omeje, K. (2008). *War to peace transition: Conflict intervention and peace building in Liberia.* Lanham: University Press of America.

Oruka, H. O. (Ed.) (1990). *Sage philosophy: Indigenous thinkers and modern debate on African philosophy.* New York: E. J. Brill.

Palfrey, J. G. (2007) "Great Puritan exodus to New England, founding of Boston" in *International World History Project (history-world. org)*. Retrieved August 12, 2009 from http://history-world.org/great_puritan_exodus.htm

Parenti, M. (2002). *Democracy: For the few.* New York: St. Martin's.

Paris, P. J. (1988). "Expanding and enhancing moral communities: The task of Christian ethics" in W. Copeland and R. D. Hatch (Eds.), *Issues of justice: Social sources and religious meaning.* Macon, GA: Mercer University Press.

Paris, P. J. (2004). *Virtues and values: The African and African American experience.* Minneapolis, MN: Fortress Press.

Paul IV (1965). *Declaration on religious freedom (Dignitatis Humanae).* (St. Paul Editions). [Online]: Available: http://www.vatican.va/

Pavlischek, K. J. (1994). *John Courtney Murray and the dilemma of religious toleration.* Kirksville, MO: Thomas Jefferson University Press.

Peterson, D. (1996). "Liberia: Crying for freedom" in *Journal of democracy*, 7(2), 148-158.

"Pilgrims and Puritans: Background" in American Studies at the University of Virginia: *xroads.virginia.edu*. Retrieved from http://xroads.virginia.edu/~CAP/puritan/purhist.html ; 12 August 2009.

Pilzer, P. Z. (2007). *The new wellness revolution: How to make a fortune in the next trillion dollar industry.* Hoboken, NJ: John Wiley and Sons, Inc.

Pobee, J. S. and G. Ositehu. (1998). *African initiatives in Christianity.* Geneva: WCC Publications.

Powell, H. J. (2001). "The Earthly Peace of the Liberal Republic," in M. W. McConnell, R. F. Cochran and A. C. Carmela (Eds.). *Christian perspectives on legal thought.* New Haven, CT: Yale University Press.

Rauschenbusch, W. (1912). *Christianizing the social order, 49, 66.* New York: The Macmillan Company .

Razaana, A. (November 2004). "But where are all Africa's women?" in *Business in Africa*, 40-41.

Rawls, J. (1971). *A theory of justice.* Cambridge, MA: President and Fellows of Harvard College.

Rawls, J. (1993/1996). *Political liberalism.* New York: Columbia University Press.

Religion*, n. Webster's new world dictionary.* Retrieved June 5, 2009 from http://www.religioustolerance.org/rel_defn.htm

Republic of Kenya. (July to August 2007). *Kenya Vision 2030.* [Online]: Available: http://www.planning.go.ke/index.php?option=com_docman&task=cat_view&Itemid=69&gid=64&orderby=dmdate_published

Reference List

Republic of Kenya. (October 2007). *Kenya Vision 2030.* [Online]: Available: http://www.safaricomfoundation.org/fileadmin/ template/main/downloads/Kenya_VISION_2030-final_report- October_2007.pdf

Republic of Kenya, Ministry of State for Planning. (2008). *Millennium development goals: Status report for Kenya 2007.* [Online]: Available: http://www.planning.go.ke/index.php?option=com_ docman&task=cat_view&Itemid=69&gid=64&orderby=dmda te_published

Republic of Kenya, Ministry of Gender, Sports, Culture and Social Services. (November 2000). *National gender and development policy.* [Online]: Available: http://www.onlinewomeninpolitics. org/sourcebook_files/Resources.2/Tools-%20Gender%20 Policy%202000.pdf

Reuters (March 11, 2008). "Small loans offer hope to women, says U. N." in *The standard*, 19, Col 1-5.

Ritschl, A. (1900). *The Christian doctrine of justification and reconciliation.* New York: Charles Scribner's Sons, 12.

Rotberg, R. I. (2004). *When states fail: Causes and consequences.* Princeton, NJ: Princeton University Press.

Rotberg, R. I. (July/August 2004). "Strengthening African leadership" in *Foreign affairs, 83* (4).

Rubin, D. (et al.). (March 28, 2008). *A gender assessment of sustainable conservation-oriented enterprises* (SCOE). U. S. Development and Training Services.

Saito, K. A., H. Mekonnen and D. Spurling. (1994). "Raising the productivity of women farmers in sub-Saharan Africa" in *World bank discussion papers, 230.* Washington, DC: The World Bank.

Saito, K. A. and C. J. Weidermann. (1990). "Agricultural extension for women farmers in sub-Saharan Africa," in *World bank discussion papers, 103.* Washington, DC: The World Bank.

Senghor, L. S. (1964). *On African socialism.* M. Cook (Trans.). London: Pall Mall Press.

Seshamani, V. (2009). *A Hindu view of the declaration of Zambia as a Christian nation.* Retrieved May 16, 2009 from http://www.jctr. org.zm/bulletins/sesh%20on%20hinduism.htm

Sharp, T. (2009). *The happiness handbook: Strategies for a happy life.* Sydney: Finch Publishing.

Skolfield, E. (2007). *The religious battle behind the headlines: Islam in the end times.* Ft. Myers, FL: Fish House Publishing.

Slick, M. (2009). "Nicene Creed" in *Christian Apologetics & Research Ministry (CARM).* Retrieved August 11, 2009 from http://www. carm.org/christianity/creeds-and-confessions/nicene-creed-325-ad

Soelle, D. (1974). *Political theology.* Philadelphia, PA: Fortress Press.

St. Augustine (c. 415/1887). *The city of god.* Marcus Dods (Trans.). From Nicene and Post-Nicene Fathers, First Series, Vol. 2. Philip Schaff (Ed.). Buffalo, NY: Christian Literature Publishing Co., 1887. Kevin Knight (2009) (Ed.) for New Advent. [Online]: Available: http://www.newadvent.org/fathers/1201.htm>

Swope, M. R. (1997). *Lifelong health.* New Kensington, PA: Whitaker House, 139.

Taylor, C. (2003). *Varieties of religion today: William James revisited.* Cambridge, MA: Harvard University Press.

Terry, L. D. (2002). *Leadership of public bureaucracies.* Armonk, NY: M.E. Sharpe, Inc.

"Umutomboko Ceremony." Retrieved June 16, 2009 from http://www.chiefsof zambia.homestead.com/mutomboko.html

United Nations. (1948). *Universal declaration of human rights.* [Online]: Available: http//www.un.org/en/documents/udhr/

United Nations Development Program. (2009). *Human development report.* UNDP Website [Online]: Available: http://hdr.undp.org/en/humandev

UN General Assembly. (2009). [Online]: Available: http://www.un.org/peace/africa/Diamond.html ; accessed 21 July 2009.

UN Human Rights Committee. (UNHRC). (April 25, 2006). *U. N. human rights committee: Third periodic report of states parties due in 1998, Zambia.* CCPR/C/ZMB/3, [On-line]: Available: http://www.unhcr.org/refworld/docid/45c30b7f0.html

UN Human Rights Committee. (UNHRC). (June 30, 1998). *International covenant on civil and political rights: third periodic report of Zambia due on 30 June 1998.* Retrieved December 29, 2011 from http://www.unhcr.org/refworld/publisher,HRC,,ZMB,45c30b7f0,0.html

UN World's Women. (2005). *The world's women 2005: Progress in statistics* (ST/ESA/STAT/SER.K/17), United Nations Publication, Sales No. E.05.XVII.7, ISBN 92-1-161482-1.

US Department of State. *International religious freedom report on Zambia, 2006: Bureau of democracy, human rights, and labor.* Retrieved May 5, 2009 from http://www.state.gov/g/drl/rls/irf/2006/71331.htm

Villa-Vicencio, C. (1989). "Have the chickens come home to roost?" in *Religion and oppression: The misuses of religion for social, political, and economic subjugation in eastern and southern Africa.* Edicessa Symposium Proceedings.

Vinay, S. and Sugden, C. (Eds.). (1987). *The church in response to human need.* Grand Rapids, MI and Oxford, UK: Wm. B. Eerdmans Publishing Co. and Regnum Books.

Wake Forest University Web site. (2009). Retrieved August 12, 2009 from http://www.wfu.edu/~matthetl/perspectives/four.html

Walker, K. E. and A. Arbreton. (April 2005). "Improving participation in after-school programs" in *The prevention researcher*, 11-13.

Warren, R. (1995). *The purpose driven church: Growth without compromising your message and mission.* Grand Rapids, MI: Zondervan Publishers.

Weber, M. (1918/2000). *Politics as a vocation.* H.H. Gerth and C. Wright Mills (Trans.). (1972, c. 1965). Philadelphia, PA: Fortress Press.

Weingartner, E. (1999). "Human Rights," in *Dictionary of the ecumenical movement.* Geneva: WCC Publications.

Welch, C. E. (2001). (Ed.) *NGOs and human rights: promise and performance.* Philadelphia, PA: University of Pennsylvania Press.

Wesley, J. (1771). Sermon 3 titled, "Awake, thou that sleepest." Delivered on April 4, 1742. Published 1771 in *Sermons on several occasions*, in four volumes.

Wogaman, J. P. and D. M. Strong. (Eds.). (1996). *Reading in Christian ethics: A historical source book.* London: Westminster John Knox Press.

Worden, S. (2003). "The role of religious and nationalistic ethics is strategic leadership: The case of J. N. Tata" in *Journal of business ethics*, 47 (2), 147-164.

World Alliance of Reformed Churches (WARC). (2004/2007). *Accra confession.* [On-line]: Available: http://www.warc.ch/documents/ACCRA_Pamphlet.pdf

World Bank. *World development indicators.* [Online]: Available:
http://www.google.com/publicdataexplore?ds=d5bncppjof8f9
_&met_y=sp_dyn_leoo_in& idim=country:KEN&dl=en&hl=en&
q=kenyan+life+expectancy#ctype=l&strail=false&nselm=h&m
et_y=sp_dyn_leoo_in&scale_y=lin&ind_y=false&rdim=countr
y&idim=country:KEN&ifdim=country&hl=en&dl=en

World Council of Churches. (2001). *Thabo Mbeki asks churches to
promote conflict resolution in southern Africa.* Retrieved July 26,
2009 from http://www.oikoumene.org/

World Peace Foundation. (2004). *The Mombasa declaration:
The mission statement, the code of African leadership, capacity
building curriculum topics.* [Online]: Available:
www.worldpeacefoundation.org/africanleadership.html

World Religions News: *"Declaration of Christian nation must go,
submit Catholic bishops,"* Retrieved June 24, 2009 from http://
www.oefre.unibe.ch/law/icl/zaooooo_.html

Zambian Constitution 1991. Retrieved June 24, 2009 from http:/
www.servat.unibe.ch/icl/zaooooo_.html

Zambian Constitution (Preamble). (1991). [Online]: Available:
http://www.elections.org.zm/constitution/constitution_act_18.
html

Zambia National Anthem. Retrieved May 21, 2009 from http://www.
thezambian.com/zambia/anthem. aspx

Index

Index

Index

Index

United States 23, 42, 85, 91,
    104, 112, 175
Universal Declaration of
    Human Rights 6, 91,
    96, 127
USA 30, 138, 186, 208

W

Wagner 98
Warren 26
WCRC 208, 213, 214
Weber 80-81, 92
Weidemann 69
Weingartner 127
Wesley 39, 45
Western philosophy 85, 86
Western world 83, 111
Women's education 69
Women's employment 67
Women's institutions 72
Women's leadership
    skills 66
Women's ministry 13, 216,
    225, 227-229
Women's National
    Coalition 68
Women's role(s) 62-63
World Bank 38, 62, 63,
    114, 223
World Communion of
    Reformed Churches
    208, 213
World Health
    Organization 42

World Peace
    Foundation 204

Y Yaoundé 48

Z Zambia 8, 68, 108-122, 195,
    ZEC 111, 120
Zimbabwe 68, 138, 195